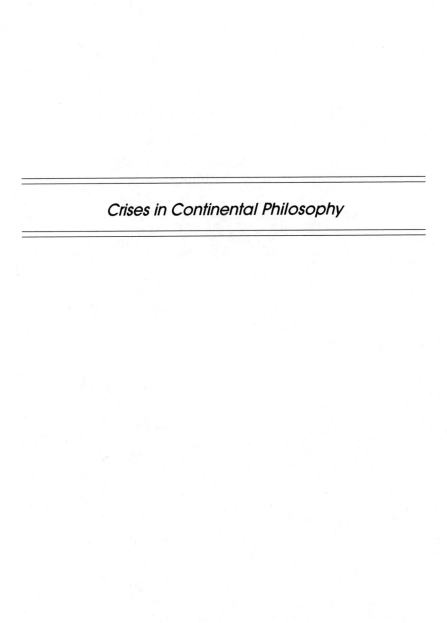

Crises in Continental Philosophy

Selected Studies in Phenomenology
and Existential Philosophy 16

Crises in Continental Philosophy

Edited by
Arleen B. Dallery and Charles E. Scott
with P. Holley Roberts

STATE UNIVERSITY OF NEW YORK PRESS

Published by
State University of New York Press, Albany

Printed in the United States of America

For information, address State University of New York
Press, State University Plaza, Albany, N.Y. 12246

Library of Congress Cataloging-in-Publication Data

Crises in continental philosophy / edited by Arleen B. Dallery and
  Charles E. Scott with P. Holley Roberts.
      p.   cm.— (Selected studies in phenomenology and existential
  philosophy ; 16)
    Includes bibliographical references.
    ISBN 0-7914-0419-6 (alk. paper). — ISBN 0-7914-0420-X (pbk.:
  alk. paper)
    1. Philosophy, Modern—20th century. I. Dallery, Arleen B.
  II. Scott, Charles E. III. Roberts, P. Holley. IV. Series.
  B804.C75 1990
  190'.9'04—dc20   90-34077
                                                            CIP

10 9 8 7 6 5 4 3 2 1

Contents

Introduction

This collection of essays addresses the moments of crisis that punctuate the course of continental thought in this century, from the founding crisis of reason, to which Edmund Husserl responded with a call for a rigorous science of phenomenology, to the current crisis of postmodernism, with its rejection of Husserl's metanarrative of history and rationality. The steps are many and discrete from Husserl's program of reformulating philosophy as a science of phenomenology to the postmodernist undercutting of philosophy's claim to a salvific role and of its attendant notions—the unified subject, objective reality, and a historical telos; these steps include Martin Heidegger's epochal history of Being, Michel Foucault's analysis of the power of cultural and disciplinary practices, and the dispersal of meanings in the philosophies of Jacques Derrida and others.

The first part of this collection, "Husserl's Narrative of the Crisis of Reason and the Life-World," comprises three essays. Rudolf Bernet's essay, which clarifies the many ways in which the world appears to the subject, takes as its focus the familiar environing-world. Bernet compares Husserl's notion of environing-world with Heidegger's examination of the limits of world in order to emphasize the contingency of the hospitality and rationality of the environing-world and to criticize Husserl's notion of the constitution of the world for its inadequacy in accounting for the ways in which the subject has a responsibility for making the world more rational. The theme of responsibility for rationality continues in R. Philip Buckley's essay, where he argues that Husserl was concerned with the crisis in Western rationality long before the publication of *The Crisis of European Sciences and Transcendental Phenomenology*, and that the motivation of this concern was an ethical one. This ethical concern also serves Buckley as a clue to understanding the quite different responses of Husserl and Heidegger to the perception of crisis. In his essay, J. Claude Evans argues for abandoning Husserl's doctrine of absolute consciousness (which, he believes, was not a discovery but, in fact, was a construction necessitated by

Husserl's account of sensations) for the sake of an account of intentionality that is more adequate to lived experience and for an understanding of time consciousness that avoids some of the problems associated with the traditional account. He also suggests ways in which this line of thought can illuminate the sources of opposing tendencies in Husserl's account of the constituting function of consciousness.

The critique of phenomenology as a science founded on the notion of absolute consciousness raises another question, addressed in Part Two, "The Possibility of Philosophy as Social Critique." Charles Harvey's essay, which opens this section, considers the question, What is it about human being that makes social criticism possible? Harvey observes that a successful answer to this question must avoid two extreme understandings of the self, the sociological and the world-purified conceptions—represented by Hans-Georg Gadamer and Jurgen Habermas, respectively—and he finds Husserl's account of the self to be more satisfactory than either of the other two. In the next essay, Kenneth Baynes first explores the different ways in which the notion of the life-world functions in the social theory of Jurgen Habermas and in Husserl's *The Crisis of European Sciences and Transcendental Phenomenology,* and how this notion contributes to Habermas's solutions to the crisis of reason and to the methodological crisis of the social sciences. He then argues that the concept of the life-world remains indispensable to social theory, even when removed from the context of the project of transcendental phenomenology. In her essay, Linda Alcoff cautions feminist theorists against too hasty an appropriation of Foucault's thought into feminist social critique. She cites Foucault's analysis of subjectivity and the further implications of his views for political practice as obstacles to any theory and practice of feminist resistance. The last essay in this section, by Thomas Thorp, focuses on Habermas's critique of Heidegger and Derrida in his *The Philosophical Discourse of Modernity* and argues that the manner in which Habermas constructs his polemic contradicts his theory of practical rationality, dependent as it is on a distinction between politically responsible argumentation and self-interested rhetoric. Further, Thorp argues that Habermas's theory of communicative action departs from the notion of political theory inherited from Critical Theory to an extent that undermines Habermas's claim that his theory is politically relevant.

The three essays in Part Three, "Subjection to Language, Power, and History," focus on the death of the epistemologically and morally autonomous subject in continental thought. Michael Clifford examines the place of Heidegger's *Being and Time* in Foucault's critique of the analytic of finitude and shows how, particularly in the notion of being-towards-death, Heidegger's work attempts to overcome the subject-object dichotomy and at the same time prepares the way for the critique of that effort. Foucault's analytics of power is the focus of the essay by Ladelle McWhorter, who rejects the interpretation that the analytics of power is a theory offering a model of power. According to McWhorter's reading, the analytics is a discursive strategy that undermines the notions of causality, identity, and foundation that underlie much of traditional analysis of power. In the third essay, Jane Rodeheffer examines the transformations at work in the notion of the call of conscience in Heidegger's *Being and Time*. She finds that these transformations make possible the movement away from the model of the conscience of a guilty subject toward the understanding of the call of language in Heidegger's later works—the call to Dasein to own its possible not-being.

Part Four, "Retrieval of Crises," comprises four essays that focus on Heidegger's response to the crisis of Western philosophy. According to Heidegger, the present crisis of Western thought can be understood only if we first retrieve the crises in Greek thought. In the first of these essays Walter Brogan turns to *Being and Time* and finds in Heidegger's discussion of Dasein's possibility of being-a-whole a parallel with Aristotle's notions of *phronēsis* and *praxis,* particularly with regard to the way in which both writers find the possibility of genuine practical life, in Brogan's words, in "a drawing back into oneself of one's ownmost potentiality." Dennis Schmidt points to the importance of the Greek conception of the relation between *physis* and *technē* in Heidegger's attempts to rethink production. Schmidt shows that Heidegger's thought moves away from an economy of representation and reproduction, but criticizes Heidegger for failing to take adequate account of *technē* as repetition, a failure with political consequences. Thomas Davis also focuses on the role of *phronēsis* in Heidegger's thought, specifically as it functions in the notion of *Gelassenheit* and the attunement of thought with its origins at the end of metaphysics. In his examination of Creon's experience in *Antigone,* Davis finds a clue to the way in which the confrontation with Greek thought might be possible. Jane Love turns to the *Phaedo* and *Phaedrus* and Plato's use of the metaphor of appetite to describe the soul's desire for intellectual contemplation. She finds that the metaphor serves both to maintain the distinction between the desires of the soul and of the body and to point toward a hidden unity of soul and body in their potential for violability and death.

Part Five, whose four essays focus on the crises of postmodernism, is aptly titled "Shattering Identities." Dorothea Olkowski follows the thought of Gilles Deleuze in his discussions of the literature of the Marquis de Sade and of Leopold von Sacher-Masoch, in which he finds a challenge to Plato's distinction between and valuation of *ikons* and their copies, on the one hand, and simulacra, on the other. According to Olkowski, in Deleuze's reading of these works the source of perversion is found to reside not in the simulacrum but rather in the nature of demonstrative and dialectical reason itself. The image of the unified self is the target of Iris Marion Young's essay, in which she uses Julia Kristeva's category of the abject to uncover the roots of unconscious prejudice toward certain groups in anxieties regarding self-identity. Political responses to such prejudice is made more difficult, she says, when prejudice is explicitly condemned on the level of discursive consciousness but unconscious prejudice remains, and when the prevailing paradigm of the mature person is one of "self-control" and unified subjectivity. Richard Boothby takes up the theme of unification and fragmentation in his examination of Lacan's treatment of Freud's theory of castration. Lacan, he says, extends the significance of castration in the Oedipal drama to the more general experience of desire and loss, and views castration anxiety as a developmental task that is intrinsically bound up with the acquisition of language. Boothby offers two examples to illustrate Lacan's interpretation: Helen Keller's account of her first encounter with language, and a child's drawings of body parts. In the final essay, Gayle Ormiston turns to Jean-Francois Lyotard's work, *The Postmodern Condition,* to explore the ways in which the postmodern is marked by the opposition and apposition of the Socratic-Platonic desire for justice and for the unknown with what Lyotard calls paganism, that is, the absence of criteria for knowing and acting. This state of linkage and disruption—of *différend*—is itself the postmodern condition of language, a condition that fractures any notion of universal knowledge, objective criteria, or foundation.

Collected together, these essays do not signify or complete a narrative history of crises in twentieth-century continental philosophy, but they do articulate multiple points or moments of crisis without cure or end.

Part 1

Husserl's Narrative of the Crisis of Reason
and the Life-World

WILLIS MONIE - BOOKS

139 Main Street
COOPERSTOWN, NY 13326
(607) 547-8363   (800) 322-2995
website: www.wilmonie.com

CUSTOMER'S ORDER NO.						PHONE		DATE 6/3/11

NAME

ADDRESS

SOLD BY	CASH	C.O.D.	CHARGE	ON ACCT.	MDSE. RET'D.	PAID OUT

QTY.	DESCRIPTION	PRICE	AMOUNT

	TOTAL	18.3C
	TAX	1.3C
		17 -

1 Husserl's Concept of the World

RUDOLF BERNET

The clarification of the meaning of *the world* was a constant endeavor on the part of Edmund Husserl. This is seen immediately in the great number of newly coined "world"-composites, such as "spiritual world" *(geistige Welt)*, "life-world" *(Lebenswelt)*, "environing-world" *(Umwelt)*, "home-world" *(Heimwelt)*, "world of interests" *(Interessenwelt)*, "universal world" *(Allweit)*, "horizon of the world" *(Welthorizont)*, "annihilation of the world" *(Weltvernichtung)*, "enworlding" *(Verweltlichung)*, etc. Although much used by phenomenologists, and used with many different connotations, the concept of "the world" as such, however, has worn out and covers many, often incompatible enterprises. Basic questions, such as what it means for the world to appear and how the subject is involved in the disclosure of the world, are often taken for granted. The result is that some phenomenologists turn toward the world, others rather turn away from it, and many remain shut up in their own worlds. Life-world phenomenologies flourish without their authors giving much thought to the fact that their descriptions of the life in the world presuppose a stance at the limit of or beyond this world. There is also a need to look more closely into the different forms under which "the world" reveals itself to a subject. In particular, the question how manifold local and self-contained worlds refer to a common and unique "open" world deserves more attention than life-world relativists are usually willing to concede.

The Phenomenological Reduction

The appearing of the world cannot be understood apart from the *phenomenological reduction.* This can seem disconcerting, in that it

3

involves a step that leads the subject, at one and the same time, to turn away from the world and to turn toward it. This is the price of a better comprehension of the appearing of the world, and the phenomenology that is consecrated to this task cannot economize on the phenomenological reduction. In transcending the things of the world, the reduction reveals at once the world as world and the subject as subject. Treating the question of the world and the question of the reduction together offers the possibility of rethinking the sense of the "reconduction" of the phenomenon to the subject and grasping better how the subject contributes to the appearance of a multiplicity of worlds.

If the aim of phenomenological reduction is to reveal the link between the diversity of worlds and the modes of life of the subject, as well as the enduring difference between the subject and its "world," then the reduction should be something else and, indeed, much more than an outmoded methodological exercise. To transgress the closed world of our habits, to assist at the collapse of a cultural world, to be excluded from a particular world that presents itself as universal, these are daily existential situations that nonetheless offer an access to the phenomenon of the world and that therefore must be considered as carrying out a phenomenological reduction. This then opens up as well the essential philosophical task concerning the safeguarding of the idea of an indefinitely open common world, which is inseparable from the idea of human rationality.

For Husserl, the analysis of the phenomenon of the world and the doctrine of phenomenological reduction are closely related. The increasing attention Husserl gave to the phenomenon of the world in his later work made it necessary for him to clarify and also modify the meaning of the phenomenological reduction. It is true that Husserl never surrendered the conviction that a phenomenological philosophy can be established only through a line of thought that in some manner turns away from the world. It is no less true that this withdrawal from the world will reveal itself more and more clearly as a necessary detour on the way to the discovery of the world. This discovery of the world is no sign of abandonment; it is rather the necessary fulfillment of the program of phenomenological reduction. It is not a question of ceasing to think in order to live; it is, on the contrary, a question of thinking the world as "phenomenon." The phenomenological view of the life-world already participates in another mode of life. The phenomenologist is awakened from the dogmatic slumber of a life that is as entangled with the world as a sleeping dog in his basket. This life in the world forgets the world because our attention is absorbed in the objects of the world; objects that appeal to our interests so strongly that they leave us without reprieve. Something must break this bondage to the things of the world, this constant entertainment, or *"divertissement,"* as Pascal calls it. The world can appear only when, somehow, our view wanders among the things of the world without having anything particular "in view." It is one and the same movement that takes us away from the world of our pre-occupations and reveals to us the order of the world.

In a letter to Hugo von Hofmannsthal of January 12, 1908, Husserl compares the phenomenological reduction to the attitude of a poet.[1] Nevertheless, the strongest motive for exiling oneself from the world of things remains for Husserl of a theoretical nature. More precisely, the point is to understand how the subject is related to the world. This can be conceived only if the subject is not itself a thing of the world and if the order of things is not foreign to the life of the subject. For Husserl, what distinguishes most radically the subject from a thing is the *intentionality* of the subject. This is, however, nothing other than the relationship of the subject to things. Thus, intentionality shows at the same time the difference and the connection between the subject and things. It also reveals the world as an order of things, because this order can appear only for a subject who relates itself to things without being overwhelmed by them. For Husserl, this means that the order of things appears to the subject as an instituted order, an order shaped by the subject. This shift from a world *for* the subject toward a world *by* the subject is made through the phenomeno-logical reduction, understood as retreat from things and as openness to their appearing. If it is perhaps possible to think the being of things independently of the subject, the same does not hold for their being-given. As phenomena, things are the concern of the subject; their logos is disclosed only to a subject; and the phenomenologist is inclined to make this subject the owner, instigator, and even founder of the logos of the phenomena. In this way of thinking, the world appears as a significant order of things in the manner it has been instituted by the transcendental subject or posited as its correlate. Rather than showing the belonging-together of the being of the world and the being of the subject, phenomenological reduction then displays a subjugated world, a world colonized by the constituting subject.

Subjugation and Annihilation of the World

This logic of subjugation dominates the first reflections of Husserl on the world, notably the notions of world view *(Weltanschauung)* and annihilation of the world *(Weltvernichtung)*. If "world view" witnesses to the subjugation of the subject to the world, "annihilation of the world" on the contrary deals with the subjugation of the world to the subject. In "world view" the subject in fact remains riveted to the world and to practical interests, to urgent problems, to vital preoccupations which make up the world.[2] In the actual functioning of "world view" the world is not grasped in itself but appears as a collection of things that are urgent to do, reasonable to hope, necessary to believe. The world of "world view" only appears as such in a second moment, in a theoretical reflection which is often animated by a project of comparing different world views and looking for their possible common ground. For Husserl, this viewed world is in no way superior to the naïvely believed-in world of the natural attitude, since a subject is lost when engaging itself, body and soul, in a particular world view, which is provisional and closed in upon itself.

On the contrary, in the "annihilation of the world" of the first book of *Ideas* the subject disengages itself radically from the world and sets it up as an objective correlate.[3] The world of things becomes a pure object of contemplation for the subject, but under such conditions that this perfect visibility of the world implies as well the possible disappearance of the viewed world. Husserl's argumentation is well known: if the phenomenological reduction consists in making every *esse* a *percipi,* one must conclude that the being-seen of the world depends on the seeing of the subject, whereas the subject is able to see itself without recourse to the world and thus depends only on itself. The result is that the being of the subject is of a higher dignity than the being of the world, as it could survive the abolition of the world, whereas the world could not subsist independently of the life of the subject. At the same time, this life of the constituting subject is not sufficient to guarantee the existence of the world in an absolute manner. The being of the world is dependent on harmony among the experiences of the subject, and this harmony is threatened by a rupture that remains always possible. Thus, the subject, which has gone to great lengths to distance itself from the world in order to acquire a good view of it, eventually views helplessly the collapse of the world it so much had wanted to see.

Husserl's criticism, twenty years later, of the hypothesis of the annihilation of the world has the immediate consequence of elevating "world view" to the dignity of an original project within transcendental phenomenology—the latter having "the capability...of actualizing the correlation between the possibility of experience and the possibility of the world under the form of a world view."[4] The error of the annihilation of the world was precisely the severing of this correlation between the seeing of the world and the world seen. The annihilation of the world goes against the sense of *intentionality,* which always carries the subject to an interest in the entities of the world and their appearing. The hypothesis of an annihilation of the world rests upon an ontological dualism (of a Cartesian type) whose two poles are the (self-evident) being of immanent consciousness and the (doubtful) being of the transcendent world; this dualism is totally foreign to the sense of the *transcendental constitution* of the world by the subject. The constituted world is neither purely within nor purely exterior to the constituting subject. If the sense of its being is said to depend on its being-given-for-the-subject, this does not mean that the appearing of the world is nothing other than an immanent experience of the subject. There is therefore a paradox in the annihilation of the world in that it finally levels the difference between the subject and the world which it was supposed to put in relief. The existence of the world is treated as if the world were a singular thing that confirms its existence in a harmonious course of intuitive appearances or, on the contrary, "explodes" when a new appearance enters into conflict with the preceding appearances. On the other hand, the subject manifests itself in a deficient and indeterminate form, as an immanent "residue" of the annihilation of the transcendent world, that is, still as a "small piece of the world" *(Endchen der Welt)*.

The hypothesis of the annihilation of the world thus does not meet the aims of the program of phenomenological reduction: it allows to appear neither the world as phenomenon, nor the transcendental being of the subject, nor the correlation or belonging-together of subject and world. The annihilation of the world does not even merit its own name, since the world (insofar as it exceeds the real existence of things) is not even taken into consideration.

Horizon and World

If the world, understood as the surplus of the perception of things, is already present in the first book of *Ideas,* it is rather in the term *halo* [*Hof*] or, more frequently, *horizon.* This notion of horizon owes its sense to what Husserl calls *horizontal intentionality (Horizontintentionalität),* and this, at least at the outset, remains marked by the preoccupations of a psychology of attention. Everything that I already or still perceive without giving it my whole attention belongs to the horizon of actual perception. This horizontal intentionality has many diverse modes: retentional and protentional horizon, which envelops the present grasping of an object; active or passive forms of motivation that prompt one to a series of (other) acts, that make the realization of one possibility of experience preferable to another, that lead to an enlargement or rather a retraction of one's field of vision, and so on. Horizontal intentionality thus establishes a continuity and a unity in one's conscious life. It anticipates future possibilities; it conserves the memory of past acts; it assures the passage from potentiality to realization; it is the principle that integrates all acts in a continuous unity of one life, of one subjective flux of consciousness. Though a principle that is essentially subjective, this horizontal intentionality has nevertheless its objective or noematic correlate—for instance, a field of vision, where certain things are closer to me than others, where certain things hitherto simply coperceived appeal to me more vividly than others, and where the possibility of the future course of my vision is mapped out.

Still one might be hesitant to follow Husserl when he calls this noematic horizon *a world (Umwelt;* IdI sect. 45). The horizon is more a dynamic principle of constituting life than an order of constituted objects. Rather than being an indefinitely open framework within which things are inserted to receive sense and come to meet us, the horizon is the shape of the present, future, and past data of my actual experience, a particular changing gestalt. With the realization of each potentiality, the entire horizon is modified. Besides lacking the objectivity and permanence proper to the world, the horizon also lacks the possibility of being truly shared. Any world, even the solipsistic world that Husserl introduces for methodological reasons, must lend itself to being shared with other subjects. A horizon cannot be shared since it is nothing else than what leads a particular constituting subject from one experiencing process to the next and, correlatively, from one object to another.

The richest approach to the phenomenon of the world can be found in those sections of the first book of *Ideas* where one discovers, opposed to the objective reality of the natural sciences, a "world of appearance" *(Erscheinungswelt;* IdI sect. 41) or a "world of experience" *(Erfahrungswelt;* sect. 47–48). This proto-*Lebenswelt* is the correlate of the open totality of possible experiences (sect. 45, 47) of an intersubjective community (sect. 48). In one and the same movement phenomenological reduction reveals the a priori conditions of possible experience and the a priori conditions of a possible world, for the reduction reveals their correlation. Nevertheless, the possible world of experience still depends on the possibility of experience. It is this possibility of experience that gives the world its meaning and its reality; it is the experience of the subject that constitutes the world. This possible reality of the constituted world should not be confused with the possible being of a *"res,"* that is, with a particular thing; the being of the world is the being of *any* possible thing. If the being of the possible world thus transcends the possibility of particular things, then one must conclude that the being of the world has a *transcendental* value. The world therefore prepares and welcomes the coming into being and manifestation of things, but this gift and mission of the world is conferred upon it by the *transcendental ego.*

This means that the logos that orders this possible world is essentially subjective. The lines of force that cut across and order the world are understood by Husserl as being *motivational* in nature. The world understood as an order of possible things is still governed by the anticipation of the experiencing subject. This is verified in reading the analyses, found in the second book of *Ideas,* devoted to the constitution of the "spiritual world."[5] It is well known that this description of the spiritual world is preceded in *Ideas II* by an analysis of the constitution of nature, consisting of physical objects and also mental states insofar as those remain conditioned by physical causality. This presentation of the spiritual world as a higher stratum of reality poorly serves Husserl's design, for it suggests that next to the world of spiritual and ideal objects is a world of real or physical objects. This is not the case, however, because for Husserl the collection of objects of nature does not deserve the name *world* and because natural objects are in no way excluded from the spiritual world. Actually, the determination of this spiritual world owes less to the metaphysical division between nature and spirit than it does to the phenomenon of expression which specifically reunites them. The things are not in themselves part of the spiritual world but become so in virtue of the way in which the subject approaches them, a way that Husserl calls the *personalistic attitude*. The spiritual world exists only as the world constituted by a community of persons; it is the communal "environing-world" *(Umwelt)* of their exchanges and interactions. In this world, things are related to each other not by causal links but in virtue of the place that they occupy within the motivational fabric of the life of a person.

The Environing-World

The characterization of this environing-world in *Ideas II* remains unchanged in the later writings of the 1920s and 1930s. The environing-world *(Umwelt)* is a limited world cut off from the more general world. This cutting-off is a function of theoretical, axiological, and practical *interests* of a person or a community of persons. The environing-world is the familiar world where everything I encounter already has a sense for me and for others. It is a "meaningful" *(bedeutsam)* world because "it carries a spiritual meaning in itself," but it is a meaningful world that remains open, in that it is "always susceptible to receiving a new sense of this type" (IdII sect. 51, p. 197). This environing-world owes its meaningfulness to the activity of a community of persons whose interest in things is aimed not only at knowledge but also at the appreciation of their ethical or aesthetic value or at their capacity to serve as means in a process of practical production (IdII sect. 50).

The meaningfulness of things of the world is thus tightly connected with the diverse ways with which the subject approaches them: In knowing and particularly in perception, the things are given as "present-at-hand" *(vorhanden)*. "In acts of evaluation...the object is given...as having a value, as agreeable, beautiful, etc." In "practical acts," the objects are able...to be apprehended as useful [*dienlich*] for serving the satisfaction of this or that need, in virtue of this or that property, and they are then the object of an apprehension as means of subsistence, as useful objects of whatever type: materials for heating, axes, or hammers, etc. For example, I view coal as material for heating, I recognize it and recognize it as useful [*dienlich*] and usable [*dienend*] for heating, as suitable [*geeignet*] and determined to produce heat.

Husserl does not hesitate to emphasize that in this relation of persons to their environing-world, the practical dimension has priority: "In its broadest meaning, we are able to describe the personal attitude...as a practical attitude" (IdII sect. 50). These passages deserve to be cited for their profound resemblance to Heidegger's analyses in *Being and Time* dedicated to the *Vorhandenheit* and *Zuhandenheit* of things of the world.

The analysis of environing-world in *Ideas II* resembles *Being and Time* in another characteristic, namely, that the environing-world envelops both familiar things and the persons occupied with these things. My environing-world contains not only "the real objects that we actually experience" and "all the things that are found [in the world] without my already knowing them but which I will be able to experience," but also "other humans [*Nebenmenschen*], animals, and...the human I denote as...being me, bearing such and such a name, constituted in such and such a way. As a human, I am part of the real environing-world of the pure ego..." (IdII sect. 27, p. 109). If the environing-world as a world of the significance of things is constituted by a pure ego, we should add that this constitution of the world goes together with a "mundanizing" or "enworlding" *(Verwelt-lichung)* of the constituting subject. Or to put it in the rigorous formulation of the *Cartesian Meditations:*

> In that I, as this ego, have constituted and am continually further constituting as a phenomenon (as a correlate) the world that exists for me, I have carried out an apperception of myself as belonging to the world [*verweltlichende Selbstapperzeption*]. This apperception makes of myself an ego in the ordinary sense, that is, a human person [situated] within the totality of the constituted world.[6]

In its ordinary or, as Husserl prefers to call it, "anonymous" life the constituting subject exists-in-the-world. It discovers its power to constitute the world long after having already been constituted as a worldly subject, that is, a "human person." The "enworlding" of itself accomplished by the transcendental ego has always already (anonymously) taken place, and the world the transcendental subject constitutes has always already been there as pregiven.

The description in *Ideas II* of the personalistic approach to the environing-world thus opens for phenomenology the rich domain that Husserl will later call *intentional anthropology,* a domain to which numerous texts in the Husserliana volumes 14 and 15 are devoted. Phenomenological anthropology studies human life in the world and can be called *intentional* because it is through intentional experience and related tendencies and motivations that human beings occupy themselves with things and one another, and also relate themselves to the framework of life common to them all, a framework that can properly be called *life-world (Lebenswelt).* This framework is neither independent of the intentional experiences that take place in it, nor can it be reduced to those experiences. All intentional relations to things and to other persons are mediated by consciousness of this familiar world. In this world, I know how to move in order to reach something far away, or how to behave in order to collaborate with a colleague in view of a common project. Every important occurrence within this familiar world relates itself intentionally to things and persons and yet transcends them in understanding them on the basis of what is already understood in advance (i.e., understood a priori), that is, the world to which they belong. Inner-worldly comportments are thus constitutive in a twofold sense: first, their intentionality brings them to things and persons; second, these comportments' transcendence reveals and shapes *the world.*

As far as the constituting intentionality of inner-worldly comportment is concerned, a distinction should be made between relations to things and relations to persons. Similar to the difference between the intentional relations to inner-worldly entities and the transcending relation to the world itself, this distinction is de jure and not de facto. In fact, a person understanding the things of the world and producing works thus enriches the world, which in turn will affect the sense of its being-with-other-persons. If our relations to worldly things are primarily practical (as Husserl emphasizes from *Ideas II* onward), it follows that being-with-others assumes primarily the form of *interaction.* In the facticity of communal life within the world, this interaction and the feeling of being-with-others *(Miteinandersein)* precedes empathy *(Einfühlung) .* Empathy is thus not at the origin of community but is rather a symptom of decay, the sign of an incomprehension among inner-worldly subjects and the mark of confrontation with strangeness.

In a text from January 10, 1931, which clearly shows traces of his reading of *Being and Time,* Husserl describes this "being-in-connection-with-others" *(In-Konnex-mit-Anderen-Sein)* in the following way: it is a manner of "living in the same world [*Hineinleben*], of being concerned in the same world [*Hineinsorgen*]," "while being constantly with one another [*miteinander*]" in the same world which becomes the world of our interests [*Interessenwelt*], the environing-world of our practical life [*praktische Lebensumwelt*]. In this manner of being, we ourselves (that is, I and the others) belong to the constituted world of objects, and this in a permanent way, whereas at the same time this "we" is subject of the world, a we that experiences the world..., knows the world and acts within the world, all of which leads to an enriching of the objective content of the world. (ZPh 138)

Husserl continues his analysis by pointing out that due to "the historicity of human *Dasein*" this "we" is "a historical community," living in an environing-world which is itself historical (139). This historical environing-world has a sense extending above and below the actual community of "we": the historical environing-world is a part of the historical world which is the world of all human beings, the world of "humanity." Humanity *(Menschheit)* is "a persistent [*verharrend*] reality of a higher order," maintaining itself "throughout the coming and going of persons, throughout the fact that people come into the world at birth [*Hineingeboren-werden*] and leave the world at death [*Heraussterben*]" (139).

The Givenness of the World

The world maintains itself and is maintained through the constitution of inner-worldly objects; and to these objects belong the communal "we" and the political and social institutions that are the incarnations of this "we." Our contribution to the maintaining of the world consists as well in the present enrichment of the world and its transmission to future generations. We shape the world we have received with a view to the future of humanity. If preserving the human world is a task and even a duty (ZPh 143–44), and if the world is a *willed ethos* for which we are responsible, then it should be added that this responsibility concerns the future of a world that has already been handed over or, as Husserl says, pregiven *(vorgegeben)*. If we transcend ourselves in our concern for the world, we do so toward that which, however, gives meaning to our existence. In self-transcendence, we open ourselves to the world, receive it as a legacy and become the temporal guardians of it. Our existence in the world in no way resembles the way in which things are present *(vorhanden)* in the world, nor should the world itself be confounded with a thing that is to be known or possessed. In this way, this openness to the world changes radically our relations to others and to humanity as such. The human community receives a new sense from this common concern for a world which transcends particular interests. This community inscribes itself in an endless chain that runs through the generations of human beings.... Human life, the unity of which is limited by birth and death, is thus traversed by the extension of the life of humanity, the unity of which is... the experience of all people [*allmenschliche Erfahrung*] and the tradition built upon it. Thus, I understand humanity as historical, I grasp how the time of the world [*Weltzeit*] ... surpasses the time of my life [*meine Lebenszeit*] and that of my fellow human beings living at the same present time [*mitgegenwärtig*]. (ZPh 169)

The familiar environing-world that is shared by contemporaries is still not the historical world of all humanity. Nevertheless, the environing-world can still only appear as already pointing to the revelation of the world of humanity. The environing-world, which transcends everything and everyone within it, can reveal itself only to a subject who is itself capable of transcending its occupation with inner-worldly objects belonging to this environing-world. That is, the environing-world appears only to a subject for whom the inner-worldly things have lost their tranquil certainty, their completely self-evident sense *(Selbstverständlichkeit)*. One could say that the environing-world reveals itself to a subject who is on the border of this world—not completely in it but also not totally out of it. We have seen that Husserl gives an existential meaning to this limit-situation of the subject when speaking of the entrance into the world at birth *(Hineingeborenwerden)* and the departure from the world at death *(Heraussterben)*. In birth, the world welcomes the person, the world is given to the person in the form of a gift, which Husserl calls *pregivenness (Vorgegebenheit)*. Throughout one's life, one is generally so avid to take possession of the riches of the world and so desirous of imposing oneself upon those with whom one should share these riches, that in fact one fails to pay attention to this gift of the world. Only in crisis situations, in which the ground seems to be slipping away, does one experience everything that is owed to the world. Nevertheless, one inevitably faces the world at the moment of departure in death, whether this consists in a desperate clinging to the world or in handing over this gift of the world to future generations.

Transcending the Limits of a Familiar World

Birth and death are events in which the secure distance between the familiar and the unknown collapses. This holds, too, for the confrontation with foreign cultures. During a journey in a foreign land, we not only see things of which we are unable to grasp the meaning, we also recognize things that are familiar to us but that clearly have another sense. Here, too, the familiar environing-world—or, as Husserl says, the "home-world" *(Heimwelt)*—reveals itself to a subject who has reached a limit, a point of intersection between a home-world that is one's own and a home-world that is foreign. The home-world is a symbolic system that lets the environing-world appear in its contingency—but also in its necessity; in its singular facticity which nevertheless is not unique; in its arbitrary and yet unavoidable transcendence. In the home-world, relativity has a certain absoluteness: the arbitrary nature of a symbolic order imposes itself in the form of an unconditional law. Husserl also asserts that we can "translate" a foreign environing-world into the idiom of our environing-world, and even that we can come to an understanding of a total and unique world that embraces all particular environing-worlds (ZPh 162). Nevertheless, such a translation will never make the foreign environing-world into a home-world for me; and I will never completely "live" in this universal "all-world" *(Allwelt)* (ZPh 624–25). If it is true that this confrontation with a foreign environing-world does not cause one to leave completely one's home-world, it is equally true that this confrontation is an invitation to take an interest in the more general world, that is, the world of humanity as a whole. The intercultural shock has in common with death the fact that it reveals at the same time both the familiar world *(Umwelt)* of a person (or a community of persons) and the universal world *(Allwelt)* of humanity.

For Husserl, the environing-world and the "all-world" *(Allwelt)* reveal themselves as transcending one's being-in-the-world and yet also as yielding meaning for an understanding of one's own existence-in-the-world. Thus, it can be readily said that for Husserl the transcendent relation to the world is the most profound determinant of the meaning of the being of the individual person. Husserl understands the life of this human being as a constitutive activity. If the world appears as such, and if the sense of the world is to be constituted by human beings, then the world must appear to them *as being constituted* by them. The phenomenologist is thus confronted with the task of describing how and in what type of human comportment the world reveals itself as being constituted. I believe that the numerous analyses that Husserl devoted to normality and abnormality in the apperception of the world are responses to this preoccupation regarding the letting-appear of the world as being constituted.[7] It is surely no mere coincidence that, once again, it is in our relation to the unfamiliar and foreign that the sense of the being of the world reveals itself.

The "abnormals" who interest Husserl are above all the mentally ill, children, and animals. These abnormal subjects belong to the same world as the normal subjects, and they comport themselves as having a certain apperception of this common world. They are thus not merely inner-worldly entities; nevertheless, they appear as abnormal because normal subjects do not comprehend them. Indeed, normal subjects understand neither the way in which the common world reveals itself to these abnormals, nor how these abnormals contribute to the shaping of this common world. Their place in the world is obscure, because, on the one hand, they are recognized as subjects having an apperception of and even participating in the constitution of the common world, yet, on the other hand, the meaning of their participation remains enigmatic. They are not subjects "like me" *(meinesgleichen)* with whom I can agree on the meaning and destiny of the historical world in which we live together. Their incomprehensible contribution to my world has the result that a part of the meaning of this world remains undetermined and unknown to me (ZPh 627). This stretch of strangeness within my familiar world reveals by contrast the world of which I understand the meaning *as* being my world, that is, as a world the sense of which I am able to appropriate in constitution. The experience of the lack of meaning functions as an appeal to meaning. The world of the abnormals, limited and closed in upon itself and thus inaccessible, reveals by contrast the normal world as a world of infinite openness, as a work in progress, as the risky and adventurous quest for meaning. Rather than being the residue of the order of the world, the disorder of abnormality evokes, on the contrary, the active quest and constitution of the ordered world. This constituted world is above all the intelligible world that governs the rational exchanges among human beings.

It is in view of this common rational world that the deviation of abnormal comportments reveals itself. The comportment of a child is said to be abnormal because a child does not yet contribute to the constitution of the rational meaning of the human world. Maturation is precisely the process of appropriation or reconstitution of the meaning of the world, which will make the child into "my equal" *(meinesgleichen)*. The case of animals is different. They are excluded from our rational world, but they constitute their own world according to the species to which they belong. Nonetheless, as the world of certain pets fits advantageously into the human environing-world, Husserl seems to suggest a partial contribution to the constitution of the human world on the part of the animals: "One might object that in the case where animals are considered as relating themselves to the world, to the same as ours, they might sometimes contribute to the constitution [*mitkonstituierend*] of the world as world. When one understands a dog sensing the hunt, the dog as it were teaches us something we did not already know. The dog enlarges the world of our experience" (ZPh 167). This possible comprehension of the animals' contribution to the constitution of my environing-world (which is, to be sure, not yet the rational "all-world" [*Allwelt*] of humanity) depends on a sort of similarity between the animal and the normal human subject. Just as in the case of apperception of a foreign human subject, this similarity primarily concerns the corporeality *(Leiblichkeit)* of the animal (ZPh 625–26).

As far as the "crazy" or "insane" are concerned (that is, *Irrsinnige, Wahnsinnige, Verrückte),* Husserl does not deal with these at any great length. Nevertheless, these cases, as with all cases of behavior related to the unconscious, are particularly interesting. My parapraxes surely contribute to the constitution of my life-world *(Lebenswelt),* even if I do not recognize myself in them. The psychotic delirium, the logic of which remains foreign to me, is however of the same material as my rational apperception of the world and thus contributes to a clarification of the meaning of my world. So we must concede that there are human comportments, the meaning of which I cannot grasp even though they appear to me as participating in the constitution of the human world. The unconscious and delirium thus constitute an improper world, which is nevertheless neither behind, below, nor beside the proper world of rational subjects. This improper world bursts into and blooms in the midst of the proper world. This proper world does not thereby become an improper world but appears as a world shot through with strangeness, as a haunted house, as a mine field. The proper world of rationality is never an established fact. It is precisely this fragility that lends the world its value.

The appearing of the human world, whether it be the familiar home-world of a social group, or the "all-world" of humanity, or the disquieting world of madness, is certainly a phenomenon unlike others. It is hospitable, but its hospitality reveals itself most clearly when we "miss" the world, for example in anxiety or in facing death. The same can be said for the rationality of this world, which reveals itself only when it is threatened. Should we conclude that the appearance of the world is always a dramatic event? Does it unavoidably reveal the profound isolation of a human subject that has been expelled from the secure ground of its familiar surroundings? This seems to be what Heidegger is saying in the period of *Being and Time* when he opposes the phenomenon of the environing-world *(Umwelt)* to the phenomenon of the "world" *(Welt).*

The World of Dasein

The environing-world is for Heidegger the everyday world, which Husserl calls *life-world (Lebenswelt).* In ordinary life, Dasein is submerged in the things of the world, and Dasein's constant preoccupation with these things leaves no occasion for questioning the meaning of this world. Even relations with other human Daseins are inscribed within the framework of these preoccupations and thus amount to mere associations of collaboration. If Dasein were to take notice of the environing-world in the midst of such occupations, it is still only to be assured of the arrangement of things and persons in view of the efficacy of its own future actions. The environing-world is viewed in circumspection *(Umsicht)*. This circumspection is actually an "inspection" by the owner, who assures himself or herself of the presence of everything contained in the familiar world. Among the things of the world is Dasein itself, and other human Daseins. Without confounding things and persons, this concernful circumspection nevertheless embraces them in one single view as beings in the world. Seeing the world and not merely the things *of* the world, Dasein still remains too tied to inner-worldly preoccupations to consider the world as such. To have the world appear as such, one must leave the environing-world or at least transport oneself to its limit.

Being and Time analyzes the leaving of the world that allows the world to appear—or, rather, the worldliness of the world—by means of a phenomenological description of *anxiety:* "The state of anxiety discloses, primordially and directly, the world as world."[8] In anxiety, the familiar environing-world collapses, and the world imposes itself upon Dasein in all its strangeness: "Anxiety . . . brings Dasein back from its fallen absorption in the 'world'. Everyday familiarity collapses. Dasein has been individualized, but individualized *as* Being-in-the-world. Being-in enters into the existential 'mode' of the 'not-at-home' [*Un-zuhause*]. Nothing else is meant by our talk of 'uncanniness' [*Unheimlichkeit*]" (SZ 189; BT 233).

This analysis of anxiety shows us in an exemplary manner the ambiguity of this "leaving the world" through which the world manifests itself as world. First, we see that the world we leave and the world manifested by this leaving are different. This difference is even indicated by the terminology: we leave the environing-world *(Umwelt)* and face the "world" *(Welt)*. Second, the world revealing itself in anxiety concerns only the being of Dasein itself. The exchanges with inner-worldly things or persons are suspended. Dasein's understanding of the environing-world and of the being of entities that Dasein is not, does not count anymore: the world and the being-in-the-world of Dasein itself are "nothing ready to hand [*Nichts von Zuhandenheit*]" (SZ 187; BT 231–32). The world of Dasein owes its phenomenalization to an "annihilation of the world," understood as abolition of the environing-world. Third, the world of Dasein that manifests itself in anxiety isolates Dasein from everything that is different from itself, even other Daseins. The strangeness of this world is a proper form of strangeness and not a foreign strangeness. It is true that Heidegger insists on the gift of the world, on the fact that the world imposes itself upon Dasein in affecting Dasein, that is to say, in the form of "state-of-mind" *(Befindlichkeit)* or the remarkable "mood" *(Stimmung)* that is called *anxiety*. Nevertheless, in the isolation by which Dasein gains access to a proper understanding of its own being, anxiety becomes a type of self-affection. If, rather than constituting the world, Dasein receives the revelation of the world as world, it is still true that it receives this gift of a given world from itself.

This description of the disclosure of the world in *Being and Time* is remarkably similar to the one provided by Husserl. The world reveals itself when its obvious and familiar presence is disrupted and it reveals itself to a subject that has turned away or has been expelled from the world. Heidegger's "anxiety" accomplishes some sort of phenomenological reduction or even an "annihilation of the world."[9] The disclosure of the world is thus dependent upon the self-transcending comportment of the subject, on a theoretical or existential "project." No wonder, then, that for both Husserl and Heidegger the world shows itself as having been "constituted" or at least "shaped" by the subject.[10] Not only does it take a special sort of subjective comportment to let the world reveal itself, but in this revelation it becomes clear also that the meaning of the world depends on the subject. Nevertheless, and despite all these analogies, Husserl and Heidegger fundamentally differ both in the way they understand the world-revealing and the world-shaping comportment of the subject, and in the way they characterize the belonging-together of the subject and the world. These differences made themselves felt as soon as Husserl and Heidegger tried, in 1927, to put in common their conception of phenomenology for the *Encyclopaedia Britannica.*[11]

The Constitution and Gift of the World

For Husserl the possibility of the revelation of the world depends on a particular attitude, on a specific sort of action, on a will and sense of responsibility on the part of the subject. For Heidegger, too, at least in *Being and Time,* the world discloses itself only for an authentically existing subject, but this authentic existence is not a matter of voluntary decision or ethical responsibility. In anxiety, Dasein undergoes the manifestation of the world; it is unexpectedly overwhelmed by it. The appearance of the world stops the busy life of human activities. Emmanuel Levinas's description of insomnia—when, in the darkness of the night and while absolutely nothing happens, one is realizing with fright that "there is" *(il y a)* unceasingly being—is a good illustration for such a passive experience of the world.[12]

But there are certainly other, less dramatic ways in which the world gives itself and in which we receive its gift. Jan Patocka, in his early text entitled *Le monde naturel comme problème philosophique,* has emphasized with particular force that if the revelation of the world requires "movements tending. . . towards the limits," this does not necessarily mean they take the form of anxiety or of an isolation of the subject: The step they accomplish leads, one could say,

> behind everything that exists, in order to find there the possibility of being human in ways other than everyday life; there is thus a change of the world, not of its content. These movements are characterized by the fact that it is impossible [possible?] to establish oneself in them; there is in them a time of rest or rather dwelling, . . . the philosophers in awe, the artist in admiration, others in hatred, some in love.[13]

In love, for example, "it is possible to become for another thrown existence a warm hearth transforming the anxiety of the uninhabitable into a possibility of acceptance. Without acceptance, there is no human existence, for we are not only thrown into reality, but also accepted. . . . "

The human being that is "accepted" by the world receives this world as a gift. It is true that there is no gift without a donation and a donator, no given world without encountering other human persons and their works. But it is also true that works of art, for example, that disclose the world give more than an artist could ever give; the given world has a meaning that goes beyond what was given to it by a person or even by the infinite community of all human beings. As we have seen, Husserl did not remain blind to the phenomenon of a pregiven world. However, this world, which is given to us as having already been there, as receiving or accepting us, is a world with a meaning that other, former subjects have "constituted."[14] In its pre-givenness the world reveals a meaning that was bestowed on it by other subjects, known or unknown, explicitly or anonymously.

Husserl's concept of constitution does not quite allow for a satisfactory phenomenological account of the *transcendence* of the world. Despite the important amendments this concept underwent when Husserl discovered the constitutive function of noematic phenomena, when he investigated the constitution not only of singular objects but also of the world, when he took into account passive and anonymous forms of constitution, Husserl continued to consider "constituting" a *subjective* achievement and the "constituted" its *objective* result. It is true that in his "intentional anthropology" Husserl gave much attention to the being-in-the-world of the human person and thus to forms of comportments where the subject and its world are intimately intertwined. Nevertheless, as we have seen, the constitution of the world belongs to a pure Ego that, while constituting the world, "enworlds" itself to become a human person. The entanglement between the person and its world is a constituted form of entanglement. The constituted world is a world posited by the transcendental subject "in front of" itself. The world thus opposed to the transcendental subject as its correlate is a pregiven world with a meaning the subject can fully appropriate since it is a meaning it has already bestowed on it, anonymously or historically. The subject gives everything to the world and the world gives the subject only what it has received from the subject; the disclosure of the constituted world celebrates and brings into full light the constitutive achievements of the subject. Husserl's notion of constitution thus does not suffice to provide a full understanding of the different forms in which the subject contributes to the manifestation of the world, and it is unable to account for the gift of the world to the subject.

In my opinion, Husserl is most convincing in what he says about the human way to enrich the historical world, to take care of it in view of future generations, to make it more rational. I also think that Husserl is right to say that pointing to the universal world *(Allwelt)* of humanity is a matter of philosophical responsibility. In doing so he successfully resisted the temptation either to sacrifice the plurality of home-worlds *(Heimwelten)* to the unity of the "all-world" or to abandon the rational quest for human equality in favor of a celebration of cultural relativism. Husserl's "all-world" should, of course, be understood as the philosophical telos of humanity and not as the realization of a world market indistinctly governed by one-dimensional technological rationality in all the countries of the world. Making everyone a "citizen of the world" in no way implies making uniform the different styles and contexts of human life. For Husserl, the most valuable contribution philosophy can make to the common work of the constitution of the world is to guide the march of history toward its telos of a world that would be fully rational. Still, there exist other ways of participating in the constitution of the world by modifying, enriching, preserving, enlarging, and improving its meaning. These various modes of the constitution of the world might all go together with a feeling of satisfaction or gratitude for what humanity in its historical development has achieved. Should we then conclude that whatever is revealed in the disclosure of the world reveals itself in the form of a meaning constituted by us? In the event that the world effectively discloses itself in such a manner, is that enough to affirm that we then can totally appropriate its meaning to ourselves? Is every meaning of the world a meaning constituted by us, and is every constituted meaning the result of a deliberate action that lends itself to being "reactivated" with perfect fidelity? Is the meaning of the world always a human meaning, and is the human meaning of the world open to a totally comprehensive "reprise"?

The World and the Subject

The world that reveals itself in birth and death, in anxiety, insomnia, religious devotion, artistic admiration, in hatred and love is much more than a "human-made" world. It can, and often does, appear as both inhuman and unmade. Not that this world would not concern us as human beings or that we could not do anything about it, but it is more than we can achieve and it is less familiar than what we know. The human shaping of the world is preceded and guided by a disclosure of the world that reveals the essential limits of all human endeavor. Rather than revealing itself as a human achievement, the world reveals that human existence is interwoven with the blank pages of what is inhuman. Human beings receive the revelation of their transcendence from the world rather than—through the effectuation of a phenomenological reduction—actively bringing the world to show itself.

The disclosure of the world interrupts the identification of human beings with their familiar surroundings. The world reveals that, considered as subjects, human beings do not belong (in-)to the world. This is, of course, not to say that the subjects, to which the world is disclosing itself, exist outside or independently of the world. The appearing of the world rather shows both: the essential belonging-together of the subject and the world and their essential difference. The belonging-together of the subject and the world is a form of entanglement that reveals a difference, a form of interdependence that excludes reciprocity. The appearing world shows itself as being strange and inhuman and at the same time as being in need of humanization and appropriation by the subject. The subject, in its turn, discovers that although its entire life takes place in the world, it is itself not a worldly being, and that although it is different from the world, it is also in charge of the world. Its shaping of the world contributes to the revelation of the otherness of the world, and caring about this foreign world is the proper meaning of the life of a human subject.

2 A Critique of Husserl's Notion of Crisis

R. PHILIP BUCKLEY

One reason given by Martin Heidegger at the outset of *Being and Time* for launching the project of fundamental ontology is the observation that although everybody uses the word *being* and seems to grasp the meaning of this word, there is in fact no proper understanding of being.[1] For Heidegger, self-evidence often masks unintelligibility, and a so-called common understanding is often a sign of a lack of understanding. Could not something similar be said of the word *crisis?* To be sure, one can hardly avoid the word these days. Not only does it abound in periodicals and newspapers (as Umberto Eco has remarked, "crisis sells well");[2] but also in the learned journals of medicine, political science, economics, art, law, literature, and philosophy, barely an edition appears without discussion of a crisis of one sort or another. One is tempted to be suspicious, to laugh at the apparent collective malaise of academics, and to surmise that many of the crises addressed are rather remote. Or perhaps we might begin to wonder whether what we have here is a crisis of the word *crisis.* On the other hand, as afflicted academics (for what institution is more in crisis than the university?), we might want to look carefully at the word *crisis* and what it entails. Are there really crises in all the aforementioned regions? If so, how are these regional crises related to one another? Is there one fundamental crisis that somehow underlies all these separate crises? And if so, why should we not view these crises (both the regional and the universal) as positive—as a normal phase in the development of each field and of humanity as a whole? This chapter proposes no definitive answers to these far-reaching questions. The hope is merely that by reflecting on some underemphasized aspects of Husserl's and Heidegger's thought regarding crisis, we will better be able to see certain presuppositions still at work in many uses of the word—and in doing so clarify our common under-standing.

23

Edmund Husserl makes very clear in his *The Crisis of European Sciences and Transcendental Phenomenology* that a proper understanding of the present-day crisis demands historical understanding and calls for the "questioning-back" *(Rückfrage)* into the origin of the sciences which are now in such a precarious state.[3] Similarly, I believe that an understanding of Husserl's mature notion of crisis calls for a clear comprehension of the entire development of Husserl's thought. In this first part of the chapter I claim that the elements of Husserl's crisis-thought were already present in his earlier works. This emphasis goes somewhat against a common tendency to view the *Crisis* text as a new beginning. Even when proponents of this view admit that the goal of the *Crisis* text remains the establishment of transcendental phenomenology as universal science, they like to emphasize its novel tone, expressed by such concepts as life-world or historical questioning. In fact, Husserl's concern for history can be traced in manuscripts back to at least 1910[4] and gains explicit form in his articulation of genetic phenomenology in the 1920s. And certainly a primordial notion of life-world is at work in *Ideen II*.[5] However, the notion of crisis itself goes back even further. Let us briefly trace the growth and broadening of this notion, and let us do so by first isolating the major components of Husserl's mature concept of crisis and then suggesting some possible roots for these components in his earlier thought.

In the *Crisis* text itself are three identifiable and related crises: the crisis of science, understood as the *Natur- und Geisteswissenschaften* (natural and human sciences); a crisis of philosophy; and a crisis of culture in general. As far as the crisis of the *Natur- und Geisteswissenschaften* is concerned, we can once again identify three aspects or types of subcrisis. First is the notion that both the natural sciences and the human sciences contain a certain lack of self-understanding, that scientists in these fields cannot account for their own activity, that they in fact do not know why they do what they do. Despite the ever-growing efficiency of the sciences in gathering and manipulating facts, there is also an ever-growing incomprehension about what underlies it all. The incomprehension of science about its own roots, its own origin, was given expression in the debates regarding the theoretical foundations of each science. But for Husserl, these debates about foundation were merely symptomatic of the loss of the ultimate foundation for science, namely, its origin in human *subjectivity*. The natural sciences, in their worship of objective facts and numbers, are particularly guilty of ignoring the subjectivity from which the original project arose. The human sciences, insofar as the object of their inquiry *is* the human subject, appear at first less guilty of this oversight. However, here too there is no proper articulation of the subject which lies at the origin of the inquiry, and since the very task of the *Geisteswissenschaften* is precisely to move toward such an articulation, they are in fact more culpable than the natural sciences, even more stigmatized by a lack of self-comprehension. Not understanding their origin in human subjectivity, the natural sciences at least still function very well indeed; they can still achieve their results. But since the very aim of the *Geisteswissenschaften* is to understand the human subject, their fundamental misunderstanding of human subjectivity dooms their entire project.

The second aspect of crisis in the natural sciences and the human sciences is their disintegrated, disjointed, or disunified nature. Husserl had already pointed out this fact as a motive for launching the project we find in *Formal and Transcendental Logic* (1929).[6] This disunity has various manifestations: the isolation of one branch of a particular science from other branches in the same science, or more broadly the isolation of one of the natural sciences from another. One does not have to stay very long in a modern hospital to experience the truth of this description. If anything, the need for specialization pushes sciences ever more in the direction of disintegration. Even more perturbing for Husserl was the growing distance between the natural sciences and the human sciences. And most upsetting of all was the disintegration of the relationship of all the sciences to philosophy. Disintegration goes completely against the original aim of science, which was precisely to produce a unified world view, to understand things in their relatedness to each other and to us.

The third aspect of the crisis of the sciences is the loss of their meaning for human life. This is certainly related to the positivistic tendency of the sciences to resign themselves to the knowledge and manipulation of brute facts without ever raising questions of value and meaning. Ever more content to live in its world of abstractions and ideal objects, science becomes ever more oblivious to the actual world of human life. More and more historical facts are accumulated, but the meaning of history remains unquestioned; human life is prolonged, but the purpose of life is left undiscussed. We are all supposed to be very happy that the space shuttle is flying again, but what does it really mean for us, what is the relation of this paradigm of technological achievement to the fundamental yearnings of human beings, and what are the values at work here that lead a nation to sacrifice so much of its resources for this achievement? Science seems as incapable today as it was in Husserl's time of dealing with these questions.

These three aspects of the crisis of the sciences show that Husserl is not using the word in a vague manner. In its original meaning of "decision," *crisis* is in fact related to an act of splitting, dividing, cutting off. The sciences are cut off from their own foundation in subjectivity, they are cut off from each other, and they are cut off from the questions about meaning that humans seem to persist in asking. These three aspects of the crisis in the *Natur- und Geisteswissenschaften* are also all related to a crisis in philosophy. For it had always been central to the project of philosophy to deal with the problem of foundation, to provide in fact a unifying base for the diverse sciences, and to pose the fundamental human questions regarding value and the meaning of life. For Husserl, the apparent lack of success of philosophy in fulfilling these original tasks was rooted in a lack of confidence, in its self-doubt about its primary tool—reason. Philosophy, unsure of its own foundation, was hardly in a position to go about repairing the foundations in the other sciences. Philosophy, with its diverse schools, varying methodologies, warring factions, hardly seemed a good candidate to produce unity in the sciences. Philosophy, uncertain of its most important tool, could hardly approach with much confidence the basic questions about the meaning of life.

The guilt experienced by philosophy in such a crisis state is compounded for Husserl by the fact that the ultimate result of philosophy's failure regarding its original projects is a crisis in culture at large. Given the situation of philosophy today, we may smile a little bit at the naïve presumptuousness of this aspect of the crisis. But of course Husserl is heir to a tradition in which philosophers and philosophies played dominant cultural roles. Moreover, since Husserl conceives of culture as a willed, rational enterprise, the doubt of philosophy about reason and hence the refusal of philosophy to engage in the struggle against *Schicksal* (fate) leads to a malaise in civilization and a negation of its telos. I will return to this later, for although it may seem a little farfetched to us today that philosophy could possibly be responsible for culture as a whole, it is interesting to note how the various crises I have already mentioned (and to which philosophy does have something to say) are in fact linked to larger cultural problems.

But first I will connect the various elements I have mentioned to specific aspects of Husserl's early work and in doing so indicate how the *Crisis* text is really a summary of Husserl's life of philosophizing. The first aspect of the crisis of the *Natur- und Geisteswissenschaften* that I mentioned was that of *foundation;* theoretical foundation of each science and ultimate foundation of all science in subjectivity. On more than one occasion, Husserl reflected on how his early interest in foundational questions in mathematics was determinant of his entire *Denkweg*. In a manuscript from 1930, Husserl points out the influence of Carl Weierstrass on the form and content of what was to become his life work.[7] Weierstrass's desire for a radical grounding of mathematical analysis *(eine radikale Begründung der Mathematik)* in a rigorous development of the real number system set the tone for what Husserl described as the *Ethos* of his scientific work.[8] A similar desire fueled Husserl's dream of a rigorously developed philosophical system based on secure foundations, even though his efforts to establish such a system in the 1920s and 1930s ended in failure. And in almost all of Husserl's discussions of foundation, the model provided by the debate about the foundation of mathematics was never far away.

However, in the *Philosophie der Arithmetik* (1891),[9] the question of a foundation of this particular science is in fact already linked to subjectivity. This is perhaps best elucidated by referring to Frege. Whereas Frege begins with the *objective,* one could say that Husserl was interested in the epistemic limits of our mathematical knowledge, that is to say, in a certain sense, in what our mathematical knowledge is like. Frege's approach can loosely be termed *realist,* as his interest is in the question regarding the real existence and nature of numbers. Husserl, on the other hand, is anti-realist, his interest going more toward the direct, intuitive experience of numbers. For Husserl, numbers arise out of our experience of groups and aggregates, but groups and aggregates are, as Robert Sokolowski points out, "concrete phenomena whose existence and structure are a result of subjective mental activity."[10] It may be true, as Theodorus de Boer claims,[11] that Sokolowski is too much under the spell of Husserl's own self-interpretation found in *Formal and Transcendental Logic*[12] and hence too willing to see the role of constituting consciousness in the *Philosophie der Arithmetik.* But it is also clear that for the early Husserl the problem of foundation and origin was linked to an origin in subjectivity. Naturally, insofar as this subjectivity was not clearly outlined, the threat of psychologism remained. Only with the identification of *intentionality* as the defining feature of subjectivity and the adoption of the method of phenomenological reduction could a non-psychological, that is, a properly philosophical, approach to subjective mental processes be assured.

It is easy to move in Husserl's early thought from the problem of foundation to the second aspect of the crisis of the sciences, that is, their lack of unity. For it is precisely the lack of self-comprehension regarding their subjective origin that allows the sciences to take their separate paths; moreover, this lack of proper self-understanding opens a space for the hubris of the sciences, and it yields an opportunity for a particular branch of the sciences to present itself as the actual foundation upon which the other sciences should be built or as a model to be imitated. From this hubris comes Husserl's closet of horrors—objectivism, psychologism, naturalism, positivism, historicism, relativism. Philosophy is responsible for straightening out this mess, but, as Husserl points out in "Philosophie als strenge Wissenschaft," philosophy itself is at present not in a state to do so, not merely because it is an "imperfect science," but because it is not yet a science at all.[13] Until philosophy solves its own crisis of foundation, it cannot, according to Husserl, cope with the foundational problems of the other sciences and help them to see the proper scope of their own activity and their proper relation to various other sciences.

All of this is not merely programmatic on Husserl's part. In texts such as *Ideen II* Husserl's analysis of the objects dealt with by the *Natur- und*

Geisteswissenschaften goes some way toward outlining the specificity of each realm of objects. At the same time, in the phenomenological description of the body as either *Leib* or *Körper* we see how these regions meet. In making these clear distinctions, distinctions rooted in the constitutional activity of subjectivity (and intersubjectivity!), much of the disunified state of the sciences can be overcome.

The lack of meaning for ordinary human life was the third characteristic of the crisis of the sciences. Herbert Spiegelberg suggests that the concern for values and meaning came somewhat late to Husserl, a result of the traumatic experience of the First World War.[14] I agree wholeheartedly with the emphasis placed on this event, and I will return to this shortly. But Husserl's *Vorlesungen über Ethik und Wertlehre (1908–1914)*, which has recently appeared as numer 28 in the Husserliana series, shows clearly Husserl's earlier concern with the relation between intellective acts (which are objectifying acts), on the one hand, and the non-objectifying acts of feeling and volition *(Gefühls- und Willensakte)*, on the other. Husserl is interested in the types of reason associated with these various acts and, in fact, in finding a middle ground between a solely intellectualistic theory of reason, which views the emotional and practical act spheres merely as realms of applied logical reason *(logische Vernunft)*, and an emotive theory, which considers the logical reasoning of intellective acts to be based in a valuating sort of reason *(fühlend-wertende Vernunft)*.[15] For Husserl, each of the fields approached by these theories has in fact its *own* type of reason and thus constitutes a separate discipline, so that besides formal logic, there are the disciplines of formal axiology and study of the various forms of praxis *(formale Praktik)*. What is important to note is that Husserl emphasizes the tendency in the tradition of philosophy to reduce the reason associated with acts of valuation and will to the logical reason attached to intellective acts *(die Allherrschaft der logischen Vernunft)*. But is this not already a foreshadowing of the crisis-problematic? The crisis and all its negative aspects come about because of a dominance or mis-application of one sort of reason. The world of *Geist* cannot be treated in the same way as the world of *Natur;* and central to the world of *Geist* are questions of value. These questions are suppressed when the realm of logical thinking or the world of the natural sciences is seen as the only world. Of course, insofar as Husserl's approach to the world of non-objectifying acts remains that of analogy to the realm of objectifying acts (that is, the method in these lectures is to outline the parallel structure of *Wahrnehmung und Wertnehmung* [perceiving and valuing]), one can raise the question as to how much Husserl himself remained under the spell of purely *logische Vernunft*.[16]

The interest in identifying the specificity of feeling-acts of valuation and volitional acts is perhaps not that surprising in Husserl. For indeed, a case can be made that, despite the titles of his works, Husserl's ultimate concerns are not about logic, but about ethics. Like Kant, the epistemological and logical questions occur in the first place; but this is only to pave the way for the questions about who we are, or better, who we ought to be. In tracing these elements of crisis through Husserl's thought, I am suggesting that one never has to dig very far beneath the surface to arrive at ethics. For Husserl, striving for a rational life is an ethical act. To be sure, not knowing the truth is a sign of the crisis; but perhaps the ultimate gravity of the crisis is shown in the despair of ever knowing the truth, in abandoning the search. This ethical imperative of striving for rationality, this responsibility of the individual to become more rational and hence more authentically human and in doing so to contribute to making the world more rational and more human—this theme runs through Husserl's thought from beginning to end. It is perhaps the link between logic and ethics that gives Husserl's thought its (sometimes unbearable) seriousness. When logical problems are viewed merely as puzzles to be solved, then debates in logic can seem trivial indeed. But when the proper functioning of rationality is not only the humanizing goal of every individual but also determinant of culture as a whole, then the improper functioning of rationality is indeed a crisis situation.

Philosophy's responsibility regarding culture as a whole had already been clearly stated in "Philosophie als strenge Wissenschaft," where Husserl says that his argumentation is "based on the conviction that the highest interests of human culture demand the development of a rigorous scientific philosophy."[17] The problems of foundation of unity, the inability of science to deal with questions of meaning—these aspects of the crisis have widespread social and cultural ramifications. Nothing indicated this more clearly for Husserl than the First World War and its aftermath. The division between technological science and its origin in human subjectivity is never more evident than when technology leads to the massive destruction of human subjects.

The ensuing political, economic, and social crises of Weimar Germany touched every aspect of life, even the lives of professors of philosophy in provincial Freiburg. As Husserl writes in a letter to Winthrop Bell on December 13, 1922, he is very happy to be a millionaire, but given the fact that the 1.5 million (marks) per year that he was earning actually amounted to 1/10 of his previous salary, the situation was not exactly rosy. Even more depressing, he admits that he wrote the *Kaizo* article, "Erneuerung," for money![18] This same article begins by explicitly claiming that the present "sorrowful" age is simply a more refined continuation of the devastation of the war. But in a rather pointed reference to Spengler, Husserl claims that we need not sit passively by in this crisis situation, nor does he accept the claim that decline is the inevitable fate of the West. Indeed, for Husserl, if the West is to stay human at all, it must continue in the struggle for the ethical ideal of a rational life. No matter how unobtainable this ideal may seem, it is precisely in the striving for the ideal that one reaches the level of true humanity. This brief essay, which charts the route that this struggle should take, in fact outlines completely the *Crisis* text. Indeed, as schematic as the *Kaizo* articles may be,[19] they indicate clearly that all of the elements of Husserl's crisis-philosophy were well in place by the early 1920s.

At the very least, the recognition of these constant elements of Husserl's crisis-thought points out the rather unsound nature of the lingering myth that Husserl's *Crisis* text was somehow a response to his experience of reading *Sein und Zeit* in the summer of 1929. If anything at all, reading Heidegger showed Husserl how deep the crisis was, penetrating even into what he refers to in a footnote found in the *Crisis* text as "the so-called phenomenological schools."[20] In this same footnote, which clearly implicates Heidegger and Scheler, Husserl identifies the basic error of these thinkers, namely, their persistence in remaining within the old, naïve, natural attitude. In rejecting the transcendental reduction, these thinkers were, in Husserl's eyes, rejecting the only possible solution to the crisis and, in fact, making the crisis worse. If anything, reading Heidegger only spurred Husserl on in his own direction and hardened him in his rejection of what he calls, in a letter to Roman Ingarden, "the fashionable turn to a philosophy of *'Existenz'* and the surrendering of the ideal of philosophy as a rigorous science."[21]

Far more remarkable than any influence Heidegger might have had on Husserl is the similarity between Heidegger's description of the crisis and that of Husserl. Given such similar descriptions, the radical difference in their solutions to the crisis becomes even more worthy of attention. Some of Heidegger's most explicit comments on the crisis occur in the first paragraph of the lecture course from the summer semester of 1925 entitled *History of the Concept of Time: Prolegomena.* In introducing the subject matter of the course as nature and history, Heidegger points out that we are reminded immediately of "the domains of objects which are investigated by the two main groups of empirical sciences," namely, the *Natur- und Geisteswissenschaften.* But this does not mean for Heidegger that we should be limited by the way in which a science deals with a subject matter. First, Heidegger is suspicious that the way in which a science deals with its subject matter might not actually give us that subject matter in its originality. The aim of phenomenology is to get at the things themselves, and this means gaining access to these realms in the way they are given to us *prior* to the sciences. And Heidegger already speculates that the "separation of the two domains may well indicate that an original and undivided context of subject matter remains hidden."[22]

The second reason Heidegger gives for not treating these domains in the same fashion as the sciences treat them is precisely because these sciences are in crisis.[23] The two aspects of the crisis are, first, the sense of alienation that people have from the sciences and, second, the internal relation of a particular science to its subject matter. In short, a crisis of meaning and a crisis of foundation. The examples that Heidegger gives for the problem of a science seeking its foundation and hence a more secure approach to its own subject matter are mathematics, physics, biology, history, and theology. These examples are repeated almost verbatim in the third paragraph of *Being and Time*.[24] But all is not lost! The crisis of the empirical sciences reveals the need for a priori science, for more originary investigation, in fact, for phenomenological philosophy. This, too, is not so different from Husserl, for whom the crisis also seems to have had a certain inevitability rooted in the history of reason; but this inevitable occurrence is redeemed by the philosophy for which the occurrence itself had set the stage.

Thus, in Heidegger's account, which stresses the positive nature of the crisis (that is, the fact that it makes clear the need for phenomenological philosophy), we have a summary of the three aspects of the crisis of the sciences that were constant in Husserl's thought: disintegration, in this case a disunity that perhaps hides a primordial unity; the lack of meaning of the sciences; and the problem of foundation. It is interesting to note that a case could be made (and I believe I have already hinted at this with my comments on ethics) that for Husserl the most important of these aspects was the lack of the sciences' meaning for ordinary human life, the dissonance between the shape that the scientific project had assumed and what he calls "the vital need" of humanity.[25] Heidegger, however, mentions this "existential" aspect of the crisis only in a passing reference to Weber; he clearly identifies the problem of foundation as the most important or revelatory: "The real crisis is internal to the sciences themselves, wherein their basic relationship to the subject matter which each of them investigates has become questionable. The basic relationship to the subject matters is becoming insecure."[26] One can easily guess why Heidegger attaches such importance to this aspect. It gives him the opportunity to talk about philosophy's relation to its subject matter, which is neither an object nor a realm of objects but being itself. The solution to the crisis can only be achieved when we uncover this original ontological realm, which is prior to such ontic distinctions as nature and history. The fact that all philosophy (or the "science of Being,"[27] as it is called in the *Basic Problems of Phenomenology*) is enunciated here in the context of the problem of foundation, is suggestive of the early Heidegger's conception of the project of fundamental ontology as foundational. Indeed, as a response to a crisis situation, it really is not so different from the form of Husserl's foundational project. Nevertheless, it is a different sort of approach to foundation, a different sort of cure for the crisis than Husserl had foreseen. Heidegger's critique of Husserl's approach to the crisis, which they both see, is that the attempt to overcome objectivism by a turn to subjectivity is doomed to failure, for rather than letting appear the primordial realm which is given before the distinctions and abstractions of the sciences, the turn to subjectivity actually comes down rather decidedly on one side of a distinction. In doing so, rather than helping to overcome all of the separations that are aspects of the crisis, it remains entangled in these separations.

In the early Heidegger we therefore have an agreement with Husserl's description of the crisis, and also agreement that the separations involved in the crisis must be overcome by seeking a more primordial ground, but disagreement over how to reach this goal. Very shortly after *Being and Time,* however, a Heideggerian critique of Husserl's crisis-philosophy can be formulated much more sharply and in a far more encompassing manner. For example, in the lectures from winter semester, 1929-30, Heidegger is critical of the philosophical attempt to "diagnose" the crisis.[28] In a certain sense, the positive view that Heidegger had held of the crisis begins to dissolve: the crisis becomes far less felicitous. As Heidegger says in 1935: "The spiritual decline of the earth is so far advanced that the nations are in danger of losing the last bit of spiritual energy that makes it possible to see the decline (taken in relation to the history of 'being') and to appraise it as such."[29] The crisis appears now to be much more a burden than a possibility. This shift tells us something both obvious and important: crisis-philosophy, that is, philosophy's attempt both to describe and to cure a crisis, arises only when one believes that there is a cure—or at least that it is not too late to start searching for one. This in turn tells us something rather startling about Husserl's phenomenology. For if we accept the fact that Husserl's thought is a sort of crisis-philosophy from beginning to end, and that at the same time crisis-philosophy always implies a prescribed cure, then we must conclude that for Husserl there was never such a thing as purely descriptive phenomenology, but that there were always traces of prescription in his thinking. On the other hand, crisis-philosophy, which works on the presupposition of finding a cure, seems to be no longer present in the postwar Heidegger. The movement by Heidegger away from what we have termed *crisis-philosophy* is undoubtedly linked to the *Kehre,* to the inner dynamic of Heidegger's lifelong effort "to think Being." One could also suspect external factors, namely, the experience of the war and of National Socialism. It is clear to see that the language of crisis-philosophy, which is the language of renewal, rebirth, regeneration, unity, can be easily confused with certain aspects of the language and pseudo-philosophy of National Socialism.

This denial of crisis-philosophy by Heidegger is the acknowledgment that, as he says in the *Der Spiegel* interview, "in the realm of thought there are no authoritative statements."[30] This is not to say that the crises suddenly disappear, nor that philosophy no longer has anything to say about them. Husserl's in-depth analysis of the modern crisis of the sciences is as valid today as it was fifty years ago. In the same *Der Spiegel* interview, Heidegger is certainly able to comment negatively on the smooth functioning of technology, which leads to ever more functioning, without ever gaining a touch of self-comprehension.[31] The movement away from crisis-philosophy does say, however, that philosophy can never fully overturn the crisis brought about by the lack of self-comprehension.

Philosophy is thus for the later Heidegger not in the business of crisis management. It is in the business of trying to think of the crisis nonauthoritatively, of interrogating the genesis of crises, of criticizing the language in which crisis-discussions take place. Crisis-philosophy gives way to philosophy as critique. In critiquing the crisis, that is, in examining its structures and limits without ever pretending to master it, philosophy itself may perhaps escape from the hubris that gives rise to so many crisis situations.

3 The Myth of Absolute Consciousness

J. CLAUDE EVANS

From Aristotle through Augustine to Descartes, Kant, and Brentano, one of the essential marks of consciousness has been its intrinsic reflexivity or self-awareness. In Descartes and Brentano such immediate self-awareness is explicitly distinguished from a reflective thematization or objectivation, and for this reason Aron Gurwitsch studied it under the very appropriate rubric of *marginal consciousness*.[1] Edmund Husserl was one of the very few philosophers not only to identify this phenomenon but also to offer an analysis of it. The key to his approach is the insight that self-awareness is essentially bound up with time consciousness. To take a simple example, if I see something happening, Husserl would distinguish three different levels of constitution:

1. "The things of experience in Objective time," that is, the event in objective space and time.

2. What Husserl calls "the constituting multiplicities of appearances of different levels, the immanent unities in pre-empirical time," that is, my intentional act of perceiving, including the sensations that function in this perception.

3. "The absolute, temporally constituting flow of consciousness":[2] this is the level of absolute consciousness, the level at which the perceptual acts of level 2 are experienced or lived through, the level of the awareness of those acts, a level that can and must be structurally distinguished from the level of immanent acts.

It took Husserl many years of work to discover the phenomenon of absolute consciousness and develop his account of it. Similarly, its

35

reception and acceptance by phenomenologists has been very slow. But since the early work of Thomas Seebohm and John Brough's study of the emergence of absolute consciousness in Husserl's early writings, Husserl's account of absolute consciousness has been studied, accepted, and developed further. Robert Sokolowski has played a prominent role in the more recent episodes of this rather dramatic story.[3]

I want to put this entire success story in question. I shall try to explain why Husserl thought he had discovered the phenomenon of absolute consciousness and why he was wrong to think that he had made such a discovery. I shall argue that many of Husserl's fascinating and subtle analyses of time consciousness are governed by a presupposition that systematically distorts them and thus produces what he took to be the "discovery" of absolute consciousness. Absolute consciousness is a myth— a very subtle, coherent, and seemingly compelling myth, but a myth nonetheless.

Husserl's early investigations of time consciousness were concerned primarily with the perception of succession, and this led to the development of the revolutionary analyses of retention and protention. But already at a very early stage of his work on time consciousness, for example in the lectures on time consciousness of 1905, Husserl's attention was focused not on the perception of objective succession but rather on succession in "the immanent time of the flow of consciousness" (ZPZ 5/ PhT 23). The reason for this focus is to be found in what Husserl would later, with reference to the *Logical Investigations,* call a *one-sided focus on the noetic.* In line with this early conception of phenomenology as the study of the immanent phenomenological data of consciousness, the "exclusion [*Ausschaltung*] of objective time" announced in section 1 of the Lectures of 1905 is not a phenomenological or transcendental reduction, but rather an "abstraction"—as opposed to a bracketing—"of all transcending interpretation," an abstraction that reduces "perceptual appearances to the given primary contents" (ZPZ 5/ PhT 24; translation altered). Thus, Husserl's phenomenology of time consciousness took as one of its primary tasks the description of the experiencing or consciousness of primary, immanent contents or sensations.[4] The phenomenology of time consciousness becomes primarily the phenomenology of *inner* time consciousness.

Now, in the *Logical Investigations* Husserl did discuss the experiencing or living through *(erleben)* of immanent contents, denying a distinction between sens*ing* and sens*ed* for sensation: "There is no difference between the experienced or conscious content and the experience itself. What is sensed is, e.g., no different from the sensation [i.e., the sens*ing*]."[5] Looking back at the *Investigations,* Husserl had to admit that the earlier analyses remained naïve in the sense of taking certain phenomena for granted. Since in the *Investigations* he "moved *within* the frame of inner consciousness," that is, took the temporality of immanent contents for granted, he found no sens*ing*, only sens*ed* contents.[6] But the temporality of the contents must itself be investigated as a phenomenon, and when this is done, Husserl's understanding of sensations severely limits what he can offer as a descriptive account.

In Husserl's account, sensations, or what he called *hyletic data,* are *non-intentional* immanent components of consciousness. Since they are non-intentional, there is no possibility of accounting for their phenomenal temporality simply by referring to their status as sensed contents. Husserl has to investigate not just the "living through" of sensations but the consciousness of sensations. Since (and this is Husserl's crucial presupposition) we are aware of sensations as moments of the stream of consciousness, there must be a sens*ing*, an immanent perception or inner consciousness: "Every lived experience [*Erlebnis*] is 'sensed,' is immanently 'perceived' (inner consciousness)" (ZPZ 126/PhT 175). This account would hold generally for every lived experience, be it an act of perception, remembering, or imagining, or a sensible content: to experience that act is to have an inner consciousness of it (see also ZPZ 127/PhT 176). What Husserl here calls *inner consciousness* and even immanent perception would be the level of the absolute, time-constituting flow of consciousness (ZPZ 73/PhT 98).

Now, I want to suggest that, given Husserl's conception of sensations as non-intentional, really immanent parts of consciousness, the descriptive account of absolute consciousness would be absolutely convincing. When I look at an object, my experience would include non-intentional, really immanent *(reell)* visual sensations. Since I would be *conscious* of these non-intentional contents, when I reflect phenomenologically on this experience I would seem to find an absolute flow of inner consciousness which must be distinguished from the sensed contents it makes present.

Thomas Seebohm argues that the choice of an immanent hyletic datum as the guiding thread for the analysis of time consciousness is arbitrary. Seebohm notes that Husserl himself later criticized the focus on hyletic data, that is, on an abstract moment of the primordial flow of consciousness,[7] but Seebohm argues that this objection does not overturn the general validity of the analyses themselves, since Husserl could just as well have used acts or the ego-pole—both of which also belong to the unity of immanent temporality—as his point of departure. The point of the "Lectures," Seebohm notes, is not to analyze hyletic data but rather to analyze the appearing temporal duration itself.[8] I want to suggest that, on the contrary, it is the doctrine of immanent hyletic data that leads Husserl to *postulate,* not discover, an absolute consciousness of intentional acts and that his often very subtle descriptions are of necessity formed by this postulate. What seemed to be a discovery is a myth, a construction in the guise of pure description.

Now, if I am right that the assumed presence of non-intentional immanent components of consciousness leads us to "find" absolute consciousness, there is in fact an alternative to this "discovery": we can follow Jean-Paul Sartre and Aron Gurwitsch in rejecting what Gurwitsch calls Husserl's "dualistic" theory of perception, which accounts for perception in terms of (i) the intentional animation of (ii) non-intentional contents. (In spite of Husserl's progressive critique of various applications of the schema, "content of apprehension-apprehension [*Auffassungsinhalt-Auffassung*]" [ZPZ 7/PhT 25], he never abandoned it in his analysis of perceptual consciousness of the world.) The arguments involved here are familiar and I do not want to cover well-known ground by rehearsing them here.[9] Instead I shall restrict myself to pointing out some of the consequences of such a rejection.

If immanent hyletic data are rejected, we still face the problem of describing the manner in which consciousness is present to itself. Husserl had quite a bit of difficulty with his account here, since his model for absolute consciousness was perceptual consciousness, absolute consciousness being initially specified as immanent perception (ZPZ 126/PhT 175), but he realized very early that this absolute consciousness or experience is not really consciousness of an object and thus is not really perception.[10] However, the specification of a distinct level of absolute consciousness as the explication of what it means to live through *(erleben)* an act continues to bear the mark of its origin in the perceptual model. In addition, the flow of absolute consciousness would itself have to be lived through, experienced, but we cannot analyze the sense of being experienced by regressing to a new level of consciousness, in which this level would be experienced (a possibility Husserl did consider, as we shall see), without the danger of falling into an infinite regress. Thus Husserl must show that "the absolute flow of consciousness constitutes its own unity" (ZPZ 378), and that "the self-appearance of the flow does not require a second flow; it constitutes itself as phenomenon in itself" (ZPZ 83/PhT 109). In other words, on Husserl's account, absolute consciousness is the locus of a radical *self-constitution:* the absolute flow must *appear* as a flow in and to itself.

Now, if we accept Husserl's concept of immanent hyletic data, his analysis of absolute time-constituting and self-constituting consciousness seems convincing. But I want to argue that if we reject hyletic data, we have to ask why the self-constituting functions of consciousness are attributed to absolute consciousness rather than to the stream of intentional consciousness of the world. Two things are noteworthy here. In the first place, the fact that consciousness is essentially consciousness of the *world* often seems to be forgotten in Husserl's concentration on the constitution of hyletic data in absolute consciousness. One might reply that this appearance is misleading, since hyletic data are only a dependent part, a moment, of a larger intentional whole. But there are a number of texts that suggest that Husserl held the view that, as Sokolowski puts it, "sheer sensation can exist as a concrete state of consciousness" (HM 127n).

Second, once we have become aware of what Husserl calls the *double intentionality of retention*—double in the sense that, for example, both (i) the just-heard sound *and* (ii) the just-past-*hearing*-of-that-sound are retended—we have to ask why Husserl would attribute this only to retention in the absolute flow of consciousness and not to the level of act intentionality, of intentional experience of the world. If we are dealing with immanent hyletic data, then we seem to find the double intentionality of retention in *absolute* consciousness. But if there are no immanent hyletic data, then I would suggest that we find a double intentionality of retention at work in our consciousness of the world: (i) a thematic constitution of the world (with its marginal retentional horizon of the just-past) with (ii) a marginal self-awareness that is a self-constitution of the unity of the stream of consciousness itself. In short, the assumed presence of immanent hyletic data leads Husserl to "find" a constitution of immanent contents and acts that is not self-constitution, and this leads him to model his account of inner consciousness on outer consciousness. But this is a construct, not a discovery, and the essential and unique marginality of the self-awareness of consciousness is lost. Husserl attempts to do justice to this marginality by recognizing that we do not really have either objects or perception here, but these remain negative qualifications of the original model, and they cannot lead to the insight that this is a marginality of self-constitution.

Abandoning the theory of absolute consciousness enables us to give more accurate descriptions of intentional achievements than are possible within Husserl's framework. Consider memory, for example. If we try to work within the framework of absolute consciousness, it may seem plausible that, as Husserl argues, in the absolute flow "in a certain way [a given phase of the flow] presentifies [*vergegenwärtigt*] the point of time which it was earlier conscious of in the mode of the now by making present [*vorstellig macht*] the primal impression" (ZPZ 376).[11] In other words, a just-past phase of a tone would be retended by retending the just-past phase of the primal impression of that tone and "looking through" it to its intentional correlate. This would lead naturally to an account of memory primarily in terms of the re-presentation of, for example, perceptual acts rather than things seen, the latter being made possible by the former. "In re-presenting my perception of the tree by my window, I re-present the window tree as well, as it appeared at that time" (HM 148; see also 147).

Now, it is important to see that this Husserlian account of retention involves a rejection of the theory of the double intentionality of retention: Husserl's account is inconsistent with his own best insight. Rather than a double intentionality, we would have a double achievement of the unitary phenomenon of retention. This would mean that to retend the past phase of an event in the world would be *to retend the just-past primal impression of the just-past perceiving of the just-past phase of the event.*[12] The retending phase of the absolute flow would "look through" the retended phase of the flow to the retended past phase of the perceiving and in turn through it to the past phase of the event. The machinery is getting terribly creaky. By the same token, concerning memory Husserl seems closer to the mark when he characterizes it not in terms of the recollection of perceiving but rather in terms of the "consciousness of having-been-perceived" (ZPZ 57/ PhT 81), which in turn makes possible what Husserl calls "a reflection in memory," a "memory of the earlier perception of the event" (ZPZ 58/ PhT 81–82).

What is going on in these accounts is, I submit, a prejudice in favor of immanence (the phenomenological counterpart to what Maurice Merleau-Ponty called the *prejudice of the world*), which turns one's intentional experience of the world into one's awareness of oneself as experiencing the world, rather than viewing one's self-awareness as being marginal to one's experience of the world.

If we cease trying to describe perceptual retention in terms of the framework of absolute consciousness, things get much simpler and, I think, much closer to lived experience. Perceptual consciousness involves both (i) marginal consciousness in the form of retention of past phases of the event perceived and (ii) an even more radically marginal consciousness in the form of the retention of past phases of perceptual consciousness itself. Rather than retending the just-past object phase through the retention of the just-past perceptual phase, the latter retention is marginal to the former. Thus, I would claim that my account is more adequate to our retention of past phases of objective events *and* that it is more adequate to the marginal retention of past phases of the consciousness of those events.

Another example of the problems presented by absolute consciousness can be seen if we look at Husserl's account of sensation. In a famous passage Husserl claims that "sensation [*Empfindung*], if we understand this as consciousness [i.e., the primal impression of absolute consciousness] (not the immanent, enduring red, sound, etc., i.e., the sensed), likewise retention, remembering, perceiving, etc., is *untemporal,* viz., nothing in immanent time" (ZPZ 333–34)[13] and that "the flow of modes of consciousness [in absolute consciousness] is not a process, the now-consciousness is not itself now" (ZPZ 333). Husserl claims that absolute consciousness is non-temporal, and yet on his own account we are forced to describe absolute consciousness as a flow, using a nomenclature derived from that which is properly temporal (ZPZ 375; ZPZ 75/PhT 100); thus, we can and must say that a certain phase of the flow *"belongs* to a now...which it constitutes"(ZPZ 371). The absolute flow is a "quasi-temporal order of the phases of the flow"; it is a "pre-phenomenal, pre-immanent temporality" (ZPZ 381).

Careful attention to Husserl's analyses can show why he has a problem with the temporality of absolute consciousness here. If the primal impressional phase of absolute consciousness is the awareness of the present phase of immanent objects, and if the double intentionality of retention in the absolute flow is marginal awareness of (i) the past phases of the immanent object and (ii) past phases of primal impression itself, it is clear that there would be no immediate awareness of the primal impressional phase itself, even though the double intentionality of retention is supposed to constitute the unity of the absolute flow itself. This is, I think, what Husserl was wrestling with in his varying use of such terms as *non-temporal, pretemporal, and quasi-temporal.* Indeed, it bothered him so much that he wondered whether we must not acknowledge yet another level of consciousness, an *"ultimate* consciousness [*letztes Bewusstsein*]" in which "the current phase of inner consciousness [i.e., what he had been calling *absolute consciousness*]" comes to consciousness (ZPZ 382). He realized that such a consciousness would necessarily have to be an "unconscious consciousness" (ZPZ 382), if an infinite regress is to be avoided. This would mean that my perception of an event would involve (i) an unconscious awareness of (ii) my awareness of (iii) my perceiving (iv) the event. That Husserl could even consider this idea demonstrates graphically just how unstable his entire construction had become.

Thus, Husserl's account necessarily implies that there is, as it were, a "blind spot" at the very core of consciousness, a primal impression that is "awareness of...," without itself being brought to awareness other than retentionally.[14] On this account, there is no immediate marginal awareness of a current primal impression, but there is a marginal, retentional awareness of the primal impression that "belongs to" past phases of the temporal object. (This clearly contradicts the account of retending in terms of "looking through.") The field of consciousness is "centered," as it were, around a fundamental absence.[15] This is the reason why, as Rudolf Bernet recently noted, in the later texts published in number 10 of the Husserliana series "absolute consciousness...is analyzed almost exclusively in its retentional achievements" ("Einleitung," xlvii). This is also the point at which Rudolf Boehm can make the strongest case for his thesis that "consciousness is the presence [*Gegenwart*] of the past."[16]

This analysis of Husserl's problems with self-constitution has some interesting consequences. Thus, as I understand him, Bernet argues that, according to Husserl, in the transition from one retention to the next we become aware of the transition from a just-just past to a just-past primal impression, and not of the transition from a just-past to a present primal impression. Our consciousness of the flow of absolute consciousness is essentially delayed, subsequent, after the fact *(nachträglich)*.[17] If time consciousness is essentially "non-coincidence with oneself—the transition," as Emmanuel Levinas says of perception,[18] then the self-appearing of the flow of consciousness seems to have its origin in retention.

But this account remains incomplete, the phenomenon of the transition *(Übergang)* unclarified, without a look at protention. Levinas has called protention a *foresensing,* which, as he puts it, "includes the imminence of *its own* sinking back into the immediate past of retention" (DHH 152–53; my emphasis). Thus, Levinas finds a double intentionality of protention, which complements Husserl's double intentionality of retention, and this is crucial, since the reflexivity involved here ("the imminence of *its own* sinking back") does present us with a radically marginal awareness of the flowing present of consciousness itself. For this reason perceiving is itself experienced as being now and not merely as belonging to a now which it presents.

Although I cannot discuss this at any length here, I would suggest that protention can function in the manner described here only if we see that the fundamental phenomenon of the consciousness of time is not the continual upsurge of the present, but rather the continual living into the future. Husserl's discussions of time consciousness—at least those published in number 10 of the Husserliana series—focus on a consciousness that observes a changing flow of events and not a consciousness that is actively engaged. However, Ludwig Landgrebe has emphasized Husserl's discovery in the 1930s of what Landgrebe calls a *primal striving.*[19] Husserl speaks of a "universal drive-intentionality [*Triebintentionalität*] which unitarily constitutes every primal present and which *presses on* from present to present in such a way that all content is content of the fulfillment of these drives and is intended prior to its achievement."[20] As Husserl writes in the same text: "Primordiality is a system of drives" (ZPI 594). This primal striving is essentially corporeal and belongs to a "primitive founding stratum of egoless flowing" (ZPI 598). Husserl explicitly recognizes that this notion of drives involves a modification of his earlier theory of inner time consciousness (see ZPI 594–95).[21]

If we follow out this line of analysis, we will come to the phenomena that Husserl calls *Empfindnisse* in the second volume of the *Ideen.*[22] In his essay "Intentionalité et sensation," Levinas has drawn attention to these *Empfindnisse,* which he finds interesting precisely because they are indeterminate with regard to the distinction between sens*ing* and sens*ed.* "The analysis of sensations as *Empfindnisse* signifies precisely the collapse of the schema and opposition [between the inner and outer]" (DHH 157). It is here that the analysis of time consciousness has to begin, not with the analysis of *inner* time consciousness but rather with a field that is not yet polarized in terms of the inner and the outer, a vital field. And it is here, I suggest, that we find a much more concrete mode of living in the present.

Finally, the rejection of the theory of absolute consciousness has another consequence. The phenomenology of the absolute flow seems to present us with a striking exception to Husserl's oft-repeated insistence on the strict parallel between phenomenological psychology and transcendental phenomenology,[23] since the non-temporal, pretemporal, or quasi-temporal structure of absolute consciousness can find no place in mundane time. Thus, the concept of absolute consciousness seems to offer a solution to what Husserl in the *Crisis* called "the paradox of human subjectivity: being a subject for the world and at the same time being an object in the world."[24] The solution would consist in specifying a level of subjectivity such that, in Sokolowski's words, "the life that is led in this domain is *in no way* a mundane life" (HM 135). It is exhausted by its function of presenting the mundane and is itself in no sense mundane; it is *of* but not *in*. Here the analysis of the transcendental, constitutive function of consciousness has given way to a metaphysical subject. In contrast, the solution in the *Crisis* hinges on a specific way of thematizing consciousness such that its constituting function can be articulated (Kr 184/ Cr 180–81). On this understanding, transcendental consciousness is not a hyperempirical consciousness, but rather, as Aron Gurwitsch put it, the "constitutive function of consciousness."[25] This is, I think, the main thrust of Husserl's phenomenology, and I think that the speculative, metaphysical nature of absolute consciousness indicates that the theory has abandoned the domain of phenomenology. This is not to say that Husserl was not tempted by the heady air of speculative solutions (see, for example, ZPI 608–10), but it is surely no accident that he never published these speculations, since they leave behind the realm of pure phenomenology to which Husserl devoted his life.[26]

Part 2

The Possibility of Philosophy as Social Critique

4 Husserl's Complex Concept of the Self and the Possibility of Social Criticism

CHARLES HARVEY

What must human being be like in order to engage in social criticism? One way to answer this question is to say that human being must be just like it is, because in almost all cases of being human the human being engages, to some greater or lesser extent, in social criticism: it complains, it protests, it strikes, it critiques. So, say what human being *is* like, and that answers the initial question.

This response is, of course, too simple. But it does make a point philosophers should not forget, namely, that social criticism is a relatively common actuality; hence it is surely a possibility. Part of the task of the social philosopher, then, is to describe what it is about human being that makes this actual state of affairs a possible one. That is what I hope to begin to do in this chapter. Before doing this, however, I would like to provide an overview of two horns of a dilemma between which theories of social criticism must steer, and highlight some recent exchanges stemming from the desire to avoid these horns. Then, borrowing from Husserl, I will try to describe the self that steers between these horns and that makes social criticism both a possibility and an actuality.

Sociological and World-Purified Conceptions of the Self: The Phenomeno-logic of the Problem

Since the nineteenth century, recognition of the social-psychological genesis of persons has been made ever more inescapable by the birth and burgeoning of the social sciences. This understanding of persons as *products* of their social-psychological environment has had as a conceptual consequent the belief that persons lack reflective distance from the environment from which they emerge. In the words of Michael Sandel, if the self is a sociological being, if it is a conditioned being "all the way down," then "there is no point of exemption, no transcendental subject capable of standing outside society or outside experience."[1] And if this is so, self and society merge, and there is no privileged position for an objective, critical perspective on society. Contra George Herbert Mead, there is no "I" unexhausted by "me." Contra Thomas Nagel, there is no "view from nowhere." And the transcendental partner, in the "empirico-transcendental doublet" named by Foucault, vanishes.[2] The person thereby becomes an empirical "single" dancing with other purely empirical "singles" in the ballroom of purely socialized selfhood.

But intractable problems concerning personal identity and social criticism arise from this extreme sociological conception of the self. If the self turns out to be only the collection of its social, psychological, and physical attributes, if it is only the collection of attributes x, y, and z, rather than something that has these attributes, then there is no conceptual space between "it" and its attributes; there is no separation between subject and situation, a separation necessary for conceiving the subject as distinct from its situation.[3] If all the distance between a self and its attributes vanishes, then the "self" collapses into its attributes, and change in them is equivalent to change in "it." Every change in "my" situation would mark a change in my identity and my identity would blur indistinguishably into my situation. It would become impossible to separate what is me from what is mine; the distinction between "me" and "mine" would vanish. In the most extreme version of this position, the phenomenologically incomprehensible position is reached in which subject and situation cannot be distinguished. And clearly, if this were the case, the possibility of critical distance between self and society would be lost. Social criticism would be impossible.

On the pole opposite this extreme sociological position is the conception of the self as strictly non-empirical and world-purified. This conception claims that the self is the zero-point of all understanding but is not itself a thing among things understood. That is, the world-purified self can make an object of other things, although *it* is not and cannot be made an object.[4] Because of its radical detachment it is said to be able to stand above and beyond the society or culture it might criticize, and this society or culture would be just one object among the many objects upon which it might focus its critical gaze.

But there is also a problem concerning personal identity and social criticism for this conception of the self. The obvious difficulties for a conception of the self that would claim a radically world-purified status are the problems of interest, empathetic understanding, and embodiment. If the person's sense of self is not tied into societal values, *what* provides the sense of self to the self? If one were not interested in the societal values that one criticized, *why* would one engage in criticism? If one did not embody such values and was not embodied by them, *how* would one empathetically understand them (empathetic understanding being necessary for effective criticism)? Affirmatively stated: one's understanding of oneself is inextricably tied to the values one holds dear. One's self-understanding and one's understanding of society refer back, inevitably, to one's interests, which are themselves intertwined with one's embodiment in the culture and tradition of which one is a part. A self detached from all this would simply have nothing to say.

As Michael Walzer notes, if an outsider managed to become an effective social critic of some alien community, it would mean that he or she had somehow managed to get on the inside of the community criticized.[5] This might happen through the use of imagination, but more likely it would happen through the gradual embodiment by the critic of that community's actual values. In any case, if one were too detached from those values, criticism would not take place; or if it did, it would not hit its mark; or if it did, it would likely do so without swaying those criticized precisely because it was so detached and nonempathetically related to the community criticized (ISC 64). And to a radically world-purified self, all communities would be alien communities.

Walzer thereby emphasizes the fact that social criticism is such a common occurrence that some special form of mental gymnastics effecting radical detachment hardly seems prerequisite for it (ISC 36). Social criticism, he writes, is really more "the educated cousin of common complaint" than the offspring of a special scientific perspective (ISC 65). And although some detachment and stepping back is necessary for a view of society, stepping back to "nowhere"—radical world-purification— would not give us a better, objective perspective; it would leave us with no perspective at all. It would place us too far from the ballpark to comment on the game.

We can conclude this problem-setting portion of the paper by drawing two simple conclusions from the extreme positions considered.

First, if the self is simply a collection of social-psychological attributes, then there is no measure of detachment between "it" and "its" society. If there is no measure of detachment between "it" and "its" society, then social criticism would be impossible. But social criticism is not impossible. Hence, there must be some measure of detachment between self and society.

Second, if the self is simply a culturally unencumbered, world-purified spectator, then the concrete connection necessary for critical comment and commitment would be absent. If the concrete connection through content and commitment were absent, concrete critical comment on society would not be actual. But concrete critical comment on society is actual. Hence, there must be some deeply rooted, empirical bonding between self and society.

Since social criticism is actual, then, an adequate conception of the self, necessary for an adequate understanding of social criticism, must account for both a deep degree of connection between self and society and some measure of detachment between the two.

The Self and Social Criticism: Recent Variations of the Problem

I must now risk blurring the fine logical distinctions just drawn and consider some recent exchanges concerning social criticism, specifically those between Hans-Georg Gadamer and Jurgen Habermas, and more recently between Habermas, on one side, and Francois Lyotard and Richard Rorty, on the other. I wish to show how these debates arrive at the position just described.

The debate between hermeneutics and critical theory, which pre-occupied continental philosophy throughout the 1960s, was a variation of the problems just described.[6] At the center of this exchange was a concern for the possibility of gaining a critical perspective on one's own society and culture. Gadamer and Habermas each vied for the right to claim that his philosophy was the most adequate for such a perspective. Supporting each position was a particular conception of the self. Generally, Gadamer's position leaned more toward the sociological conception of self as a socially conditioned being, and Habermas's position strained to achieve a world-purified conception of self with its ideal of detachment. For Gadamer, the self was the current manifestation of an inherited tradition, the now-point at which that tradition reinterpreted and understood itself. Habermas, on the other hand, although not totally unsympathetic to Gadamer's position, wished to maintain a world-purified, "quasi-trans-cendental" residue of selfhood that would leave some critical breathing room between self and society. The virtue of Gadamer's position was its insistence upon the connection of self to society; the virtue of Habermas's position was its insistence upon the need for some disconnection between the two.

Since this exchange in the 1960s, the debate over the self and social criticism has shifted—but only a little. In the 1980s, in the writings of such postmodern philosophers as Jean-Francois Lyotard and Richard Rorty, the possibility of Habermas's hoped-for philosophically privileged perspective has come under fire.[7] And as with the Gadamer-Habermas exchange, so too with these more recent exchanges about social criticism: the logic of the relations between self and society lies at their heart. But although it is no accident that Lyotard and Rorty deny the possibility of a privileged position for social criticism and also pronounce the "death of the self," to pursue the extremist language here is to pursue a red herring. What is really significant in these writings is that the postmodern critics do not deny the possibility of social criticism but only the possibility of a philosophically privileged social criticism. Likewise, although they deny the notion of a philosophically or spiritually special kind of self, they do not deny the notion of a "self" in the everyday sense of personal identity. Lyotard and Rorty admit that social criticism goes on but deny that a special kind of self is necessary for its occurrence.[8]

I will not argue with this position because I think that it is right. With Michael Walzer, I think that social criticism is such a common occurrence that it cannot require a unique, philosophically privileged kind of consciousness for its occurrence. As Rorty suggests, what the coal miner does when he strikes against working conditions, what the teacher does when she strikes over pay, what the housewife does when she bucks against her household's restrictions, and what the philosopher does when he or she writes a "critique of political economy," are variants of a common occurrence—namely, social critique.[9] The differences here are differences in degree of sophistication, not differences in some kind of specialized interior selfhood.

However, although I do not wish to challenge the content of these postmodern claims, I do think that this content pushes postmodern philosophy to a position it would like to avoid—namely, the position of transcendental philosophy. Here is why: The postmodern conception of self lands squarely between the sociological and world-purified conceptions of self, squarely between the Gadamerian and Habermasian tendencies. Since postmodern philosophy acknowledges engagement in social criticism, it must also admit that the self can be neither a totally tethered (sociological) entity nor a fully detached (world-purified) one. Because the self recognized by postmodern thinkers does, in fact, engage in social criticism, it must be located in the logical space between the sociological and world-purified extremes we have considered. This is because to be so located is required for social criticism. Hence, to acknowledge, as do Rorty, Lyotard, and Walzer, that (1) social criticism occurs, and (2) that it requires no philosophically unique form of self, is not to banish the task of describing the self that does in fact do social criticism; instead, it is to invoke that task. But this is a transcendental task: it is the task of asking for the conditions of the possibility of social criticism, and it is a task that remains even after the critique and rejection of philosophically privileged perspectives.

Hence, we ask once again: What must human being be like in order to engage in social criticism? What must it be like in order to occupy the space between the sociological and world-purified conceptions of self? How do we describe it? We have learned this much: (1) Whatever "it" is, it must account for both a deep degree of connection between self and society and for some measure of detachment between them. And (2) these logical parameters must be the parameter-characteristics of the ordinary, every-day self, since there is no special kind of philosophical self necessary for social criticism.

With these characteristics in mind I begin my appeal to Husserl.

The Self and Social Criticism

To make my argument I will identify three senses of the self described by Husserl. Two of these closely match the two extreme notions focused on thus far, whereas the third makes sense of these two and mediates between them.

The three senses of self that dominate Husserl's work are (1) the sense of self as an empirical reality, (2) the sense of self as a "world-purified" or "empty" self, and (3) the sense of self as a historically and socially constituted and constituting entity that knows itself as such, that is, the sense of self as "transcendental." In what follows, I will argue that the empirical sense of self is the self-sense of a conscious being experiencing itself as connected to its social world, that the sense of "emptiness" and mere relationality is the self-sense of a conscious being experiencing itself as disconnected from its social world, and the sense that one is both connected and disconnected, both constituted and constituting, is the transcendental sense of selfhood. I will argue, also, that each of us is all of these.

In the *Logical Investigations* Husserl described the empirical self as a not-so-special empirical content in a network of relations of empirical contents.[10] This self experiences itself as a thing among things, a cognitive content among cognitive contents without special or privileged status. In this vein, Husserl described as the self what he would later label the *naïve* or *worldly self*. Its primary characteristic is involvement with the world of its concerns. This self-sense exists unthematically for itself in a centrifugal relation to the events of the world. It is the self-sense that dominates most of us, most of the time; it is the prereflective lived sense of being an empirical reality amongst empirical realities. Considered by itself, this self-sense is indicative of a connected consciousness, a consciousness at one with its world, and it is indicative of the involved, interested, and socially conditioned self earlier described. Those who argue that this is the nature of the self, *simpliciter,* focus on this one characteristic of selfhood as though it existed by itself.

By 1913, however, Husserl had come to realize that this empirical self was never "by itself," not even when it was with only itself. He had by then experienced the sense of Paul Natorp's descriptions of the self as a "pure ego," meaning by this the sense of self as *inalienably other—even in relation to itself as an empirical reality.* In the words of Rimbaud, Natorp and Husserl had discovered that "'I' is an Other"—even to "me."

This sense of self as perpetually other than that to which it relates, arises from the relatively common experience of our non-absorption in or by our activities and involvements. When most intense, this experience can be described as a vivid sense of self-absence in relation to otherness, a sense that one is not part of the objective totality to which one is related. It is this not uncommon experience that illustrates the sense of disconnected selfhood. This is the sense of self as standing away from society even while living within it—the sense of self that tends to be most vivid prior to and during moments of critical consciousness. Indeed, this "alienated" self-sense is virtually synonymous with critical consciousness, and to some it has seemed synonymous with being a person. But those who say that this is the essential nature of the self, *simpliciter,* also focus on *one* characteristic of self-conscious experience as if it existed by itself. But again, it does not.

Although Husserl would not want to remain for long at a Kantian level of deductive reasoning, it can be argued that since the two senses of self that have generated and guided our problematic thus far *are senses available to each of us,* then there must be a connecting self-sense in order for each of us to think these characteristics as characteristics of a single self. In other words, the reason these dual senses can be senses of a single self is that the dual ways of being a self that constitute each self, are just the dual *senses* of self that constitute each self-conception. But how can these dual senses constitute each self-conception if there is no unified self-sense that unites them? Answer: they could not. Whence the need to postulate a transcendentally unifying self-sense in the Kantian mode, and whence Husserl's need to describe the experiences that constitute this unity. Consider his descriptions.

Husserl recognizes four key characteristics of the transcendental sense of self: (1) the sense of being inseparable from the processes that make up one's life, (2) the sense of being what one is solely in relation to systems of world-directed intentionality, (3) the sense of being a non-empty, content-laden, center point of identity that (4) senses itself as a growing and abiding network of past acts that have become habitualities.[11] Now, if there is a single way of expressing the sense of these various senses it is something like this: The transcendental sense of self is the sense of oneself as a content-laden, spatial, and historical point of intentional interface with the world.

To experience oneself in this way is to experience oneself as both a passive inheritor of a previously existing world, and an active point of transmission and transformation of that world. The sense of oneself as transcendental is the sense of oneself as a new channel for the intentional re-formation of the meanings, values, and beliefs that the world has given to one. Partnered with this sense is the sense that one will now, inevitably, meld these meanings, values, and beliefs in new ways with that world. In such conditions, of course, not only one's own past but the past of one's society and culture run through the intentions that one directs toward the present and future world.

So, where lie the empirical and world-purified senses of self in relation to this transcendental self-understanding? As I have noted, the predominant sense of self is the empirical sense of being a reality amongst realities, of not being strange, odd, or foreign to the world. This sense of self is the self as a "merger" with the world, where world- and self-content combine. But this sense is an achievement of forgetfulness. It is an achievement of diminished awareness, made possible by the passive inheritance and acceptance of previous persons' acts of transforming and transmitting the meanings of their society and culture so that these meanings have now become mine. The conditioned sense of the self that merges with the world can so merge because the meanings of the Other have become the meanings of me—in a sense, "I" have become "them." Living together under a common protective umbrella of reified meanings has allowed each of us, most of the time, to be just what he or she is. But it is precisely when the sense of self as world-purified or as a historical-intentional self-world interface emerges that this empirical sense of self is revealed as a forgotten achievement. And it is the transcendental self-understanding that sees this empirical sense as one-sided.

The empty sense of self, on the other hand, as the sense of being a contentless, purely spectatorial relation to the world, indicates the other extreme pole of forgetfulness of historically constituted and constituting subjectivity. This sense of being a world-purified self is the sense of being a substrate of habitualities *without the habitualities.* Because it lacks content, this world-purified sense is a sense of not being at home in the world—the sense of separation from one's society, culture, and history. In short, it is the sense of not being dictated to by the social habitualities that have made one what one is. As with the empirical sense, this sense is indeed a necessary component of the self-sense that allows for social criticism, but it allows for a criticism that is effective only because the self that criticizes experiences itself as separated from a world to which it also necessarily belongs. Hence, this empty sense of self is also an achievement of forgetfulness. As is the case with the empirical sense of self, the world-purified self-sense forgets its constitutive inheritance—it forgets the social-historical content that makes it what it is—but instead of forgetting itself by losing itself in the world, it forgets itself by losing the world that is part of itself. Once again, the sense of self as a historical-intentional self-world interface allows us to see this world-purified self-sense as a partial and dependent sense.

Hence, what Husserl called the *empirical ego* in his early writings and what he called the *pure ego* in his middle writings are two apsects of the self-experience of each of us. They are, in fact, just the senses that promote the one-sided sociological and world-purified conceptions of self. They are not, however, indicative of unique, philosophical, or independent types of selfhood; they are, rather, senses of the ordinary self as it, at different times, appears to itself. In Hegelian terms, these self-senses are incomplete forms, each a partial moment in an ever-changing unity—but each, also, a partial form that can, at any time, emerge as the dominant sense of self. In the popular jargon of the day, these aspects of the self are appearances of the self in terms of descriptions that capture only part of what they describe. They are one-sided descriptions, one-sided self-understandings that some-times convince us that we are only what they proclaim. But as we have seen, each of these senses—the empirical-sociological sense and the world-purified sense—are phenomenologically sense*less* without the transcen-dental sense of self as a historical and intentional, self-conscious interface with the world.

By the end of his life Husserl had come to realize that the descriptive unity of the sense of self is approximated only when the socio-historical sources of these senses are recognized. And once these sources are made conscious, the "self" is recognized to be the multifaceted living point of interaction between society, culture, history, and the present world. It is then that the person can be understood to be the passive and active transformational fabric that Husserl called the *transcendental ego*. This so-called ego is the self-conscious recognition that each of us is an intentional web of inherited meanings that actively transforms those meanings in the very process of transmitting them. And because we are the inheritors and intentional reweavers of our past world, and because we are the dual and oscillating sense of being within and without that world, it is possible, indeed it is sometimes necessary, to criticize that world which to a large extent *we are*.

5 Crisis and Life-World in Husserl and Habermas

KENNETH BAYNES

Two Forms of Crisis and the Return to the Life-World

In *The Theory of Communicative Action* the concept of the life-world has become an even more prominent feature of Jurgen Habermas's social theory than it was in his earlier writings.[1] Habermas refers to it as the symbolically prestructured nexus of social action that arises in conjunction with the mutually shared interpretations of their situation by social actors, and it functions as an indispensable correlate to his concept of communicative action.[2] So conceived, the life-world is subject to crises that are experienced by its members to the extent that the communicative infrastructure sustained by it is threatened by the expansion of instrumental or functionalist reason—a process Habermas refers to as the *internal colonization of the life-world.* At the same time, since its institutions embody the structures of a (communicative) reason that is opposed to instrumental rationality, the life-world is also the principal resource or means for surmounting such crises.

In view of the central importance assigned to the concept of the life-world in Habermas's social theory, its role can be profitably compared to the one it serves in Husserl's *The Crisis of European Sciences and Transcendental Phenomenology* in two broad respects. First, Habermas, like Husserl, turns to the life-world in response to the crisis of Western reason and its threatened disappearance from the world. Husserl's words describe equally well the strategic posture Habermas adopts toward recent harbingers of postmodernism:

> In order to be able to comprehend the disarray of the present "crisis," we had to work out *the concept of Europe as the historical teleology*

of the infinite goals of reason; we had to show how the European "world"[read: modernity] was born out of ideas of reason, i.e., out of the spirit of philosophy. The "crisis" could then become distinguishable as the *apparent failure of rationalism.* The reason for the failure of a rational culture, however, as we said, lies not in the essence of rationalism itself but solely in its being rendered superficial, in its entanglement in "naturalism" and "objectivism".[3]

For both Husserl and Habermas, there is a reason not exhausted by the reason of the sciences that can help orient human individuals in the world and that makes it possible still to speak of them as responsible moral agents. Under the rubric *rationalization of the life-world* Habermas pursues this first role of the life-world as an alternative to Weber's thesis of modernization as a process of societal rationalization culminating in the "iron cage" of the bureaucratic state and capitalist economy.[4]

Second, according to Husserl, the life-world is also introduced in response to a more narrowly conceived "theoretical crisis" concerning the foundation and validity of the sciences.[5] A return to the life-world as the pregiven fundament of meaning is supposed to provide philosophy with a perspective from which it can criticize the positivistic or objectivistic self-understanding of the sciences, and it should supply the sciences with a validity they would otherwise lack. It should, according to Husserl, provide the "eidetic contours" of the domains of reality to be explored by the special sciences without, however, calling into question the empirical results of those sciences.[6]

Although, at least for Husserl, this requirement holds for both the natural and the social sciences, in this chapter I will focus on the relation between philosophy (or phenomenology) and the social sciences.[7] Even in this case, the claim that phenomenology should ground the social sciences without impugning their empirical findings is contentious and threatens either, on the one hand, to deprive philosophy of any critical relation to the empirical sciences or, on the other hand, to instate philosophy as a final arbiter or judge whose task is to assign to each of the sciences its proper domain of inquiry.

Evidently cognizant of the precariousness of such a formulation, Maurice Merleau-Ponty proposed that the relation between philosophy and sociology be conceived as one of "reciprocal envelopment":

Philosophy is nature in us, the others in us, and we in them. Accordingly, we must not simply say that philosophy is compatible with sociology, but that it is necessary to it as a constant reminder of its tasks; and that each time the sociologist returns to the living sources of his knowledge, to what operates within him as a means of understanding the forms of culture most remote from him, he practices philosophy spontaneously. Philosophy is not a particular body of knowledge; it is the vigilance which does not let us forget the source of all knowledge.[8]

Merleau-Ponty's proposal, however, is not Husserl's, and Husserl's close disciple and pioneer of phenomenological sociology, Alfred Schutz, would no doubt have regarded this solution as a conflation of the constitution of sense with the constitution of being.[9] Phenomenology explores the eidetic structures of meaning as correlates of consciousness or "lived experience"; the particular sciences, by contrast, study the "ontic" objects to which those intentional acts refer.[10] The same concepts may appear in both intellectual enterprises, but in the former they are viewed strictly as the achievements of transcendental consciousness, its acts and their correlates—*noeses* and their *noemata*. For Schutz, accordingly, "the most serious question which the methodology of the social sciences has to answer is: how is it possible to form objective concepts and an objectively verifiable theory of subjective meaning-structures"?[11] to which we may add, What are the respective contributions of philosophy (as phenomenology) and sociology toward the realization of this possibility?

I would like to suggest that Habermas's particular recourse to the life-world in connection with this second, "theoretical" crisis locates him somewhere between Schutz's notion of a preestablished harmony between philosophy and science and Merleau-Ponty's notion of reciprocal envelopment.[12] According to Habermas, the task of philosophy, as "the guardian of reason," is to articulate critically the universality claims implicit in various programs of theoretical research and to relate the rationality assumptions contained in them to those already operative in everyday communicative practices.[13] In contrast to his alternative to Weber's thesis of modernization as societal rationalization, Habermas develops his response to the theoretical crisis of the (social) sciences in connection with a reformulation of Weber's model of "rational interpretation" as the proper method for social inquiry. He describes his reformulation as one that yields "methodologically shocking consequences" (TCA 1: 111). In particular, it gives rise to the "disquieting thesis" that the interpretation of action cannot be separated from the interpreter's taking a position on the validity of the claims explicitly or implicitly connected with the action (TCA 1: 107). The interpretation of action (as well as its products) requires making clear the reasons that actors would give for their action (or could possibly give within their social and historical setting); but

One can understand reasons only to the extent that one understands *why* they are or are not sound, or why in a given case a decision as to whether reasons are good or bad is not (yet) possible. An interpreter cannot, therefore, interpret expressions connected through criticizable validity claims with a potential of reasons (and thus represent knowledge) without taking a position on them. (TCA 1: 116)

According to Habermas, the gentle force of a quasi-transcendental argument thus obliges the interpreter to "equip" actors in the object domain with the same formal suppositions of rationality that she herself employs (TCA 1: 118–19). In the final analysis, rational (i.e., objective) interpretation requires treating social actors in the object domain as equal participants in a discourse about the validity of one another's beliefs and practices. There is, however, no possibility of "replacing" the performative attitude with the "scientific attitude," as Schutz maintained, only the possibility of a "withdrawal of one's qualities as an actor," as Habermas has somewhat obscurely expressed it (TCA 1: 114).

In the following remarks, I want to explore the way in which the concept of the life-world contributes to Habermas's solution to both dimensions of the crisis, that is, how it informs both his response to the general crisis of reason and his response to the methodological "crisis" of the social sciences. After briefly recalling the status and function of the life-world in Husserl's *Crisis,* I will consider how this concept is deployed by both Schutz and Habermas in an attempt to ground the social sciences. What I hope to show is that the concept of the life-world remains indispensable to social theory, even after it is separated from the project of transcendental phenomenology endorsed by Husserl and Schutz.

The Life-World in Husserl's *Crisis*

Despite the wide dispute concerning the various meanings Husserl associated with the concept of the life-world, scholars seem generally agreed that two different senses, corresponding to two different basic attitudes, are most important: the life-world as a pregiven mundane world and the life-world as an originary horizon.[14] In contrast to the objectified world of the sciences, Husserl speaks of the mundane world of everyday life. This is the sense of the life-world as something pregiven, taken-for-granted, and always familiar to us (CES 123–24). It is the world of *doxa,* from which the sciences arise and on which they finally depend for their validity. Even within this notion of life-world as a pregiven fundament of meaning, however, Husserl makes a further distinction between the precategorial (and hence pretheoretical) world of perceptual experience and the sociocultural life-world into which flow cultural achievements (including the sciences).[15] In view of the diversity and changes within the latter, one can speak of a plurality of life-worlds, although Husserl believed it was nevertheless possible to identify a general structure that these worlds share (CES 139, 142). In connection with comparative historical studies and the empirical sciences, phenomenology should even be able to arrive at descriptive regional ontologies of this common world, that is, an analysis of the essence of *ta onta*.[16]

However, Husserl also expressed a certain dissatisfaction with such a project. "Rather than spend our time here, we prefer to move on to a task which is much greater" (CES 142). In connection with this further task Husserl speaks of the life-world as *horizon*. We are not conscious of this world in the same way we are conscious of things within the mundane world, or even of the plurality of life-worlds. "The world does not exist as an entity, as an object, but exists with such uniqueness that the plural makes no sense when applied to it. Every plural, and every singular drawn from it, presupposes the world-horizon" (CES 143). However, the thematization of the life-world as horizon raises difficulties not found in the attempt to describe general features of the life-world from within the natural attitude. Here we encounter the problem of suspending or bracketing the facticity of all historical investigations and uncovering the universal a priori of history as the condition of their possibility.[17] There is also the question of what sort of evidence could be provided to show that what is uncovered is not merely the contingent features of the investigator's own historical standpoint.[18]

Husserl, of course, believed that the universal validity of the life-world as the a priori of history could only be secured through an additional, transcendental, epochē or reduction. The task of philosophy as a rigorous science consists in demonstrating that the world-horizon can be seen as an accomplishment of transcendental subjectivity (CES 151–52, 333–34). What is also well known is that some of Husserl's most promising disciples refused to follow him along precisely this path from the life-world back to transcendental subjectivity—Martin Heidegger's hermeneutic phenomenology and Merleau-Ponty's analysis of the embodiment of consciousness in the world being among the most notable alternatives.[19]

For purposes of our own comparison, therefore, what is of most interest is not so much Habermas's own rejection of Husserl's philosophy of consciousness but the way in which he hopes to continue *by other means* Husserl's project of securing the general structures of the life-world (TCA 2: 135, 143). The stage for such a comparison can be set by briefly reviewing Schutz's analysis of the life-world from the standpoint of a descriptive phenomenology and by noting some of the problems to which it gives rise.

Schutz and Habermas on the Life-World and the Social Sciences

Alfred Schutz has provided the most detailed clarification of the general structures of the life-world from within the natural attitude.[20] Although he apparently always held out the possibility of conducting a further transcendental reduction, he nevertheless chose to remain at the level of descriptive phenomenology.[21] From this perspective the life-world exhibits several general features: First, the mundane world of everyday life is experienced from the outset as a sociocultural as well as a spatiotemporal world. Moreover, the life-world is experienced as constant and generally valid: "I trust that the world as it has been known by me up until now will continue further and that consequently the stock of knowledge obtained from my fellow-men and formed from my own experiences will continue to preserve its fundamental validity" (TCA 2: 132). Although different segments of the life-world can become problematic in light of changing definitions of the situation, as a whole it cannot be called into question.

Second, the knowledge that social actors have of this world is fundamentally practical; it is the sedimentation of typifications built up by the social actor in accordance with various systems of relevance; and it consists of varying degrees of familiarity determined by the actor's own biographical situation. Schutz illustrates this sort of knowledge by comparing it to an individual's knowledge of the city in which he lives: the individual knows parts of the city well, other parts not at all; in any case, his knowledge is generally sufficient for knowing how to get on in the world.

Finally, Schutz's analysis of the typified character of an actor's mundane knowledge is what accounts for the possibility of social scientific knowledge: although the types constructed by the social scientist are "of a different kind" than those constructed by the actors themselves, the basic process is not fundamentally different (CP 1: 61). Furthermore, the "second-order concepts" which the social theorist develops are "constructs of the constructs made by the actors on the social scene" (CP 1: 59). To be sure, according to Schutz, the inquirer qua scientist must "replace" her biographical situation in the life-world with that of the "scientific situation." Schutz describes this as a "leap" in which the scientist transcends her own action context as well as that of the actor she is observing. "The theorizing self is solitary; it has no social environment; it stands outside social relationships" (CP 1: 253). In adopting this "radical change of attitude" the scientist also agrees in principle to submit the second-order concepts to the same standards of scientific rigor and logical consistency required by any empirical science, thereby securing their objectivity.

Several of the problems raised earlier in connection with the question of the foundation and validity of the social sciences can now be formulated more precisely in relation to Schutz's program. First, concerning the relation between philosophy and social science, we might ask, What sort of division of labor does Schutz have in mind, especially since both presumably occupy what he describes as a "theoretical attitude"? Schutz attempts to draw this distinction in two different ways, both of which are finally unsatisfactory. On the one hand, he sometimes draws a distinction between the study of meaning and the study of being, linking phenomenology to the former and the particular sciences to the latter (CP 3: 47–48). While this *may* have some plausibility for the natural sciences, it is problematic for the social sciences since its object domain is the life-world, understood as the world constituted by the intersubjectively shared meanings of its social actors. To insist on such a distinction between meaning and being would seem to amount to a disregard for the symbolic character of the sociocultural life-world as such.

A second way in which Schutz attempts to distinguish between phenomenology and empirical social science is by regarding the former as concerned exclusively with questions related to the "logic of discovery," while viewing the sciences as concerned with the confirmation of those discoveries. Some of Schutz's discussions of how the social sciences are built upon "first-order" concepts through the addition of "second-order" concepts that must be submitted to rigorous testing and validation move in this direction, as does his generally sympathetic response to the characterization of the scientific method by Ernest Nagel and Carl Hempel (CP 1: 62). However, such a division of labor would undermine the possibility of philosophy qua phenomenology taking a critical position vis-à-vis the social sciences.[22] The question of the relation between philosophy qua phenomenology and social science thus remains unresolved within the framework of Schutz's program.

A second problem mentioned earlier concerns the relation between theoretical knowledge (of either the phenomenologist or the social scientist) and the knowledge possessed by social actors themselves. It was a strength of Schutz's program—expressed in his Postulate of Meaning Adequacy—to insist that social science must begin with a description of the world from the participant's perspective and thus to call into question the assumed superiority of the observer's perspective (CP 2: 85). However, when Schutz goes on to describe the perspective of the social scientist as one marked by a radically different attitude, one that lifts the scientist out of both her own and the actor's life-world, these gains are jeopardized. The relation between the "systems of relevance" that define the "scientific situation" and the systems of relevance that define the mundane world of both the scientist and the actor in the object domain remains unclarified. There is also the question of whether the theorist does not "overrationalize" the practices and beliefs of the actor when these are incorporated into her own "second-order" ideal-typifications.[23]

In light of these difficulties, Habermas has proposed that the phenomenological description of the life-world might be better accounted for within the context of his own theory of communicative action (TCA 2: 130). This suggests that although he accepts much of Schutz's descriptive analysis of the life-world, he seeks to establish its relevance for the social sciences by means other than a final appeal to the accomplishments of transcendental subjectivity and a traditional conception of theory. The life-world is described as a "culturally transmitted and linguistically organized stock of interpretive patterns" from the outset, and its general structures and "rationalizability" are accounted for in connection with his theory of communicative action (TCA 2: 124). Moreover, his own attempt to modify Weber's model of "rational interpretation" has a slightly different emphasis from that of Schutz. The performative attitude of the participant is not relinquished in favor of a putatively superior theoretical attitude; rather, the criteria for determining the objectivity of an interpretation can already be found within the communicative practices of everyday life (TCA 1: 123).

Communicative action designates a form of social interaction in which actors unreservedly coordinate their actions on the basis of a mutually shared interpretation of their life-worldly situation (TCA 1: 86, 101). It can be contrasted to both instrumental action (or a goal-oriented intervention in the physical world) and strategic action, in which actors draw upon, but do not subordinate their action-plans to, mutually shared interpretations of their life-worldly situation. In acting communicatively, individuals more or less naïvely accept as valid the various claims raised with their utterances or actions, and mutually suppose that they each stand ready to provide reasons for them, should the validity of those claims be questioned. Because of this intimate connection between validity, reasons, and action, communicative action must initially be approached from the internal perspective of the participant. Communicative action is connected to domains of validity that can be understood only "from the inside," that is, by those who as (virtual) participants are able to give and assess the reasons for an action (TCA 1: 112). In a slightly more technical sense, and one tied more specifically to modern structures of rationality, Habermas states that individuals who act communicatively self-reflectively aim at reaching understanding about something in the world by relating their interpretations to three general types of validity claims connected with three basic types of speech acts: a claim to truth raised in constative speech acts, a claim to normative rightness raised in regulative speech acts, and a claim to authenticity or truthfulness raised in expressive speech acts (TCA 1: 316).

The concept of the life-world is then introduced as a necessary correlate to the concept of communicative action. On the one hand, communicative action always takes place against the background of the life-world as horizon. On the other hand, the life-world is itself replenished and reproduced through communicative action, that is, through the interpretive accomplishments of actors who seek to reach agreement about something in the world. In modern societies, Habermas argues, the attainment of mutual understanding relies less upon normatively regulated forms of interaction based on tradition, and more upon a risk-filled search for a consensus that makes use of the "categorial scaffolding" of formal world-concepts which correspond to the three basic validity claims, namely, the objective world of facts, the social world of legitimate norms and orders, and the subjective world of needs, intentions, and experiences (TCA 1: 70, 340).

This description of the life-world also anticipates another distinction that Habermas draws more sharply than Schutz. On the one hand, the life-world is a *resource* drawn upon in communicative action. As a resource, it remains in the background as a pregiven or already interpreted stock of knowledge. On the other hand, as a *topic* about which communicative actors seek to reach agreement, elements of the life-world are thematized as problems.[24] Habermas frequently draws this distinction in terms of a contrast between life-world (resource) and world (topic) and in connection with a spatial metaphor:

> While the segment of the lifeworld relevant to the situation encounters the actor as a problem which he has to solve as something standing as it were in front of him, he is supported in the rear by the background of his lifeworld. Coping with situations is a circular process in which the actor is two things at the same time: the *initiator* of actions that can be attributed to him and the *product* of traditions in which he stands as well as of group solidarities to which he belongs and processes of socialisation and learning to which he is subjected.[25]

In *The Philosophical Discourse of Modernity* Habermas warns that this description of a circular process should be accepted with caution: Actors are not products of the life-world in the sense that the latter can be viewed as a self-generating process that has a life of its own. Rather, individuals (and groups) reproduce the life-world through their communicative action; and the life-world as resource is "saddled on" the interpretive performances of its agents.[26] Thus, although Habermas resists reducing the life-world to the noematic correlate of transcendental consciousness, he also resists reifying it in ways that obscure its roots in the communicative acts of concrete individuals and groups.

The correlation of the life-world with the concept of communicative action also enables Habermas to clarify the general structures of the life-world over against the plurality of concrete life-worlds without recourse to a priori intuitions. When viewed as resource, the life-world can be structurally differentiated in connection with the three basic components of speech (propositional, illocutionary, and intentional) into culture, society, and personality:

> I call *culture* the store of knowledge from which those engaged in communicative action draw interpretations susceptible of consensus as they come to an understanding about something in the world. I call *society* (in the narrower sense of a component of the lifeworld) the legitimate orders from which those engaged in communicative action gather a solidarity, based on belonging to groups, as they enter into interpersonal relationships with one another. *Personality* serves as a term of art for acquired competences that render a subject capable of speech and action and hence able to participate in processes of mutual understanding in a given context and to maintain his own identity in the shifting contexts of interaction.[27]

Similarly, when it is considered as a topic about which actors seek to reach agreement, Habermas distinguishes among three worlds in connection with the three basic types of speech acts and their corresponding validity claims. The objective world of facts, the intersubjective world of norms, and the subjective world of intentions and experiences designate collectively the cultural *(geistige)* products of cumulative learning processes vis-à-vis claims to truth, rightness, and authenticity (TCA 1: 77–84). In communicative action, elements of the life-world may be taken up as problems and thematized under one or more of the validity claims, although this always occurs against the background of a largely unthematized, taken-for-granted stock of interpretive patterns.

Conclusion

We are now in a position to summarize the importance of the concept of the life-world for Habermas's response to both aspects of the crisis of reason mentioned earlier, that is, to the threatened loss of human freedom and significance with the scientific-instrumental rationalization of everyday life, and to the more narrowly conceived theoretical crisis of the social sciences.

In modern societies the symbolic reproduction of the life-world has become increasingly less dependent upon traditional norms and interpretive patterns, which are relatively immune from criticism, and more dependent on a risk-filled search for consensus that relies on the cooperative interpretive achievements of those who engage in communicative action. Societal rationalization thus does not refer solely to the expansion of instrumental rationality to ever more aspects of social life, as Weber supposed, but also to a widened scope for self-reflective processes of cultural reproduction, social integration, and socialization in light of highly abstract norms and formal argumentative procedures. With respect to these latter processes, one can speak of a communicative rationalization of the life-world along three dimensions: first, in terms of a greater structural differentiation of the three components of the life-world;[28] second, in terms of a distinction between form and content; and third, in terms of a greater reflexivity of symbolic reproduction (TCA 2: 145). The complete rationalization of the life-world, accordingly, can be specified in connection with the counterfactual ideal or "vanishing point" associated with each of its three structural components: "For culture, a condition of the constant revision of traditions that have been thawed, that is, have become reflective; for society, a condition of the dependence of legitimate orders upon formal and ultimately discursive procedures for establishing and grounding norms; for personality, a condition of the risk-filled self-direction of a highly abstract ego-identity" (PDM 345; translation modified).

Such a communicative rationalization of the life-world is by no means inevitable, nor does it signal an irreversible process. The crisis of reason associated with the modern age is, in fact, posed as a question of whether systemic processes of instrumental or functionalist reason (in the form of the capitalist economy and technocratic bureaucracy) will continue to erode or displace the communicative rationality of the life-world—a phenomenon Habermas describes in a reworking of Marx's notion of commodity fetishism as the "internal colonization of the lifeworld" (TCA 2: 322, 332–33).

The general contours of Habermas's response to the theoretical crisis concerning the foundations and methodology of the social sciences can also be summarized in connection with his communication-theoretic concept of the life-world. This response, it will be recalled, is found in his claim that the interpreter must "equip" actors in the object domain with the same suppositions of rationality that she herself employs, coupled with the "disquieting thesis" that the interpreter cannot avoid taking a position on the validity-claims implicit in the actor's beliefs and practices.

First, the distinction between life-world as a background resource and life-world as a topic that actors thematize indicates how communicative action and, in particular, the three formal-world concepts introduced with it contribute to the reproduction of the symbolically prestructured life-world. Although understanding takes place against the taken-for-granted background of the life-world, in communicative action the formal-world concepts present a scaffolding by means of which actors reach mutual understanding about the world. This scaffolding can also be used by the social inquirer in constructing rational interpretations of social action. In answer to the question, Why ascribe rationality suppositions to actors? Habermas insists that this is unavoidable once one accepts the view that the object domain of social science is the symbolically constituted life-world.[29] In formulating "rational interpretations" of action, the inquirer and the actor become embroiled in one (counterfactual) "universe of discourse."

Second, in reference to the relation between philosophy and science, Habermas distinguishes between a material or empirical sociocultural concept of the life-world and the formal communication-theoretic concept of the life-world (TCA 2: 135). Although the latter provides a framework in connection with which interpretations are developed, the proper object of social science is not this stylized concept of the life-world, but the everyday life-world constituted by the narrative interpretations of social actors and objectified in social and cultural institutions. The empirical social sciences are also assigned the further task of clarifying the specific ways in which the conditions of material reproduction constrain the general institutional forms of mutual understanding (TCA 2: 187).

Finally, even this sociocultural concept of life-world does not exhaust Habermas's model of social theory. He argues further that an adequate social theory requires a two-level concept of society, that is, one that not only treats society as a symbolically mediated life-world accessible from within the performative attitude of a participant, but one that can also consider the way in which "norm-free" subsystems of purposive rationality (e.g., the market economy and the bureaucratic state) can contribute functionally to either the maintenance or the destabilization of the life-world in which they are anchored. In contrast to the process of social integration, which is achieved through the interpretive accomplishments of social actors, the process of system integration associated with these subsystems operates, so to speak, behind the backs of social actors (TCA 2: 150). However, this distinction between society as system and society as life-world, as well as the related one between social and system integration, has been one of the most criticized features of Habermas's recent social theory and, for our present purposes, can be left to one side.[30] In this chapter I have merely sought to establish the continuing relevance of a concept of the life-world for addressing the crisis of reason initially sketched out in Husserl's *Crisis* as well as its indispensability for any critical social theory worthy of the name.

6 Feminist Politics and Foucault: The Limits to a Collaboration

LINDA ALCOFF

Feminist theorists are becoming increasingly interested in the work of Michel Foucault.[1] His concepts of discipline, bio-power, and the networks of power-knowledge practices have proved genuinely fruitful for analyzing the various ways in which women are inscribed in structures of gender domination.[2] Such theoretical successes may encourage feminists to attempt more wholesale appropriations of Foucault, beyond merely applying his concepts or categories of analysis. Some have already argued that feminist theory needs to be informed by Foucault, or post-structuralism in general, in order to correct its tendency toward an ahistorical essentialism and to guide its development of resistant strategies.[3]

This chapter will argue that a wholesale appropriation of Foucault by feminist theorists is unwise. Certain key Foucauldian claims pose obstacles for an effective feminist emancipatory project—and, indeed, perhaps for any emancipatory project. I will explore two such obstacles or points of disjuncture here: the first concerns Foucault's analysis of subjectivity and the second concerns the prescriptive implications his views have for political practices. My intent is not to close down the collaboration between feminism and Foucault's texts but to demarcate some possible limits to such a collaboration.

The usual political criticism made of Foucault is that neither his archaeology nor his genealogy allows any possibility for normative commitments or judgments. It is said that no claim about present injustice can be consistently defended by a Foucauldian because Foucault's analyses of power are "normatively neutral" and his work undermines all possible grounds the identification of injustice requires—for example, a concept of human nature that is then seen as thwarted, a concept of natural sexuality that is seen as repressed, a notion of human rights that are being violated, and so forth. It follows from the Foucauldian view that subjects are discursively constituted that an institution cannot be criticized because it is oppressing or repressing the "natural" rights or desires of individuals, nor can such rights and desires be used as a yardstick to measure the degree of oppression in a society. Thus the usual justifications given for accounts of injustice are unusable, and it is unclear at best with what a Foucauldian might replace them. Moreover, given Foucault's thesis about regimes of truth, it has been argued that no claim about injustice could be privileged by a consistent Foucauldian simply because there is no truth.[4] This chapter will not pursue these lines of argument, however. I will not argue that an appropriation of Foucault is problematic for feminist politics because he can provide no grounds for normative claims. Rather, my argument will be that what one might call the political ontology of Foucault inhibits the development of an adequate theory of resistance and that it undercuts the possibilities for an effective resistance to domination. Let us begin with Foucault's ontology of subjectivity.

The Problem of Subjectivity

Foucault makes two claims about subjectivity that are pertinent here: one is that subjectivity is in some significant sense constituted by a discourse, and the second is that the development of subjectivity has increased domination. First let us look at what he means by these claims.

Foucault says that "subjects are gradually, progressively, really and materially constituted through a multiplicity of organisms, forces, energies, materials, desires, thoughts, etc." Therefore, "the individual is not to be conceived as a sort of elementary nucleus, a primitive atom."[5] Here Foucault is continuing but extending the attack on the Cartesian notion of the subject developed most importantly in this century by Martin Heidegger, where Heidegger argues against the notion of a privileged subject that can pass judgment on knowledge from a supposedly neutral, rational, and disengaged position. For Heidegger the subject is necessarily historically situated, and there is no privileged neutral standpoint that can serve as an epistemic tribunal or metaphysical grounding of belief. Heidegger thus effects a particularizing and historicizing of the subject. Foucault's notion just expressed, that the subject is constituted rather than elementary, produces a similar effect: the subject can no longer serve as an absolute ground of knowledge, as a transcendental historical figure, or as an ultimate justification for moral theories.

Foucault goes further than Heidegger, however, by arguing that we need to eliminate and not merely situate the subject. In "Truth and Power" he says:

Historical contextualization needed to be something more than the simple relativisation of the phenomenological subject. I don't believe the problem can be solved by historicising the subject as posited by the phenomenologists, fabricating a subject that evolves through the course of history. One has to dispense with the constituent subject, to get rid of the subject itself, that's to say, to arrive at an analysis which can account for the constitution of the subject within a historical framework. And this is what I would call genealogy, that is, a form of history which can account for the constitution of knowledges, discourses, domains of objects, etc., without having to make reference to a subject which is either transcendental in relation to the field of events or runs in its empty sameness throughout the course of history. (P/K 117)

Thus Foucault's position on subjectivity is more nominalist than that of his predecessors: for him subjectivity is causally inefficacious, historically constructed, even a kind of epiphenomenon of power/knowledge.

It is important to note that it is not simply the transcendental notion of subjectivity that Foucault is opposing, that is, a subject that is trans-historical and universal, but the notion of a subject as a being with a kind of primordial interiority that is autonomous or spontaneous in some ontological sense. This is why Foucault says that historicizing the subject is insufficient and that we must dispense with the constituent subject altogether, that is, a subject that founds knowledges, grounds morality, and causes events. What his analysis undermines is the conceptualization of the very internal life of consciousness that has been taken, within the Cartesian tradition, to be the ultimate authority, a level of reality about which we can have more direct knowledge than any other and that generates a knowledge least open to interpretation and illusion. For many epistemologists since Descartes the internal life is a series of self-presenting states that alone of all our experience need no corroboration for their validity and cannot in fact be invalidated. On their view, it is possible to invalidate all of those beliefs that refer to externality, even those beliefs present to us with clarity and distinctness, but we cannot invalidate the internal experience of clarity and distinctness itself.

Though he is not the first to do so, Foucault takes issue with both the Cartesian and the phenomenological traditions in this regard. Both the interiority of consciousness and our notion of consciousness itself is considered by Foucault a historical-cultural product and thus open to significant alteration. His claim is that there is no level of experience that can be taken as a bedrock or irreproachable layer of reality to which we have uninterpreted access or on the basis of which we can build a stable foundation for knowledge. He does not argue against the claim that our internal experiences are actually experienced by us, but denies that they can serve as any kind of privileged, authoritative starting point for epistemic validity or as a basis for social theory. And this is because these experiences are themselves the product of social phenomena and institutions of discursive practices. In short, we are effects, not causes. Foucault's project, then, has been to place in relief this constitution of subjectivity and to analyze its effects.[6]

Foucault further argues, in "Two Lectures," that our constitution as individual subjects is an effect of power strategies: "it is. . . one of the prime effects of power that certain bodies, certain gestures, certain discourses, certain desires, come to be identified and constituted as individuals. The individual, that is, is not the *vis-à-vis* of power; it is, I believe, one of its prime effects" (P/K 98). His extensive historical studies are intended to demonstrate how this works, that is, how the modern form of power

> applies itself to immediate everyday life which categorizes the individual, marks him by his own individuality, attaches him to his own identity, imposes a law of truth on him which he must recognize and which others have to recognize in him. It is a form of power which makes individuals subjects. There are two meanings of the word *subject:* subject to someone else by control and dependence, and tied to his own identity by a conscience or self-knowledge. Both meanings suggest a form of power which subjugates and makes subject to.[7]

Foucault's argument thus turns Hegel on his head (again) and rejects the view that expanding one's freedom involves achieving or developing further oneself as an autonomous subject. For Foucault, the achievement of subjectivity has meant that we have become manipulable bodies with internalized self-disciplining guides that direct our behavior. We have been subsumed into the dominant system of power/knowledge, particularly, the discourse of the human sciences, which can then more effectively and efficiently produce docile and skilled bodies. Subjectivity has made us more, not less, vulnerable to domination.

Foucault tries to show historically that since the increased interest in the internal life of the subject—in the subject's intentions, desires, and needs—we have actually lost ground in the battle against domination by becoming kinds of beings that are more amenable to discipline and bio-power. The human sciences exert their claim to expertise over us and their right to translate the truth about us to ourselves through the use of this conception of interiority, which serves the role of internal warden and guide as well as opening up the need for a whole army of mediating experts for the purpose of interpretation. The effect of subjectification has been our subjection. Therefore, if we are interested in subverting the forces of domination, we must, as he says, "refuse what we are."[8]

Can these claims augment the development of an effective feminist political practice?[9] In my view, if Foucault's analysis of subjectivity is correct, a feminist emancipatory project is in trouble. Foucault's account, though it may contribute to an understanding of women's oppression, also poses obstacles for feminist practice. Because of this, it behooves us to look long and hard at his account before we accept it. And, I will argue, if we do so, we will see that Foucault's case is not airtight. Let us take up this last issue first.

The constitution of subjectivity is not as internally homogeneous, monolithic, or one-sidedly pernicious as Foucault makes it out to be, even within our own historically situated discursive formation. The liberal version of subjectivity, which involves individualism and a deep self separated from the social, may have been the dominant version in the West, but at least since Hegel there have been other contenders who construct subjectivity both socially and in ways that are resistant to scientific objectification (e.g., Hegelian, hermeneutic, and Critical Theory traditions). Foucault's analysis does not take sufficient account of this multiplicity and diversity in either the construction or the effects of subjectivity but tends to treat it as homogeneous. However, it can be argued that, some of the time, thinking of ourselves as subjects can have, and has had, positive effects contributing to our ability effectively to resist structures of domination. Subjectivity can accord a sense of agency and authority over one's actions, needs, interests, and desires. It can create an obstacle to the instrumental appropriation of one's self for externally articulated ends. It can produce at least the potential for an ontological space in which the reflective reconstruction of one's social environment can take place, a site of relief from determinism and manipulation. In short, even though it may be a discursive construction, the notion that one is a subject can engender a repositioning of one's perspective from other to self (a very important act for women at this historical point) and a vigorous awareness of the possibility of critical reflection on demands that issue explicitly from an external source. What I am arguing here is that the concept of subjectivity can help women gain critical distance from the expectations foisted on them by husbands, family, and social milieu. Such an account of the potential of subjectivity does not compel us to accept the liberal notion that an individual's needs, desires, aspirations, or self-understandings are unconstructed, autonomous givens existing as pre- or extrasocial entities. The point of contention here is not over *that* claim but over the claim that our constitution as subjects is an event that has been and will continue to be unrelentingly negative and at odds with the program of resistance to domination.

A feminist emancipatory project has a pragmatic interest in making a space in its political ontology for resistant subjects who have some degree of old-fashioned agency and are *able* to reflect and reposition or renegotiate their positions within their social or discursive contexts. Some feminists who use Foucault argue that Foucault factors just such a resistance into his description of power.[10] Chris Weedon, for example, argues that the Foucauldian subject is a "social agent, capable of resistance and...able to reflect upon the discursive relations which constitute her and...to choose from the options available."[11] A Foucauldian feminist practice will articulate new subject-positions from which to strategically resist and desist from structures of domination. That is, in Weedon's view, through collective processes women can maneuver within the dominant discursive practice in such a way as to decrease their subjection to disciplines of domination. I have no argument with Weedon's prescriptions for feminist practice, but it remains unclear to me whether the potential for agency she accords to women can really be made consonant with Foucault's political ontology.[12]

Foucault paints a picture in which the constitution of subjectivity is the work of a totalizing power and results in a "totally imprinted" body.[13] This appears to leave no trace of free space or room to maneuver. He does say that there is resistance—and in fact argues that there can be no power where there is no resistance. But he does not locate the source of this resistance within the construction of subjectivity, and at times specifically argues against this. For example, in *Discipline and Punish* he says, "It is not the activity of the subject of knowledge that produces a corpus of knowledge, useful or resistant to power, but power-knowledge, the processes and struggles that traverse it and of which it is made up, that determines the forms and possible domains of knowledge."[14] Foucault identifies *sites* of resistance, as opposed to sources, primarily in subjugated discourses.[15] But two problems beset this identification of resistance in subjugated discourses. A discourse is said to be subjugated and therefore a site of resistance to the extent that it disrupts hegemonic systems of power/knowledge or is incapable of being subsumed within them. But this is insufficient to establish that such discourses effect a resistance to domination. For example, some subjugated discourses are fascist and yet at odds with the dominant discourse in their context. Foucault gives us no means to discriminate politically between subjugated discourses. Further, Foucault never says that subjugated discourses arise out of a conscious, reflective agency that chooses to resist, as Weedon implies. As usual, Foucault gives us no causal story about the emergence of subjugated discourses, and certainly does not accord it to resistant subjects. Foucault therefore does not sufficiently theorize resistance: his identification of subjugated discourses does not establish their politically emancipatory character nor does it help us understand where or how they arise and how, therefore, they might be abetted.

It is politically significant and very troubling that there are no categories of oppressor or oppressed in Foucault's political ontology.[16] He describes power as "a machine in which everyone is caught, those who exercise power *just as much* as those over whom it is exercised."[17] In "Power and Strategies," he says, further, "There is certainly no such thing as 'the' plebs; rather there is, as it were, a certain plebeian quality or aspect (*'de la 'plèbe)*. There is plebs in bodies, in souls, in individuals, in the proletariat, in the bourgeoisie, but everywhere in a diversity of forms and extensions, of energies and irreducibilities" (P/K 138). Plebeianism is a discursive construction available to all. In a certain sense this seems quite right: we sometimes can observe attitudes of subservience, for example, even among top executives. But the difference in material conditions alone between the Latina maid and the white male CEO who both work for the same corporation demands a political ontology that says more than that capitalism is a machine in which everyone is caught. Foucault's analysis of power, although it is significant and useful in some important respects, renders invisible certain inequities of power and thus creates obstacles to the development of a political ontology with different categories for relations of oppression. In "The Eye of Power" he admits that "certainly everyone doesn't occupy the same position; certain positions preponderate and permit an effect of supremacy to be produced"(P/K 156). But the issue I wish to bring into focus here is a differential access to power on the basis of which we can identify oppressors and not merely a privileged group. On Foucault's account, no one owns or holds power; power moves from bottom to top as well as top to bottom in the socioeconomic hierarchies of society, and domination exists in structured fields of relations rather than in differential access to power. Some are in positions of supremacy over others, but not in the sense of having more power to effect their decisions or control others' lives. As far as power is concerned, the different positions in the social landscape appear to be identical. Foucault states, in "Two Lectures": "Power . . . is never localised here or there, never in anybody's hands. . . . And not only do individuals circulate between its threads; they are always in the position of simultaneously undergoing and exercising this power" (P/K 98). Political struggle therefore is a war of "all against all,"[18] and thus the conceptual categories of oppressor and oppressed, to the extent that they imply a differential access to power, are inadequate and even misleading.

It is difficult to understand how agency can be formulated on this view. Given the enormous productive efficacy Foucault accords to power/ knowledge or the dominant discourse, there could be agency only if human beings were given the causal ability to create, effect, and transform power/knowledge or discourses, but Foucault does not concede to us this capacity. He declines to offer a hypothesis about the construction of the discourse itself. One reason for this must surely be his distrust of schemas of linear causality and his subsequent disinclination to look for a "cause". Another reason is that, like other structuralists and post-structuralists, in the spirit of anti-empiricism Foucault cuts discourse free of its moorings and treats it as a self-sufficient, self-perpetuating entity that performs the ontological equivalent of pulling itself up by its own bootstraps. In my view, Foucault's version of this move is significantly superior to those of others (e.g., Jacques Derrida and Jean Baudrillard) because it theorizes discourse to be more of a concrete historical materiality and less a web of signifiers. But on the issue of human agency Foucault's version leaves just as large a gap. Power/knowledge may be manifested in people's speech and actions, but these are ontological epiphenomena, not causes. And unless they are at least partial causes, I fail to see how there can be agency within this kind of analysis. If we are the effects of a totalized power/knowledge and do not ourselves have causal control over power/knowledge, then in what possible sense can we be said to have effective agency?

One important problem with this view is that if we cannot posit agency on the part of actors in the historical drama, then it is impossible to assign responsibility for the state of things to anybody. In other words, there is no one to blame. Or, if blame can be assigned, it cannot be assigned differentially throughout the population, given that there is no differential access to power. But better yet, it is not the population as a whole that should be blamed but the system of power/knowledge, which is itself, he tells us, anonymous and polymorphous.[19] Therefore on this view feminists are misguided to claim that some men are blameworthy or that women are generally less blameworthy than men for the existence of the system of gender domination. I think such an account can only undermine an effective feminism. The effect of absolving all men of the responsibility for sexism, or of equating a rapist's responsibility with the rape victim's, can be only an increase in sexism.

My argument is not that women are mere victims or that all men should be held responsible for sexism, but that a complete denial of agency makes it difficult to posit a differential of power and responsibility throughout the population and also makes it unclear how we can theorize women's effective resistance to domination.

So my conclusion is that Foucault insufficiently theorizes resistance since he allows for no resistant agents, no differential categories in terms of access to power, and his identification of subjugated knowledges as resistant is problematic for the reasons given earlier. These problems are connected: if Foucault had an adequate theory of agency, I suspect he would have categories of oppressors and oppressed, and if he had these categories, he could probably establish which subjugated knowledges are genuinely resistant to domination. However, it may appear that if we want an adequate theory of resistance, we must stick to some type of political theory with a strong account of agency, such as liberal individualism. Are we not in a dilemma here, after all? The usual way to reveal domination is to argue that there is some inner truth about human beings that can then be used as a standard against which to identify domination and oppression and measure their extent. On Foucault's account this procedure is illegitimate, and I have already conceded his point that the subjective experiences of belief, desire, and intention are not spontaneous presocial phenomena on the basis of which "deep truths" about the "authentic" self can be formulated. On the other hand, if the erasure of agency and a "true-self" subjectivity makes the identification of domination impossible, it looks as if I cannot continue to demand an adequate theory of resistance to it. Thus there appears to be a dilemma between our political agenda and our ontological beliefs (or disbeliefs).

Fortunately, this dilemma is false: there are other alternatives consistent with both commitments. I will describe only one alternative possibility here. Frigga Haug, together with a group of German feminists, spent several years collectively engaging in what they called *memory work* in an attempt to trace and reflect upon the ways in which each of them had been constructed as a female subject with a sexualized female body. An explanation and critical evaluation of their procedure, together with a report of its results, is included in their collectively written book, *Female Sexualization.* Their project recognized the social and discursive construction of their subjectivities but attempted actively to intervene in this construction through collective reflection and analysis. Toward this end, the collective asked, How do women participate in their own inscription within structures of domination? How do we participate in our interpellation as feminized, subordinate subjects? These questions presuppose an active agency on the part of women, and this presupposition the collective defends very explicitly. Their defense consists partly in stating their feminist political agenda of developing forms of resistance, which they see as predicated on the possibility of agency. But they also argue that an ontology that does not include agency is theoretically incapable of adequately accounting for their "lived experience." For example, it cannot fully capture the ways in which women develop competence in what they call *slavegirlishness,* that is, activities directed toward improving their value as commodities. This competence, which produces pleasure for women at the same time that it inscribes them in patriarchal disciplines, involves women's active participation—in developing disciplinary techniques, promoting and reinforcing the validity of norms against which to judge themselves and others, as well as reinterpreting and developing norms. The practice of feminization involves the active participation of women, in which we maneuver and sometimes resist within a realm of imposed constraints.

The collective did not conclude from this that the liberal concept of the autonomous self is validated. They explicitly rejected the view that by turning to the subjective arena of experience the truth could be simply discovered. In fact, they argue that their memory-work project resulted in a recognition that the traditional ontology of subjects and objects is inadequate: neither category can capture the way in which women become socialized as feminine. And their description of the process constantly makes reference to difficulties unrecognized by liberal individualists: the illusive, fragmented, unconscious and semiconscious nature of subjectivity; the social, macro-level discursive determination of individual practice and experience; and the absence of any bedrock of experience that might serve as a source of critique.[20] Thus the collective's analysis cannot be reduced to a liberal account. Nevertheless, they argue that it is human subjects whose participation makes discourse manifest. In their words, "It is the fact of our active participation that gives social structures their solidity."[21] And it is their belief that this participation can come under our control to a partial extent. Through collective processes of reflection in memory work, for example, this active participation can become conscious and resistant strategies can be developed.

My own view is closer to Haug's than to Foucault's. In my view, the notion of oneself as a subject is not always a force for domination in our particular discursive context. Subjectivity can be a source of emancipatory practices in enabling us to reflect and reconstruct our historical experience and social positioning. We are not totally imprinted by history but interact with history (or the social structures constituted through our actions) in an ongoing process of construction and self-construction. The notion of subjectivity can create a means of access for our manipulation, but it can also produce a way in which to articulate our resistance to manipulation. The only way to "prove" such claims would be to give a historical account, which I cannot adequately give here, but it is striking that every successful (relatively, of course) political movement has used the discourse of subjectivity to articulate its demands. In the South during the Civil Rights Movement, marchers on picket lines would routinely chant, "I am a Man, I am Somebody; I may be Black, but I am Somebody; I may be poor, but I am Somebody." This chant used the discourse of humanist subjectivity to articulate a space for resistance and self-defined freedom from instrumental subjugation. The implicit corollary of the chant was, "I am not a nobody, a nobody that can be ignored, rendered invisible, or manipulated at will." Thus, the purpose of the chant was to assert subjectivity by the oppressed in order to claim their ability to reflect and pass judgment on their historical and social situation from a perspective that was not completely subsumed within the white man's world, a perspective from which one could create meaning and not merely adopt it. As bell hooks movingly puts it, "Forced to behave as objects in white dominated space, they clinged to the representation of themselves as subjects in segregated Black space even if it was only an illusion."[22] Even when recognized as a representation, subjectivity can abet resistance. In ignoring this dialectic of subjectivity, Foucault renders invisible the history of struggle and resistance, characterizing such attempts as uniformly ineffective and co-opted by their reliance on subjectivity. Foucault's one-sidedly pessimistic view that all humanist-inspired conceptions of subjectivity have been recuperated thus endangers our ability to take advantage of the dialectical nature of subjectivity for purposes of resistance.[23]

A more correct analysis of the humanist, Enlightenment conception of subjectivity, given Foucault's own historical demonstrations, would produce a dialectical conclusion and emphasize the contradictory nature of the way in which the emancipatory possibilities of subjectivity have been promised and then reneged upon. On the one hand, both Hegelian and Kantian treatments of the subject promise to give authority and control to the individual, to recognize and respect the individual's own perspective on his or her situation.[24] But on the other hand, as Foucault so amply demonstrates, the result of power/knowledge practices developed within the human sciences, on the basis of humanism itself, was an increase in the expert's power to mediate, interpret, and evaluate the non-expert individual's experience. The question then must be, Why has the development of humanism so often resulted in the subjection of the individual to external, instrumental authority? Why has the notion of the subject's inviolable self-understanding and perspective—functioning as the authoritative origin of needs, desires, and beliefs—been so easily transformed into an object of interrogation and manipulation for externally articulated instrumental aims?[25]

Foucault argues that the answer lies in the concept of "man the doublet," a subject/object in which domination is ensured through the very constitution of subjectivity. In other words, these constructions are two sides of the same coin, mutually interdependent and supportive. His arguments for this claim, however, are less than conclusive. Why is external objectification and domination conceptually inherent in all concepts of subjectivity and interiority? The fact that some forms of subjectivity have been used to augment domination some of the time does not establish such inherence. Foucault is persuasive when arguing that interiority has been used to create an internal warden and a means to empower expert mediators, but he ignores how it also has been used as a site of resistance and a source of authority against external manipulation. There exists a tension between these effects of subjectivity, not a relationship of entailment. Foucault certainly cannot himself argue that it is necessarily the case that all constructions of subjectivity will increase domination, since he does not accept the category of necessary truths. His arguments are always historically contingent. Given the conceptual tension between concepts of subjectivity and the domination of objectification, and given the existence of instances in which the discourse of subjectivity has been used successfully to augment political resistance, the conclusion that our constitution as subjects leads inexorably to heightened domination is premature. It is premature to argue that all political programs currently invoking a concept of subjectivity will eventually lead to increased domination. Moreover, if it is the case, as I argued earlier and many others have argued as well, that without subjectivity it is unclear how we can theorize agency or resistance, then feminists have ample motivation to maintain and transform concepts of subjectivity, rather than relinquish them altogether.

None of this is to say that dominant discursive constructions of subjectivity need no radical critiques. Both Critical Theory and post-structuralism contribute important critiques which deserve careful study. Cartesian and liberal individualist conceptions of the subject should be rejected. In particular, the notion of the subject as an autonomous agent should and can be replaced with a concept of subjectivity as constructed in a social space, where the locus of subjectivity is not in the individual but in the social unit. However, this does not require rejecting all versions of subjectivity. A mediated conception of subjectivity that conceives its locus as residing partly in a social space, but that also maintains some ability for the individual to reconstruct and reinterpret from his or her own vantage point, has a long tradition, from Hegel through G. H. Mead and now to feminist theorists such as Teresa de Lauretis and the *Female Sexualization* feminist collective. It is a false dilemma to portray the situation as a choice between liberal individualism on the one hand and a total constructivist account that erases agency on the other, or between liberal subjectivity and no subjectivity at all. It is possible to have an account of subjectivity that both provides a social analysis of need, desire, and belief and does not conceive of these as entirely autonomous or self-created, but that also provides for some level of agency on the part of the individual.[26] It is also possible—and important—to use such an account to contribute to Foucault's own project of criticizing the discourse of expertise and the practice of instrumentality in the human sciences.[27] This critical but dialectical approach to subjectivity can criticize the ways in which subjectivity can increase our domination while maintaining a transformed and informed notion of subjectivity that makes it possible to adequately theorize an effective resistance.[28]

Foucauldian Political Practice

The second area of disjuncture between Foucault's work and feminism concerns the implications of his analysis of power for political practice. It is Foucault's thesis that power is not a possession that one person or group can hold over another and is not centralized in or monopolized by the state or some other major institution but is rather an emergent property of relations between people in which actions are incited, guided, and constrained. A discursive practice of power/knowledge operates through structuring "the possible field of action."[29] Although Foucault says that this structured field of actions can be characterized as having a coherent and unitary framework, he argues that power itself should be located in the capillaries that run throughout, and not in either an underlying foundation or central authority. This is a direct argument against the Marxist view that a socialist movement against domination should be directed at taking state power. If power resides in the capillaries, a seizure of state power may not alter the micro-level of power relations. This view has been influential among many French intellectuals, who concluded from the experiences of Soviet socialism that the seizure of state power by a Marxist party will not necessarily decrease the amount of control that hegemonic structures of power relationships have over people's lives. In fact, in Foucault's view, a competition for state power between two discourses with equal claims to universality, such as the discourse of liberalism and the discourse of socialism, will not address (or redress) the structure of power/knowledge at all. It will not, that is, subvert the structure of power relationships in the capillaries.

Some Foucauldian feminists have concluded from this that the political strategy of forming coalitions to take state power in order to restructure the society along socialist-feminist lines must be rejected. As Irene Diamond and Lee Quinby argue, it makes no sense "to seize power when power is no longer held by a clearly identifiable and coherent group."[30] What strategy should we adopt? The only defensible strategy on this view consists in practices that are *irreducibly* local, regional, and individual.[31] Anything else will merely replicate universal and therefore hegemonic structures of power/knowledge. To really disrupt and subvert this structure, Foucault says, the resistance must be decentralized and without aspirations toward reimplanting another universal structure of power relations. Furthermore, it cannot utilize the rhetoric of oppressed and oppressors. Given that power is capillary—consisting in emergent properties of relations within a dispersed field—there is neither a centralized source of power nor a location devoid of power. Power moves at equal speed and with reciprocity throughout the social framework, from the top down and the bottom up (therefore the notions of "top" and "bottom" no longer can convey a power differential). As we have already seen, on this picture it is difficult to understand how there can be a differential in responsibility for the overall structure, or any kind of hierarchy at all, much less a pyramidal organization of domination effected from the top down.[32] Given this, forces of resistance should not be directed at a centralized place because in reality there is no centralized place. Only local, individual forms of resistance are warranted.[33]

Thus, it is not the case that Foucault's views lead to fatalism or quietism: his claims that power emerges everywhere at once and that universalizing counterhegemony movements and discourses replicate domination are arguments against certain kinds of political practices but not all. At least four kinds of practices might be consistent with these claims (these practices overlap): (1) local actions that do not attempt to coordinate or build large coalitions or global strategies (so as to avoid replicating hegemonic structures and dominant discourses), (2) negative actions that seek to disrupt or subvert hegemonic discourses without offering any counterconstructions, (3) an aesthetics or ethics of everyday life, and (4) discursive interventions into dominant discourses. None of these practices should be opposed, but when they are raised to a theoretical level and given universal status as uniquely privileged forms of practice, then problems emerge.

Perhaps the most obvious problem is the contradiction between rejecting all totalizing strategies and then valorizing universally applicable dos and don'ts for activists: one cannot reject any universalizing move that seeks hegemony by reimplanting a political dogma about the only acceptable or truly progressive forms of political practice. The call for irreducibly local action is itself a kind of global strategy. And in regard to (2), I take it as a given that negative activities alone are insufficient, though I am aware that some will disagree. But the remaining practices, even in combination, are insufficient for an effective politics. In regard to (4), discursive interventions are important, but I am suspicious of their effort to valorize and privilege the work of intellectuals, especially since it is intellectuals who invariably make the arguments valorizing this kind of practice. I also remain doubtful that highly sophisticated theoretical interventions—interventions accessible only to other specialized theoreti- cians—can really be the cutting edge of resistance or affect the lives of nontheoreticians to any substantial degree. Thus, as interventions, such theoretical polemics are sideline skirmishes, to the extent that they are interventions at all. And in regard to (3), how can an aesthetics or ethics of everyday life, in whatever manner it is formulated, avoid being class- exclusive (among other things)? How can this be a sufficient politics for those who need global changes before their daily life can transcend the fight for survival? I do not here resist the movement to everyday life, as a shift of focus from major institutions to the micro-practices of "mundane" daily actions. What I resist is the notion that an emancipatory political practice can or should consist primarily or exclusively in refashioning the ethics and aesthetics of one's daily life. Foucault himself prompts me to ask here, Precisely who may participate in this, and who shall be excluded?

Despite the problems, none of these suggestions for practice should be rejected outright. But I would claim that even together they are insufficient to effect global changes. Let us take a closer look at (1), the call for irreducibly local forms of resistance. This has perhaps been Foucault's most persuasive prescription for political practice. And is it not persuasive to argue that a global strategy of resistance will duplicate the centralized structure of domination, and thus reinstate what it opposes?

I am claiming that Foucault accepts only local forms of resistance because he opposes all strategies that have as their goal the overtaking of central institutions, and because he valorizes only subjugated knowledges that resist hegemonic or dominant ones. If a discourse of liberation poses an oppositional alternative to the dominant discourse and seeks to challenge it within a claim of ascendancy on its own, it simply replicates hegemonic structures of power/knowledge without displacing them, or in Foucault's words, it seeks, at best, merely "a change of masters."[34] As we have seen, there is a problem here in being unable to discriminate between forms of subjugated knowledge: apparently Foucault's views would lead to a valorization of all of them. But it also remains very unclear how only local resistances can be effective. Does Foucault believe that these will ripple throughout the system, causing structural damage and dislocations? If Foucault does believe the latter, what differentiates this strategy from a global strategy? What will a qualitative progressive change look like? If we have no idea what it will look like or whether it is possible, what can motivate resistance? And without categories of oppressor and oppressed, how shall we direct our strategic practice, how will we determine who are our allies?

Foucault's valorization of only local forms of resistance follows from his political ontology of a dispersed field of micro-relations saturated with power at every point. This ontology is inaccurate. There may exist no simple pyramidal form with power concentrated at the top, but there are hierarchies and concentrations of power relations that contribute in different degrees to the operation and reproduction of the system as a whole. Power does not emerge with equal dispersion throughout an undifferentiated open field but in a field structured by economic and political hierarchies. Surely, for example, it is implausible to argue that women's use of cosmetics and thus self-construction as disciplined bodies is as equally productive of power as the cosmetics industry's creation, manufacture, and ideologically informed advertising of cosmetics. It strikes me that a power differential exists between consumers, even en masse, on the one hand, and the boardrooms of major industries, on the other. Surely Foucault is right to argue that the distribution of power does not *merely* move from the top down, but surely he is wrong to say that power emerges without qualitative distinctions among these qualitatively diverse locations.

However, it is not necessary for it to be the case that power exists primarily or exclusively in the institution of the state or the major economic institutions for it to be strategically advisable for feminists to seek power over these institutions, not merely to change personnel, but to dismantle and transform the state institutions for the purpose of social reconstruction. Foucault is certainly correct that power does not reside simply in the state, but it does not follow from this that an important part of our resistant strategies should not be the taking of central political and economic institutions. In order to reconstitute the existing structure of power/knowledge operative in a given society, we need to be able to alter the structure not only of the centralized institutions but also of the micro-level institutions. And this can be effected at least partially through the state apparatus. We can agree with Foucault that power exists throughout the social fabric, that it emerges within micro-practices, but we still must ask how we can effect a disruption or restructuring that will realign these micro-practices. Depending exclusively on individual or local changes seems as hopelessly utopian as the view Foucault counters, which places all its hopes exclusively in the major institutions. We can and should multiply the sites and strategies of our resistance (and this is an important advance of Foucault's position over some readings of Marx); however, these multiple sites and strategies should not be left unconnected but organized as coherently as possible into global strategies of resistance. Unconnected local resistances cannot succeed against global, highly organized structures. The analogy of the by-now-immortalized Vietnamese guerilla war against United States bombs and tanks should be instructive. Guerilla warfare is highly localized, abstaining from frontal assaults out in the open on central locations. However, guerilla warfare is also coordinated and strategically planned. Foucault's emphasis on local struggles makes a needed departure from narrow attachments to a frontal assault imagery found in some apocalyptic versions of revolution. But the Vietnamese also made such a departure, without having thereby to relinquish all possibility of coordination or global strategy.

Foucault's valorization of local, individual resistance has been especially persuasive to many feminists in the 1980s who look back at the last twenty years of feminist social movement in the United States and see few nationally organized activities yet persistent and recalcitrant feminist struggle in countless local and individual locations. The fact that the movement has survived and even flourished despite constant media invocations of its demise, together with the radical feminist critique of centralized organizations, supports the belief that, just as Foucault says, local practice is the most effective means of resistance. However, while sharing the concern over the ways in which global strategies and centralized organizations themselves can become instruments of oppression, I am also concerned about the ways in which local and individual actions can be easily recuperated or subverted. Certainly feminism has survived and grown, but there is more female poverty and more sexual violence today than at the movement's inception. In the mainstream, feminist politics have been recuperated into career advancement for a small segment of women and women's increased productivity for capitalism. The strategy of local and individual political practice strikes me as especially susceptible to these reconfigurations, as well as insufficient to attend effectively to the massive problems of female poverty and powerlessness.

The danger of replicating one form of domination with another is a serious one, and I include myself among those who believe that there are lessons to be learned from the failures in the Soviet Union thus far to maximize effective democracy in the lives of the general population. But the lesson is one of democratizing our methods of achieving state power, increasing local autonomy, formulating a more inclusive discourse, and recognizing the multiplicity of the sites and strategies of resistance, rather than an unwillingness to contest for discursive dominance or a failure to engage in constructive practices along with destructive ones. Feminists already too often are unwilling (sometimes sounding as if they think it would be too presumptuous) to make the radical demand for state power. I am not suggesting that feminists alone should hold state power, but that we too often shy away from directly competing with and challenging the existing dominant parties, or from participating in a coalition of groups that attempts to create a counterhegemonic political opposition. If we are not willing to present an alternative possibility, we cannot seriously effect a restructuring of society along feminist lines. This does not entail falling into another dominating structure of power/knowledge. In fact, the process of mounting a political opposition movement can and should be informed by Foucault's and others' analyses of power and the many ways in which movements of liberation can be subverted. However, it is false to present as our only choices (1) staying at the level of local, individual struggles or (2) attempting to take over without transforming the dominating structures of state power. The opposition movement should seek the overtaking of centralized structures in a way that is maximally democratic and accountable, so as to refashion the major institutions in society so that their business as usual will not require the torture, killing, and domination of human beings. Individual, local practices will not be effective toward this end. Merely defending subjugated knowledges without contending for ascendance leaves a vacuum that will be filled by our enemies if it is not filled by us. Therefore, the solution to the problems Foucault sees with regard to hegemonic power/knowledge systems is not to restrict ourselves to the local sphere but to formulate a more inclusive discourse than traditional liberalism and to develop a political practice that maintains the maximum local autonomy possible.

Clearly this argument does not pertain solely to feminists but to all opposition movements for liberation. However, there is a strong tendency within the feminist movement in particular to decline to push our demands to this step. It is a tendency that, I fear, will receive theoretical consolidation from Foucault's texts if their limits are not placed in full relief.

7 Derrida and Habermas on the Subject of Political Philosophy

THOMAS R. THORP

Is "the subject" the proper subject of a political philosophy? Two divergent currents in Jurgen Habermas's thought confront this question. First of all, Habermas insists upon the political relevance of his thought, characterizing it as a resumption of the unfinished Enlightenment project. Yet the Enlightenment prospect of an autonomous rationality expressed itself as a philosophy of the subject, and it is precisely this notion of the subject that Habermas criticizes as the common foundational flaw of both traditional and critical philosophy. The paradigm of a philosophy of consciousness is, on the one hand, the heart of the Enlightenment project. On the other hand, Habermas insists that his own reconstruction of the project of an autonomous rationality begins with a rejection of the notion of the knowing subject as the principle of reason.

The second current, in Habermas's recent work, that confronts the question of the status of political philosophy is his criticism of the antihumanist, post-structuralist, postmodern discourses. Habermas argues that the postmodern discourse rejects reason itself in a perverse and irresponsible continuation of the Nietzschean celebration of the paradoxes of reason. Habermas understands the relation between his own neo-Enlightenment project and the Heideggerian and Derridean postmodern discourses as a relation between a contemporary theory of rationality that takes political problems seriously and a postmodern discourse that has perversely given up any attempt to bring the resources of philosophy to bear on political issues. It is the aim of this chapter to contest each of the points of this argument. By forcing a strict comparison between, on the one hand, the theory of communication and argumentation on the basis of which Habermas asserts the political efficacy of his own position and, on the other hand, the actual form of argumentation that Habermas employs

87

in his critique of the postmodern discourse, it should be possible to disturb the self-certain understanding of the subject of political theory that grounds Habermas's contentions. I will proceed by developing two arguments that I outline here:

First, there is an unacknowledged price to be paid for the evidently polemical condemnation Habermas mounts against the particular brand of postmodernity exemplified by Heidegger and Derrida. Habermas's presentation, in *The Philosophical Discourse of Modernity,*[1] does not even pretend to be a serious examination of *the work* of either thinker—a claim that is fully substantiated only if these readings are held to the same standard of scholarship Habermas himself has demonstrated again and again in the series of *Streite* that have determined the course of his career.[2] Habermas's reading of Heidegger and Derrida is, rather, a carefully constructed polemic designed to reveal the political cost of what he takes to be the postmodern abandonment of rationality. Rather than attempt to establish the textual inadequacy of Habermas's reading—a gambit that would have to locate itself within a rationality debate defined already by the misreading one would refute—I prefer to take up the challenge at the level at which it is offered, at the level of a certain polemical assessment of the proper subject of political philosophy. It is, after all, Habermas who argues, who insists, that there is a real political effect associated with the philosophical gesture called *deconstruction.* "This neoconservative leave-taking from modernity is directed, then, not to the unchecked dynamism of societal modernization but to the husk of a cultural self-understanding of modernity that appears to have been overtaken" (PDM 3–4).

Is the postmodern discourse as exemplified by Heidegger and Derrida properly characterized as a "neo-conservative leave-taking" of the actual process of modernization, one that takes refuge in empty refutations of a straw-man rationality? More to the point, can Habermas offer such an argument in a manner that does not overstep the very basis for the charge? If the charge of neo-conservative paganism rests upon Habermas's contention that rigorous and politically responsible argumentation can and must be distinguished from rhetoric that disguises its private interests, then the argument would be endangered if Habermas could not establish the distinction without violating it. I will argue that Habermas's reading of Heidegger and Derrida contradicts in practice—and according to a certain necessity—his theory of practical rationality. I will argue, that is, that the polemical reading offered as a critique of the postmodern discourses constitutes a telling refutation of Habermas's claims concerning the nature of practical discourse and its power to distinguish illicit expressions of self-interest from rational argumentation tied to validity.

Second, Habermas's theory of communicative action amounts to a virtual abandonment of the concept of political theory that he inherited from Critical Theory. Habermas substitutes a theory of rationality for an account of practical reason and a theory of social development for a critical theory of society. If an examination of Habermas's work puts in question the traditional sense of what a political theory is supposed to be, then, in a sense that needs to be carefully defined, the criteria of what constitutes a political theory are up for grabs.

Habermasian Polemics

Following Weber—if not very far—Habermas opens *The Philosophical Discourse of Modernity* with the general thesis that the forms of societal modernization should be seen as processes of rationalization.[3] Postmodern discourses, the argument contends, are guilty of ignoring or dissolving this connection.

> The theory of modernization performs two abstractions on Weber's concept of "modernity." It dissociates "modernity" from its modern European origins and stylizes it into a spatio-temporally neutral model for processes of social development in general. Furthermore, it breaks the internal connections between modernity and the historical context of Western rationalism, so that processes of modernization can no longer be conceived of as rationalization, as the historical objectification of rational structures.... But as soon as the internal links between the concept of modernity and the self-understanding of modernity gained within the horizon of Western reason have been *dissolved,* we can relativize the, as it were, automatically continuing processes of modernization from the distantiated standpoint of a postmodern observer. (PDM 3)

Habermas is arguing that the postmodern discourses have erroneously taken the phenomena of societal modernization to be self-regulating processes independent of the self-understanding of Western reason, which therefore appears obsolete.

This criticism of the postmodern *dissolution* of the bond between modern rationality and societal modernization depends, of course, upon the assumption that the bond is real. For Habermas that claim is beyond question, since to deny that modernization is rational would entail denying the possibility of a rational diagnosis of the process. Habermas's distinction between the rationality of systems and the rationality of the life-world is designed to reassert the fundamental rationality of social history even as it recognizes that appearances seem to suggest anything but a progressive alliance of history and reason. Habermas is contending that the postmodern account dissolves this alliance due to its failure to recognize the fundamental processes behind the appearances. The consequence of that failure, then, would be a destructive postmodern discourse that ends up confirming the status quo because it gives up the possibility of rational critique.

In short, Habermas contends that the postmodern discourses have lost all faith in the power of a reflective rationality to explain and govern the development of the life-world. They fail to recognize the continuing relevance of the modernization-is-rationalization formula. Because they identify rationalization with purposive rationality they take the inadequacies of that limited aspect of reason to be a failure of reason itself. Following Nietzsche's diagnosis of the undifferentiated exhaustion of Western reason, Habermas argues, the postmoderns throw out the baby with the bathwater.

Notice that Habermas attributes to his opponents a reading of modernization and rationalization that he claims to be transparently inadequate. This is the polemical ploy that organizes the readings of Heidegger and Derrida. The rationale behind the vehemence of that polemic is clear here as well. If Derrida has failed to note the distinction between life-world and system rationality, and if Derrida has chosen to follow Nietzsche's rejection of the notion of rational argumentation, Habermas feels justified in arguing that Derrida, like Heidegger before him, has simply chosen to ignore the post-Nietzschean developments in philosophy and the social sciences. Habermas sees this stubborn disregard for the contemporary literature as a politically indefensible refusal on the part of the postmodern discourse to acknowledge the intellectual lessons of the Second World War.

Habermas's distinction between system and life-world rationality is designed to address these political and philosophical imperatives. The analysis of system recognizes the apparent reduction of reason to reifying means-ends analyses. Yet the distinction itself acknowledges, Habermas contends, the increasing rationality of the life-world that preserves the possibility of rational practical decision.

In such an overdetermined, politically charged atmosphere it is easy to see how the polemic against Derrida's deconstructive strategy is determined by Habermas's criticism of Heidegger. Habermas argues that Heidegger's early thought amounts to a failed attempt to break away from the epistemological model of the subject by replacing Kantian or Husserlian (inter)subjectivity with a concept of world as existential background. And Heidegger's later works are presented as a self-conscious attempt to rationalize the involvement with National Socialism in a manner that might preserve his philosophical insights.

First of all, Habermas diagnoses Heidegger's lectures of the late 1930s and 1940s as a straightforward attempt to protect the existential phenomenology of *Being and Time* from the political reading he gave to those existential themes when he interpreted them in terms sympathetic with National Socialism.

> Because he identified "Dasein" with the Dasein of the nation, authentic-capacity-to-be with the seizure of power, and freedom with the will of the Fuhrer, and because he had read into the question of Being the National Socialist revolution... an internal and not easily touched up connection between his philosophy and contemporary events was established. A plain, political-moral revaluation of National Socialism would have attacked the foundations of the renewed ontology and called into question the entire theoretical approach. But if, on the contrary, the disappointment with National Socialism could be elevated beyond the foreground sphere of responsible judgment and action and stylized into an objective error, to an error gradually revealing itself in history, the continuity with the point of departure of *Being and Time* need not be endangered.... He interprets the untruth of the movement by which he had let himself be dragged along not in terms of an existential fallenness into the "they" for which one is subjectively responsible, but as an objective withholding of the truth.... Thus was born the concept of the history of Being. (PDM 159)[4]

I cite the argument at some length to show that Habermas's interpretation is entirely consistent with the relatively innocuous claim that Heidegger remained, in *Being and Time,* indebted to the tradition of epistemology grounded in a principle of subjectivity even as he worked to overcome it. Habermas's account offers no evidence to contest the suggestion that Heidegger managed to break away from that tradition only when, in the course of his Nietzsche lectures, he began to read metaphysics as the systematic process of making sense of the epochal forms in which the question of Being was posed.[5] There is no textual argument offered by Habermas to support his polemical claim over any number of other possible accounts that would not need to reduce philosophical arguments to issues of personal guilt. Habermas's reading does not rest upon a novel reading of Heidegger's texts but, rather, reflects Habermas's own political agenda. As such the question raised by Habermas's interpretation is not whether the polemical reading is true but whether such a reading can be defended in the Habermasian vocabulary of truth understood as a system of specifiable validity claims.

Second, however, Habermas's account of the writings that follow the *Kehre* is internally inconsistent. Habermas explains the "turn" in Heidegger's thought as an objectification of error designed to assuage personal guilt. On the one hand, Habermas insists that Heidegger alters the existential account developed in *Being and Time* to preserve the underlying truth of the system from the fascist reading he had given it in 1933. Having discolored his "entire theoretical approach" by defining it in terms serviceable to National Socialism, Heidegger would have to develop, according to Habermas, a new account called the *history of Being*. The argument asserts that Heidegger aims to attribute his personal failures to truths about the essential dissimulating nature of truth. Habermas explains this complex strategy by attributing to Heidegger two motivations. First of all, Heidegger would be attempting to excuse his own failures of judgment. Second, Heidegger would have to restate, or recontextualize, his earlier philosophical insights in a manner that isolates them from the taint of their earlier association with National Socialism. This characterization says that the account of the history of Being is developed with the intention of preserving the philosophical heart of the system that it replaces. But note that if the story about the history of Being is supposed to replace the systematic heart of *Being and Time,* then it makes little sense to argue that the motivation behind the change was the desire to protect the (now abandoned) earlier existential account. However, the attendant argument was that Heidegger develops the history-of-Being account to "objectivize" his own lack of political judgment. This argument assumes, simply, that Heidegger was concerned primarily with his own personal failure, and that he devoted his mature thought to expunging at all cost his own political error, even as the world around him was calling out for some account of *its* own failure.

Nuanced and interesting as Habermas's account of Heidegger's *Kehre* certainly is, it is not the conclusion of an argument as Habermas himself has defined the term.[6] I need not argue that Habermas's reading is false; the point is that his claims are not falsifiable. In other words, the polemical reading of Heidegger's error and the account of his later writings as a reaction formation raises fundamental questions regarding Habermas's own theory that all rational uses of speech can be expressed as validity relations.

Operating at the level of motivations and substituting thereby surmise and suggestion for argumentation, the discussion removes itself from the realm of contestable validity claims. Habermas's intention is, clearly, polemical; that is to say, the intention is to give a plausible summary account of the relation between Heidegger's personal, political, and professional careers, to offer a persuasive account of the meaning—here this means just the political significance—of Heidegger's life and work. Outlining the political consequences of Heidegger's developing notion of rationality is not, in itself, an unimportant or inappropriate task. Given my own polemical purposes, this approach is significant because it amounts to the introduction of a polemical form of argumentation at a critical stage in Habermas's attempt to demonstrate that the postmodern discourses substitute polemic for argumentation. If such a polemical element were essential to the process of political argumentation, then Habermas's own procedure would constitute a fundamental exception to his claims about the forms of argumentation.

With respect to Derrida, Habermas's reading in *The Philosophical Discourse of Modernity* is less personal but no less a polemic. Habermas argues that Heidegger's mature notion of truth—the one identified by Habermas as a strategy designed to protect Heidegger from his own guilt—identifies "truth" with "a happening that is not at our disposal" (PDM 162). Habermas asserts that Derrida has inherited from Heidegger a notion of truth, indeed of history, which notions wholly determine the Derridean concept of deconstruction despite Derrida's radically distinctive "network of metaphors." Derrida, who demonstrates, Habermas is willing to concede, finer sensibilities than Heidegger, is nonetheless guilty by association. Derrida, the argument says, has translated Heidegger's idealized version of history into an account of language that need not respond to any but idealized textual imperatives. Habermas argues that Derrida simply identifies all speech with the rhetorical force of literary (idealized) language and, consequently, subverts the political significance of language directed toward the resolution of actual problems or disputes (PDM 204).

But this reading of Derrida really is a reading by association, since virtually none of Derrida's writings are considered. By association then: Having posited history as an objective and ideal realm, Heidegger and Derrida, the argument says, have detached the issue of rationality from the milieu of actual processes of social modernization. The upshot, Habermas claims, is twofold: (1) The deconstructive discourse is idealistic. It has given up its relevance to any rationality debate. Insofar as reason is detached from rationalization, the postmodern account of reason is left examining an empty husk rather than a living process. (2) The deconstructive discourse is (neo)conservative. Insofar as rationality is detached from the actual processes of modernization, those processes, left unchallenged, essentially are confirmed. These, at any rate, are the conclusions that constitute Habermas's polemic.

Habermasian Politics

Habermas's work constitutes a shift from traditional Critical Theory in favor of a theory of rationality. Habermas has always insisted that his own thought be measured against a certain radical intention. His thought is radical in two senses. It borrows from the tradition of Western Marxism, principally from Lukacs, Horkheimer, and Adorno, both a political intention and fundamental understanding of the rationality problematic.

Lukacs had to develop an account of the essential identity of revolutionary agency (the proletariat) and the subject of history (the proletariat) in order to provide the necessary theoretical assurances regarding the historical inevitability and legitimacy of class action. For Lukacs, the motor of history would have to be a particular form of life, the concrete life-form of a particular class. This nomination of the consciousness of one class within the socio-historical situation to be the simultaneous subject and object of history amounted to a fundamental identification of theory and the process of concrete history.[7] Adorno and Horkheimer, writing only twenty years later, recognized that the only significant role for theory was to announce and encourage an element of resistance to the very process of historical rationalization that Lukacs, expressing the very essence of Hegelian Marxism, had worked to ground. Which is to say, Horkheimer and Adorno took the identification of modernization and rationalization quite seriously—they continued the Weberian element picked up by Lukacs—but they no longer could recognize in that rationalization process any guarantee of the advent of social freedom.

The Frankfurt School's break with the teleological conception of history has at least two fundamental theoretical consequences. First, the theoretical identification of matter (i.e., the social conditions of material reproduction) and will (class consciousness) is broken. Second, and consequently, theory can no longer describe itself as the expression of the laws of social oppression and their dialectical unfolding as inevitable social liberation. In a dialectical irony the Frankfurt School theorists are recognized as the heirs of Marx precisely because they forced the question of rationality out of its home in the laws of history. Thereafter, which is to say, ultimately, with Habermas, a theory of rationalization adequate to the social-historical phenomena of modernization would have to ground itself methodologically, discursively. The power of a certain critical science replaces the critical power of scientifically conceived history. But if Horkheimer and Adorno continued to insist that theory identify itself with the oppressed class—even though it was no longer possible to identify that class as the agents of history—Habermas broke that specific relation of theory to oppression.

With Habermas the object of a critical social science would be the processes of mediation at work in the two "worlds" that can no longer be simply identified: the world of matter, of nature, where rationality is purposive, and the life-world, where rationality would have to guard a respect for will, for the unconditioned.[8] Habermas inherits from the

Frankfurt School brand of Critical Theory a fundamental distrust of what had been the very ground of Marxist theory. The traditional identification of theory with the material basis of history came to be recognized as the ground of a totalizing totalitarian process of modernization that was consuming the space of values and norms as the price it exacted for its power to destroy every form of dogmatic foundationalism. Habermas agrees that the task of a contemporary theory of rationality is to respect that realm of unconditioned reflection at the same time that it recognizes the incontrovertible power of calculative, purposive rationality.

Habermas's solution to this dialectic of technical rationality is to argue, on the one hand, that the rationality of systems (technological, bureaucratic) is appropriately characterized as the calculation of efficiency with respect to accepted ends. On the other hand, he argues that the rationality appropriate to human interaction is an intersubjective process better characterized as "action" than calculation, and which Habermas calls *communicative action.* Communicative rationality is appropriate to the life-world since it guards the ability to rationally criticize the ends or goals of action—a power that the rationality of system, with its concern for efficiency, had abrogated. Habermas argues that the Frankfurt theorists could not express their insights regarding the need to resist a homogeneous totalizing technical rationality because they were unwilling to draw a distinction between the rationality of societal modernization and the rationality of a revolutionary response. To draw such a distinction would, it seemed, forgo the power of the latter to intervene in the former. The form of their faith in reason was, Habermas contends, evidence of both their powerful understanding of modernity and their fundamentally traditional attachment to a conception of rationality wholly determined by the model of consciousness, by the principle of subjectivity (PDM 129).

Habermas's model of communicative action is designed precisely to break with that paradigm of the philosophy of consciousness in order to give an account of an element of reflective rationality that is not overwhelmed by the growing power of system rationality. Affirming the observation that modernity is characterized by increasing colonization of the life-world by systems that no longer retain any reflective rationality, Habermas thereby confirms the general diagnosis of the Frankfurt School at the same time that he asserts a distinction between life-world and system unthinkable on the traditional model of rationality tied to consciousness. Habermas's claim is that we produce and reproduce, in the illocutionary bonds of communication, fundamental (universally presupposed) relations, which relations can be reconstructed—that is to say, read off of actual speech use—as validity claims.

This does not amount to saying, of course, that actual participants in a disagreement could somehow draw upon a background knowledge to definitively validate the position they might be advocating. The theory of communicative action is not an ethics; it is a theory of the rationality at work in "discourse" when it is used to reach agreement rather than to assert propositional validity, or to assert one's will. Notice that this distinction between the theory and the actual speech actions of participants in a dispute locates the theory outside every such actual dispute. The theory asserts that no participant in an actual discourse oriented to reaching agreement can fail to instantiate linguistically mediated relations to the objective world, moral standards, and an implied sincerity standard. These three relations (truth, rightness, and sincerity) constitute the logic of speech use, of communicative action. This is not a formal but a pragmatic logic: the logic of the form of intersubjective "reflection" that actually grounds every instance of speech used to reach agreement.[9] It is, of course, impossible to develop an adequate account of the theory of communicative action in this space. But this summary needs to identify those elements of Habermas's theory that would substantiate the claim that his thought remains politically responsible and that would ground the charge that the deconstructive discourse is politically reactionary or irrelevant.

Critical Theory identified itself with the objective fact of oppression, even if it no longer held to the view that the eventual overcoming of oppression was an objective fact.[10] When Habermas argues that Critical Theory could not have recognized the option of communicative action, he is asserting a most fundamental difference between the respective philosophical foundations of his theory and of Critical Theory. When Horkheimer and Adorno insisted that freedom must be rational even as they recognized that this demand would submit freedom to a technical rationality, they established that they saw no other paradigm for rationality than the conflict between nature and will. Habermas, however, aims to provide an alternative account of rationality. Because he shifts the paradigm from consciousness to communication, communication can be both unconditioned (not reducible to a means-ends calculation) and yet rational. On the communicative model, rationality is an attribute of the world relations at work behind the process of consensus formation carried out between participants in a communicative discourse. The notion of communicative rationality through consensus is saved from relativism because Habermas locates the element of reason behind the actions of the actors. He locates communicative rationality within the universally presupposed formal relations produced and reproduced within the given use of speech. Rationality is not predicated of the judgments that follow from such a discourse, nor is it predicated (except counterfactually, as a necessary theoretical illusion) of the participants themselves. Habermas does not claim that participants are inherently rational and that, given optimal conditions, argumentation in fact will produce a legitimate outcome. Habermas is not, could not be, making such a claim. The theory of communicative action has not preserved the intention of Critical Theory as expressed by Horkheimer. Habermas does not imagine that his theory could help to stimulate some nascent element of resistance to a totalizing modern rationality; and this is because he has characterized the Frankfurt School's faith in a homogeneous element of negative or resistant rationality as an error grounded in their traditional model of reason. Habermas substitutes a theoretical account of a communicative rationality for a theory capable of intervening in actual communication. By locating the moment of rationality at the level of (universally presupposed) validity relations reproduced in every communicative action, Habermas guarantees the rationality of the life-world without guaranteeing that the life-world is rational. That is to say, his notion of rationality is secure against all empirical claims regarding the actual conduct of participants who, in fact, seem to pursue polemical strategies even in a discourse ostensibly designed to produce consensus.[11]

In securing his claim to a universal rationality appropriate to reflective (not merely purposive or technical) relations to the world, Habermas has achieved one-half of the incomplete project of Critical Theory. He has, in fact, designated a nonrelative structure within the life-world that is universally presupposed in every debate about the legitimacy of a course of action or the rightness of a norm. And, it is true, this structure of communicative rationality can be described in terms of validity relations. It would follow then that rationality is not limited to mere propositional validity. Freedom, it would follow, need not be synonymous with relativism. Claims to legitimacy have their own proper logic and can be reconstructed as validity claims that are not merely assertions of power or of prejudice. Yet in securing that realm of rationality Habermas insulates his theory from every actual instance of such discourse. This argument need not assert that political judgments in the broadest sense are necessarily particular. The force of the observation, rather, is that Habermas insists that the normative force of his theory of communicative action follows from a series of claims about what would (present conditional) necessarily (a transcendental claim) occur if an actual discourse were to achieve a rationally motivated consensus. The force of the observation, in other words, is that Habermas must preserve his theoretical account of ideal or counterfactual speech from the actual process it would explain. The theory is an account of a rational procedure, not a mechanism for producing rational conclusions. Habermas insists upon this distinction. And yet he does not acknowledge that the distinction leaves fundamentally unclear his claim that such a theory is properly political. The theory of communicative action must not be confused with the practical discourse itself, which must take place between participants in a practical dispute. The theory claims a certain universality that Habermas employs in contrasting his theory to the merely rhetorical play of the postmodern discourses. The universality follows from the claim that the theory identifies certain functions necessarily at work in every use of speech aimed at agreement. And yet, as in every transcendental account, the price of necessity is the loss of particularity.

Habermas substitutes a theory of a type of rationaiity appropriate to questions of legitimacy for a Critical Theory that defined itself in terms of its power to intervene in the name of legitimacy. To put the point in Habermasian terms: The process of modernization is a rationalization process that takes place within universally presupposed aspects of the implicit background that is our life-world. Rationality, in this sense, does not function at the level of particular actions or the assessment of particular proposals. The price Habermas pays for his decision to preserve the modern notion of rationality—and that means, not incidentally, to save it from the postmodern project—is that he must locate his account at a level fundamentally behind and beneath every particular instance of action. Only the life-world itself can be rational, never this or that mode of life, this or that judgment; and this conclusion follows not from some oversight on Habermas's part but from his firm determination that the process of modernization be recognized as a process of rationalization. This may indeed be a theory that overcomes the fundamentally modern philosophical paradox still controlling the Frankfurt School, but it is certainly not a resolution that they could have accepted. It is a resolution achieved through a philosophical revolution that places the question of legitimate action and advocacy behind the backs, and inherently out of the hands, of every actor.

Subject to Reason

What exactly is the force behind the charge that postmodern thought— and specifically Derrida's version—relinquishes any political efficacy in the course of its readings of Western logocentrism? Habermas insists that his communicative approach guards a fundamental resource that the deconstructive strategy renounces. The bond between modernization and rationalization is broken, Habermas contends, by the deconstructive critique that overstates its case in its identification of the paradigm of self-consciousness with rationality itself. The result of that identification would be that the deconstructive critique, following Nietzsche, sets itself in opposition not only to the paradigm of modernity but, through the flawed identification, in opposition to Western reason itself. Habermas sees in his communicative theory of speech-action a possibility closed off by the deconstructive procedure. By recasting the problem of modern rationality in a communicative rather than subjective model, Habermas aims to preserve the potential for raising and deciding validity claims—for critically solving problems—"always already operative in the communicative practice of everyday life, but only selectively exploited" (PDM 311). Habermas aims, in short, to preserve the authority of rationality by rescuing it from its modern paradigm as the philosophy of consciousness. "Only then does the critique of the domineering thought of subject-centered reason emerge in a *determinate* form—namely, as a critique of Western 'logocentrism', which is diagnosed not as an excess but as a deficit of rationality" (PDM 310).

But what exactly is the political virtue of such a communicative approach? Habermas insists that when it is drawn into the communicative framework and out of the ontological commitments of the philosophy of consciousness, the representative relation between the knowing subject and the world can be recast as a communicative relation between speakers and a differently conceived "world."

> The "world" to which subjects can relate with their representation or propositions was hitherto conceived of as the totality of objects or existing states of affairs. . . . But if normative rightness and subjective truthfulness are introduced as validity claims analogous to truth, "worlds" analogous to the world of facts have to be postulated for legitimately regulated interpersonal relationships and for attributable subjective experiences. (PDM 313)

Why does the vocabulary of the subject, of subjectivity, reappear here, where Habermas is most intent to distinguish his own critique of the paradigm of the subject from the politically irresponsible deconstructive critique of the idea of the subject? Habermas is quite clear on this point, and it is not necessary to suggest that he, somehow, falls back into a position that he aims to criticize. The fundamental distinction between his own and the deconstructive critique of the idea of the subject is abbreviated in the phrase just cited, in a concern for "legitimately regulated interpersonal relationships," and "attributable subjective experiences." The aim of Habermas's recasting of the modern notion of the subject is to produce an account of rationality adequate to the demand that "not just constative but also regulative and expressive speech acts can be connected with validity claims and accepted as valid or rejected as invalid" (PDM 313).

Habermas insists that an account of rationality be adequate to assertions about the objective world, normative claims about the shared

social world, and the expression of subjective experiences. Only an account
of rationality adequate to assertions of validity in each of these linguistic
"worlds" could meet the unquestioned demand that Habermas claims to
carry forward from the Enlightenment and Critical Theory. Habermas's
pedigree is telling. The unquestioned demand that measures Habermas's
contempt for Derrida's approach is the same unquestioned demand that
defines and determines the account of rationality described in the theory of
communicative action. That demand—reformulated, Habermas acknowledges, in the political and academic climate of the postwar Federal
Republic—insists that any account of rationality worthy of the term must
identify itself with resistance against totalitarianism and terror. Unquestionable, then, is the alliance between philosophy and rationality and the
alliance between rationality and societal modernization. The relation
between rationality and modernization, then, requires that philosophy
determine itself in terms amenable to public validation. This notion of
validation, however, cannot be allowed to rest within the arbitrary
determinations of the "text." The deconstructive textual politics fails,
Habermas insists, because it offers no account of the necessary relation
between discourse and claims that can be validated (PDM 190). Short of
that necessary relation, philosophy would offer no resistance to expressions
of illegitimate power disguised as a legitimate consensus. The bond
between legitimacy and validity in Habermas's system does not simply
repeat the traditional "fact mirroring function of language" but, rather,
rewrites that traditional foundational gesture in a theory of language use.
However, this pragmatic approach is designed to preserve—that is, to
rescue—the normative power claimed by the traditional subjective model.
The communicative approach differs from the traditional model of
knowledge and truth by regrounding the question of rationality in the
actual interactions between participants in a conversation aimed at
consensus. But the communicative approach differs from the deconstructive model precisely to the extent that it refuses to allow the philosophical
account of that conversation to be detached from the political imperative
that requires a fundamental distinction between rational and irrational
conversational procedures. It follows, of course, that at least one fundamental issue could not be subject to the vicissitudes of the actual
conversation. Given the possibility of disguised expressions of power, of
self-interest, of pathological or self-deluded arguments—given, in short,
the irrational power of rhetoric—one fundamental element, at least, would
have to be decided prior to any "possible" conversation; and that would be,
of course, the nature of reason itself.

   In its earliest incarnations the theory of the validity basis inherent in the
everyday use of speech was labeled *universal pragmatics*. And it is the
element of universality that grants the theory, in Habermas's own view, its

political efficacy. The translation of the traditional normative and political imperatives out of their foundation in a reflexive and immanently grounded principle of subjectivity and into a communicative or intersubjective foundation assures the Habermasian neo-Enlightenment approach of its political relevance, because it substitutes for a flawed universal foundation a pragmatic process that could assure that same universality, without simply repeating it. The subject of political philosophy remains, on this model, the alliance of rationality and universality, of self-reflexive autonomy and foundational transparency. Of course, Habermas resists every attempt to categorize his work as foundational, but the actual process of argumentation in which his work is formed describes and specifies a series of systematically related political, normative, and polemical imperatives which he could contest only at the risk of contradiction.

The procedural concept of rationality proposed by Habermas takes the form of a pragmatic logic of argumentation. The logic itself becomes the subject of political philosophy, harboring as it does an entire system of unquestionable presuppositions regarding the duties and, consequently, the form of the requisite alliances between rationality, universality, and normativity. Despite his misunderstandings regarding the fundamental gestures or strategies of deconstructive reading, Habermas is quite correct to insist that no system of normative validity follows, of necessity, from its work. Is Habermas, then, justified in asserting the political impotence and irresponsibility of a deconstructive strategy? I will conclude with two very brief observations that address this question.

First, clearly, a delegitimizing function is at work in the process of textual deconstruction. This chapter has shown, for example, that where he aims to criticize the political connotations of Heidegger's thought or where he would attempt to demonstrate the political conservatism of Derrida's works, Habermas enters the realm of interpretation and speculations that cannot be expressed as verifiable claims. The process of argumentation always exceeds the parameters of an account of its essential, or possible, rationality. The only universalizable checks upon the legitimacy of polemical argumentation follow, as Derrida says, from the imperative to read. This is not simply to argue that Habermas has stepped beyond the border between argumentation and rhetoric. It is to insist, rather, that the border is not universal, but regulative. This means, simply, that in order for Habermas to describe the actual or necessary distinction between argumentation and mere rhetoric, he must appeal to a counterfactual, or extra-discursive, principle of reason. The prior condition for the determination of the distinction between argumentation and rhetoric is a reference to one element that is not, itself, subject to determination in a conversation aimed at consensus. When Habermas argues that certain universally presupposed relations are instantiated in practical discourse, he is insisting, simply, that one unquestionable element determining every such discourse is not itself subject to "validation" in that discourse.

Second, yet the delegitimating function of a deconstructive reading seems to offer no positive alternative to the system of intersubjectively presupposed validity relations that ground Habermas's new account of the normative function of language. This suspicion, more than any other, powers the Habermasians in their vitriolic attacks on deconstruction. What possible benefit could follow from what they take to be a method that would satisfy itself merely with pointing to the paradoxical relation between foundation and concepts in every theoretical system? If, as Habermas suggests, the deconstructive strategy eschews any appeal to the very binding and universal validity relations upon which Habermas grounds his claim to political efficacy, then what conceivable positive alternative could deconstruction offer? The answer, of course, is that the process of deconstructive reading intends to offer no positive position to take the place of the traditional or neo-Enlightenment positions that it delegitimates. The aim is to question the "position" itself, not to satisfy it with an alternative neo-foundationalism. And here the Habermasian responds, with some disgust, "And what of the real social and political problems?"

Recognize, first of all, that the question is flawed. It is Habermas, after all, who not only acknowledges but insists:

> My restrictive view levels down the old philosophical claims to normative theory, be it in politics or ethics....The problem with classical normative theories is that they give people the illusion that they simply need to find the theory and then act on it. Which is nonsense. The normative part of the theory should be only pro-cedural, while everything else that matters for practical purposes should be learnt from science, from social theory and not from moral philosophy....I am sorry that social theory is basically not in any shape to perform the role I say it should.[12]

As I have argued from the outset, Habermas is consistent in his conviction that the proper subject for a contemporary political or normative science is the problem of rationality itself. And this is the avenue of a Derridean response to the political challenge. To assure the political force of his account of rationality, Habermas insists that the account be adequate to the task of an absolute distinction between a rhetorical argument that employs illegitimate force and a form of argumentation that appeals only to "the force of the better argument." What is the force of the better argument? It would have to be the expression of rationality itself. It is no caricature of Habermas's position to insist that the conversation that would instantiate rationality requires that one voice in the argument be the voice of reason. Reasons must be distinguished, in principle, from expressions that parade themselves as reason but actually disguise interests, or power. The force of the deconstructive reading is limited to its ability to illustrate—never in general but only in the process of an actual reading—how every such appeal to a principle of reason subverts its own demand. The political force of the Habermasian system follows from the ability of the system to give reason a place in the account of rational conversation. But what role could the voice of reason play in the actual conversation between participants that, Habermas insists, is the only locus of a rational practical discourse? Reason could not speak as just one participant in the conversation, since the voice of reason would then be either subjected to possible contradiction or it would have to carry the argument by virtue of its own proper force, in which case there would be no actual conversation at all. Habermas's account acknowledges this dual danger by locating the force of reason behind the backs of the participants. This is what Habermas means when he insists that the theory of argumentation could not, must not, take the place of the actual conversation itself.

The condition of the possibility of the distinction between mere rhetorical power and "the force of the better argument" is that the voice of reason be, itself, excluded from the conversation that would determine its actual force. Whoever would claim to speak in the name of reason would be branded as irrational, as a demigod, and excluded. And so Habermas must assert—speaking presumably in the name of reason itself—that certain universally presupposed relations guarantee the rationality of discourse, just in case reason has no actual voice in the conversation. The voice of reason, like an irrational voice, would have to be excluded from this actual conversation because these two voices—the voice of the irrational and the voice of reason—are beyond questioning; these two voices refuse to submit to the prior minimal conditions of rational argumentation itself. The conversation will be rational just in case it meets certain predetermined and, in principle, unquestionable rational standards. But this paradox does not pretend to point to an error in Habermas's thought. The discovery and purging of fundamental errors is a Habermasian motif, a process that Derrida, for essentially political reasons, has always avoided. The paradox points, rather, to the inherently antinomic relation of reason to rationality, a relation that Habermas refuses to acknowledge. The demonstration of this necessary exclusion, in principle, of the question of reason from every discourse that would claim to legitimate its account of argumentation through an appeal to a universal logic of reason is the political achievement of the deconstructive strategy. For Habermas, the subject of a properly political philosophy would be the necessary alliance of rationality and modernization, of rationality and argumentation. The price to be paid for such an account is that the idea of reason itself be, pragmatically, beyond question. For Derrida, if I may use the name, the subject of political philosophy is the question of reason, that is to say, the question about the ability of an account of rationality to be open to the need to continue to question the notion of reason.

Part 3

Subjection to Language, Power, and History

8   Dasein and the Analytic of Finitude

MICHAEL CLIFFORD

In *Being and Time,* Heidegger poses the question of the Being of beings in terms of the being of human Dasein. *Dasein,* it turns out, "is temporal in the very basis of its Being."[1] In *The Order of Things,* though barely mentioning Heidegger by name, Foucault identifies existential phenomenology as one of the last great forms of philosophic inquiry constituting the "analytic of finitude."[2] In this chapter I attempt to show more specifically than in *The Order of Things* how Dasein, temporality, and Being-towards-death fall within the framework of Foucault's critique. We shall see that *Being and Time* to a great extent anticipates Foucault's criticisms of the analytic of finitude and in fact engenders the conditions for philosophy's move beyond it. That is, by pushing the analytic of finitude to its limits, *Being and Time* opens a space for a thought, for a mode of *thinking,* that can transgress those limits.[3]

Foucault's work takes place in the space opened by *Being and Time,* or rather, by the *crisis* of *Being and Time* reflected in Heidegger's *Kehre.* Examining *Being and Time* in the light of Foucault's critique can serve to render Heidegger's *Kehre* intelligible. However, the question is not, Why did Heidegger turn? but rather, Were the possibilities for Heidegger's *Kehre* already there in *Being and Time?* The issue is not so much whether *Being and Time* is subject to Foucault's criticisms of the analytic of finitude, but to what extent *Being and Time* made Foucault's critique possible. The question and the issue turn on understanding Heidegger's *Kehre* in terms of the relation between crisis and critique. The *Kehre* is the *hinge* between the crisis of *Being and Time* and Foucault's critique. Heidegger's *Kehre* brings the two together even as it holds them apart, providing at once the intimacy and the distance necessary to their correlation. As such, as the hinge, Heidegger's *Kehre* turns to nothing, except insofar as its meaning, its possibility for meaning, closes upon the tension and rapport between *Being and Time* and *The Order of Things,* between crisis and critique.[4]

There is a close affinity between "crisis" and "critique" that goes beyond their common etymological heritage. Both words derive from the Greek *krinein,* meaning to cut or to separate. The affinity between crisis and critique can be seen by restoring the fullness of their original meaning. In *cutting* the two are thought together; that is, the severity, the severing moment, of crisis can be realized only through a critique that enables it to be recognized *as* crisis. Crisis is a form of upheaval that separates us, that cuts us adrift, from the firm and familiar. But the possibility for crisis must have been already there in the space from which we are dislodged. Crisis, strictly speaking, is the experience of separation that occurs with the movement of upheavel within a delimited space; it is nothing over and above this experience. As an experience, crisis is impossible without an interpretation, a discourse, to give it meaning, reality, as the movement of separation. Critique makes the crisis discursive: it gives discourse to crisis, and only in so doing is the crisis made real (i.e., meaningful).

Critique actualizes the cut of crisis that has yet to be brought to thought. This is not to say that crisis may be reduced to critique. On the contrary, the effectiveness of critique lies precisely in the extent to which it not simply analyzes crisis but appropriates it, appropriates the *cut* of crisis. The cut is the power of critique, the power to mark the limits of an established space (a tradition or an entrenched mode of thought) and in so doing, to transgress those limits. Critique without the cut of crisis is mere interpretation; in fact, a discourse that merely interprets crisis, without having been shaken by it, has the effect of nullifying the crisis, of causing its elimination by explication. Genuine critique brings the critical moment of crisis forward, where it can, in the form of critical discourse, sever ties with the space from which it arose. The critical moment of crisis is actualized through the critical return of critique, a return that is also an opening to a beyond, the space opened by the cut of crisis and *delimited* by the dissecting movement of critique. In this sense, crisis and critique require one another for whatever power and density of meaning they may have. Crisis without critique is meaningless. Critique without crisis is a sham.

The relationship between crisis and critique is sometimes expressed superficially by assuming a temporal-causal connection in which crisis precipitates critique, or critique precipitates crisis.[5] The latter supposition (that critique precipitates crisis) must be wrong if critique is essentially reflective; in that case, crisis would always precede critique. But how then would we account for the opening of a new space for thought—with new tasks, new demands, new *truths*—that seems to attend necessarily every great form of critique? It is not enough to say, for example, that

Christianity emerged from the crisis of Greco-Roman rationality, or that existentialism arose from the crisis of Hegelianism, unless we can account for the cutting power of such critiques—the power of separation, of slicing through boundaries, of carving out a space in which thought does not yet anticipate its own inevitable collapse. This power, the power of the cut in critique, can have come only from crisis. The appropriation of crisis by critique has the effect of upsetting the temporal-causal aspect of their relation. In bringing the crisis forward, critique represents the *temporal lag* of crisis, the point at which the upheaval becomes an opening.

Just as we may gauge the distance of lightning by the temporal lag of its thunder, so may we trace—or retrace—the moment of crisis in the critique that it spawns. In fact, only with the emergence of critique does the crisis become visible. We saw this in Athens, whose decline was accompanied by various "crisis philosophies." Actually, these crisis philosophies turned out to be the hinge between Greek rationalism and the stoicism peculiar to Rome and the entire Christian world. We saw the tracing of crisis by critique again in Königsburg, where Kant's critique emerged out of the crisis of skepticism. Actually, it would be more appropriate to view skepticism as the hinge between Kant's critique and traditional empiricism. Before Kant, skepticism was merely a challenge to empiricism. Kant's critique revealed both the crisis of empiricism and the emptiness of skepticism, empty in the sense that it took all its meaning from the relation of crisis to critique.

Heidegger's *Kehre* has been interpreted as a kind of crisis. But the real crisis, the silent upheaval that precipitated Heidegger's turn was in *Being and Time*. Foucault's critique of the analytic of finitude (a period of philosophic inquiry running roughly from Kant to Heidegger) represents the temporal lag of that crisis. Through Foucault's critique the crisis of *Being and Time* at last is made clear. Foucault's critique reveals that *Being and Time* suffers from a "doubling movement," peculiar to the entire analytic of finitude, that results from the attempt by philosophy to ground concrete limitation on an identical subject-object; this attempt collapses under the weight of its infinite task. But although Foucault's critique is directed against *Being and Time,* to a great extent the critique is possible only because of *Being and Time.* Moreover, to the extent that Foucault's critique represents the opening of a space in which thinking can go beyond the analytic of finitude, this possibility is likewise rooted in *Being and Time*. The crisis-critique relation between *Being and Time* and *The Order of Things* may be unique in that, for the first time in the history of thought, critique may be able to carry the cut of crisis forward indefinitely, always putting itself in question, always anticipating its own crisis and collapse, always seeking to *undercut* its own provisional, crisis-laden claims to truth.

To understand how *Being and Time* not only falls under Foucault's critique, but how it made that critique possible, first it is necessary to identify the elements in *Being and Time* that place it in the analytic of finitude. The fundamental expression of finitude in *Being and Time* is *Sein-zum-Tode,* or Being-towards-death.

Being-towards-Death

In Part I of *Being and Time* we learn that the being of Dasein is *care,* or concernful Being-in-the-world. In Part II we come to understand care as *temporal.* "The primordial unity of the structure of care lies in temporality" (BT 375). Temporality makes possible the unity of existence and is understood in terms of Dasein's futurally making present in the process of having been, that is, in terms of Dasein's temporalizing of the three ecstases of past, present, and future onto the horizon of temporality:

> Coming back to itself futurally, resolution brings itself into the Situation by making present. The character of "having been" arises from the future, and in such a way that the future which "has been". . . releases from itself the Present. This phenomenon has the unity of a future which makes present in the process of having been; we designate it as "temporality." Only in so far as Dasein has the definite character of temporality, is the authentic potentiality-for-Being-a-whole of anticipatory resoluteness. . . made possible for Dasein itself. *Temporality reveals itself as the meaning of authentic care.* (BT 374)

The fundamental structures of Dasein—the basic possibilities of existence, the authenticity and inauthenticity of Dasein—all are temporal and "grounded ontologically as possible temporalizations of temporality" (BT 352). Temporality is the meaning of care. Care—authentic care, understood in terms of "anticipatory resoluteness"—is "Being-towards-death" (BT 378). Being-towards-death is the basis for the temporalizing activity of Dasein.

Death, says Heidegger, is the possibility of the absolute impossibility of Dasein. In "anticipatory resoluteness"—which is the basis for authentic Dasein, whose temporalizing activity provides the temporal horizon in which entities in the world are disclosed—Dasein understands and appropriates its *"ownmost* and uttermost potentiality for Being,"that is, its death (BT 307). If Dasein exists at all, it has already been *thrown* into this possibility. To be authentic, it must release itself from the illusions of the "they-self" and free for itself its own death.

> *No one can take the Other's dying away from him....* Dying is
> something that every Dasein itself must take upon itself at the time.
> By its very essence, death is in every case mine.... In dying it is shown
> that mineness and existence are ontologically constitutive for death.
> Dying is not an event; it is a phenomenon to be understood
> existentially. (BT 284)

Being-towards-death, as a mode of being for Dasein, "is possible only as
something futural" (BT 373). In being futural it is the basis for the
temporalization of temporality by Dasein. Temporality, then, is at bottom
Being-towards-death.

   Death, for Heidegger, is a *possibility,* the utmost possibility of
impossibility, which Dasein must appropriate resolutely to be authentic. In
confronting and appropriating death, Dasein is able to realize the radically
finite (temporal) character of existence. *"Authentic Being-towards-death
—that is to say, the finitude of temporality—is the hidden basis of Dasein's
historicality"* (BT 438). Inasmuch as death is not an event, Being-towards-
death is ontological rather than ontical; it is an existential relation toward
the possibility of death and, as such, is concerned with the meaning of
Being in general.

   Being-towards-death, understood in terms of authentic existence, is
more than Dasein's genuinely appropriating its own mortality. Dasein, as
Being-in-the-world, is the clearing of being in which beings are manifested,
that is, brought into the clearing, *disclosed* as beings. "The horizon of
temporality as a whole determines that *whereupon* factically existing
entities are essentially *disclosed"* (BT 416). Being-towards-death entails
that this disclosedness, constitutive of authentic Dasein, is a mortal
disclosedness, that Dasein is basically finite; and the disclosiveness, the
disclosing of being is thus temporal. It is, in fact, grounded upon the
temporalized temporality of finite Dasein.

   In grounding disclosed being in the temporalizing activity of Dasein,
Heidegger is seeking to overcome the subject-object dichotomy which is
fundamental in the pure transcendental phenomenology of Husserl. For
Heidegger, Dasein *is* the clearing. The being of beings is thus disclosed in
Dasein. There are no objects "out there" to be discovered by Dasein. There
is no subject as such standing in opposition to an Other. Dasein *is* its
disclosedness. Being is the disclosedness of Dasein. The subjectivity of
transcendental consciousness is thereby dissolved. "No sooner was the
'phenomenon of knowing the world' grasped than it got interpreted in a
'superficial', formal manner," says Heidegger. "The evidence for this is the
procedure (still customary today) of setting up knowing as a 'relation
between subject and Object'—a procedure in which there lurks as much

'truth' as vacuity. But subject and Object do not coincide with Dasein and the world" (BT 86–87).

Heidegger's dissatisfaction with the subject-object dichotomy stems from and belongs with his conviction that the question of Being never really has been asked adequately by prior metaphysics. Being, the question of Being, has necessarily eluded metaphysics because of metaphysics' reliance on a fundamental opposition between a *subject* whose *object* is the being of beings. But being as object can never cross the great chasm that lies between it and the seeking subject. Kant with his categories and Husserl with his pure transcendental consciousness, for example, both set up a dichotomy in which being, if it is understood at all, stands to the subject as Other, removed and unappropriated. For Heidegger, on the other hand, it is through Dasein, as Being-in-the-world, as care (rather than through a transcendental "bracketing" consciousness), that the being of beings is understood (interpretatively) as bound constitutively to the "already-there" and temporalizing activity of Dasein.

The Analytic of Finitude

Michel Foucault shares with Heidegger a general dissatisfaction with the dichotomizing tendencies of Western metaphysics.[6] Foucault's interest in the subject-object dichotomy, especially in the work of the period that resulted in *The Order of Things* and *The Archaeology of Knowledge,* is just part of his broader concern with the constellation of epistemological positivities constituting the modern episteme. *Episteme* refers to the totality of epistemological (discourse-forming) relations that characterize a given historico-scientific period. The modern episteme, ushered in by Kant and typified by Husserlian phenomenology and the emergence of the human sciences, is characterized—and, in fact, permeated—by what Foucault calls the *analytic of finitude:*

> At the foundation of all the empirical positivities, and of everything that can indicate itself as a concrete limitation of man's existence, we discover a finitude . . . it is marked by the spatiality of the body, the yawning of desire, and the time of language; and yet it is radically other: in this sense, the limitation is expressed not as a determination imposed upon man from outside (because he has a nature or a history), but as a fundamental finitude which rests on nothing but its own existence as fact, and opens upon the positivity of all concrete limitation. (OT 315)

The analytic of finitude is based on the emergence of man, in the nineteenth and twentieth centuries, as a concrete epistemological positivity, as an object of reflection. But man emerges as a kind of "double"; man functions within the scientificity of discursive formations composing the modern episteme as an "empirical-transcendental doublet"—that is, as an object of knowledge and as a subject that knows (OT 318). For the human sciences, this creates an object of discourse (man) that is fleeting and illusory. Ground and that which is grounded are double in the sense that "knowledge will be attained in [man] of what renders all knowledge possible" (OT 318). In phenomenology we see the same sort of doubling movement between man and being, wherein the *cogito* of transcendental consciousness stands against the "unthought" of pre-intended objects in the world. Here the "unthought" designates the Other. The Other is "both exterior to [man] and indispensable to him. . . . the inexhaustible double that presents itself to reflection as the blurred projection of what man is in his truth, but that also plays the role of a preliminary ground upon which man must collect himself and recall himself in order to attain his truth" (OT 326–27). What is peculiar to the empirical-transcendental doublet of the human sciences, to the fragile transcendentality of Husserlian phenomenology, to the anthropological humanism of the entire modern episteme is that they all "find themselves treating as their object what is in fact their condition of possibility" (OT 364).

In rejecting the subject-object distinction, Heidegger sought for the being of Dasein (and, in fact, Being in general) a firmer ground. He thought he had discovered such a ground in the temporality of Dasein. In fact, through Dasein, Heidegger is not only undermining the subject-object distinction; he is moving—or so he thinks—beyond *subjectivity* altogether. (Whether Heidegger actually achieves this is a point of contention among Heidegger scholars, but it is a point that must be conceded to Heidegger, as I shall attempt to show.) But does Heidegger really escape the doubles of the modern episteme? Does the temporality of Dasein allow him to escape the limitations of the analytic of finitude as it is drawn by Foucault? Foucault thinks not (at least the Foucault of *The Order of Things* in consideration of the Heidegger of *Being and Time*). In fact, for Foucault, *Being and Time* represents the "culminating example" of the analytic of finitude.[7] With *Being and Time* the double of this analytic is seen in the double movement of the "retreat and return of the origin" (OT 328–35).

"The last feature that characterizes both man's mode of being and the reflection addressed to him," says Foucault, "is the relation to the origin" (OT 328). The themes of labor, life, and language which form the modern episteme and cover the entire domain of what can be known about man, differ from the epistemological formations of previous epistemes in that they have acquired, and are characterized by, their own *historicity*. This historicity, according to Foucault, "makes possible the necessity of an origin" (OT 329). *Origin* here refers to the ground or source for all possible factical, positive knowledge of man (or the being of man). The search for such an origin, understood as bound constitutively "to a previously existing historicity," is characteristic of the modern episteme (OT 330). According to the analytic of finitude, asserts Foucault, it is in man that things find their beginning. "The analytic of finitude attempts to reappropriate the whole of history by showing that man always already has a history,"[8] that man is always already there as history's ground. The analytic thus seeks to establish some sort of ontological boundary, the origin, first in the past and then in the future, that can serve as the ground for self-reflective inquiry and for inquiry into (the being of) the world in general. But this ground always eludes us; and, in fact, the search for an origin "dooms us to an endless task," according to Foucault (OT 334).

In *Being and Time,* temporal beginning and temporalizing clearing, understood as bound constitutively to the temporality of authentic Dasein, represent two kinds of origin or source.[9] Foucault's observation that "it is always against a background of the already begun that man is able to reflect on what may serve for him as origin" (OT 330), is reflected in the Heideggerian observation that Dasein is always already there in the world. The return and retreat of the origin is seen in Heidegger's distinction between the everydayness of inauthentic Dasein and the temporalizing activity of authentic Dasein. "Being is farther than all beings and is yet nearer to man than every being," says Heidegger.[10] Origin is thus at once *there* and removed, bound constitutively to man's being and yet inaccessible to man. Observes Foucault, "Man is cut off from the origin that would make him contemporaneous with his own existence: amid all the things that are born in time and no doubt die in time, he, cut off from all origin, is already there" (OT 332).

For Heidegger, the temporality of Dasein—as that which constitutes its being—derives from, and is understood in terms of, Being-towards-death. Being-towards-death must be interpreted phenomenologically in that it *lets be,* as a projecting mode of being, the temporal stretch of Dasein. In *Being and Time,* this Dasein, which is the clearing for the disclosure of being, is essentially *human.* Human Dasein is the origin of being in that it constitutes the temporalized clearing in which beings are disclosed. Thus, the history of being is always a history of human Dasein. Although human, Dasein is not, however, to be identified with subjectivity, with a definable and identifiable "self" or human subject. "Dasein's Selfhood has been defined formally as a *way of existing,* and therefore not as an entity present at hand" (BT 312). This represents Heidegger's move away from the dichotomizing tendencies of previous forms of philosophic reflection making up the analytic of finitude, specifically, the subjectivism of transcendental phenomenology and the human sciences. But while disclosed being is a temporal phenomenon, or rather a mode of being occurring on a temporalized horizon bound constitutively to human Dasein as origin, this is an origin that Dasein cannot and yet *must* claim as its own. Dasein must claim this origin as its own if Dasein is ever to be authentic. Dasein must claim this origin as its own if the origin is ever to become the object of (hermeneutic) phenomenological reflection. However, Dasein cannot claim the origin as its own. In being, the origin always returns to Dasein, but this return is always accompanied by the concealment of being; thus, the origin retreats, is lost in Dasein's anticipation of itself *as origin*. Here we see the self-reflexive doubling movement of the analytic of finitude.

Beyond the *Kehre*

Although human Dasein is not to be understood subjectivistically in *Being and Time,* it still belongs, contends Reiner Schurmann, with the post-Kantian humanistic concern with man. In Heidegger's early writings, observes Schurmann, "what appears as originary is human existence (Dasein). All phenomena are phenomena for man.... The modalities of time as well as the manifold ways in which things show themselves are all referred back to man's existence and its basic structure."[11] Apparently Heidegger recognized this and became dissatisfied with his interpretation of Dasein, because he underwent what is generally referred to as his *Kehre,* a reversal or turning with regard to his early work. "Everything is reversed," writes Heidegger in the "Letter on Humanism."[12] With the *Kehre,* after 1930, we see a remarkable shift in Heidegger's understanding of Dasein as well as origin, which is reflected in the philosophical discourse that follows it.

Above all, Heidegger's *Kehre* represents a move away from the being of man and toward language as "the house of Being."[13] This move toward language is definitive of postmodern thought. We see this, for example, in Derrida and deconstruction, as well as in the archaeology-genealogy of Foucault. For the latter, archaeology-genealogy gives a certain autonomy to statements (as opposed to a speaking subject), to the discursive as such. Foucault wants to consider statements and sets of statements "in their discontinuity, without having to relate them...to a more fundamental opening or difference."[14]

This shift in philosophical inquiry can be, and has been, traced back at least as far as Heidegger's *Kehre,* to his changed understanding of Dasein, according to which Dasein is no longer peculiarly human. His turn to language in many ways anticipates Foucault and is characteristic of postmodern thought in general. But is there something in *Being and Time* itself that makes this turn possible, that opens a space for the possibility of a Foucault and even for a so-called later Heidegger? Is there something in the analytic of finitude, of which *Being and Time* is the "culminating example," that allows for the emergence of Foucault, for his critique of the analytic of finitude and his movement beyond it?

Perhaps the most obvious way in which *Being and Time* anticipates Foucault and the postmodern epoch is in its move away from subjectivity. After *Being and Time* philosophy can no longer take the transcendental ego as fundamental. Subject and object are revealed as the purely ontical *representation* of the ontological disclosure of being by Dasein, an existential phenomenon that is the ground for the possibility of subjects and objects and their relation to each other. Heidegger's destructuring of the subject-object dichotomy allows Foucault to call into question—and, in fact, to undermine—the privilege of man as the epistemological center of the universe. Heidegger (as well as Nietzsche) allows Foucault to ask the audacious question, "Does man really exist?" (OT 322). This is the fundamental question of postmodern thought, but it is no longer a metaphysical question. It is a question that displaces man, in the substantive sense, by looking to language, by recognizing in language an arbitrary delimitation of space in which "man" emerges as a privileged object of discourse.

Thus, although *Being and Time* may fall under Foucault's critique in that it repeats the doubles of the analytic of finitude in the return and retreat of origin, to a great extent Heidegger's understanding of Dasein as origin makes possible the destruction of the subjectival doubles that precede it. What Dasein shares with transcendental phenomenology and the human sciences is a relation to a fundamental finitude. In *Being and Time* this finitude, as we have seen, is Being-towards-death. In all the forms of philosophic reflection composing the analytic of finitude, finitude is the foundation for all concrete limitation; but nowhere is this finitude brought forward from the background and made to play such an actively fundamental role as in *Being and Time*. It is only by anticipating resolutely its own death that Dasein can be authentic. Being-towards-death involves Dasein's bearing a relation to Being in general. What is the nature of this relation? It is a relation of *questionableness,* a mode of being that puts being *in question.* The question of the Being of beings is the fundamental question of *Being and Time*. The being of Dasein is linked to Being in general, not by the privilege of a knowing subject but by the question of Being. Thus there is no simple origin to be assigned to Dasein; rather, origin is a question that must be asked of Dasein. By developing the question of origin, which is a question of Dasein's relation to Being in general, the issue of subjectivity is set aside.

The effectiveness of *Being and Time* lies in its ability, its resolve, to ask the question of the Being of beings without attempting to answer it. This is also Heidegger's departure from traditional metaphysics, which always seeks to answer the question, to put a closure to thought. The question of Being is a question called forth by Dasein's own finitude. Thus *Being and Time* pushes the analytic of finitude to its limits, traces it to its utmost possibility: the possibility of impossibility, of death. But perhaps finitude itself needs to be called into question. And of course this is exactly what Foucault does in *The Order of Things*. He recognizes the fundamental role, even privilege, of finitude in structuring *Being and Time,* and, *in a move that is typically Heideggerian,* he calls that privilege into question.

This "calling into question," even more than his deconstruction of subjectivity, is Heidegger's true legacy to later thought. It is a move that, along with the Death of Man, is "nothing more, and nothing less, than the unfolding of a space in which it is once more possible to think" (OT 342). Heidegger's *Kehre* is a turn toward a space that opens onto the possibility of perpetual critique, a critique that constantly calls itself into question, that courts crisis with every step—a crisis-thinking, a thinking perpetually in crisis. This possibility is the Nietzschean in Heidegger that he was never able to suppress, the Nietzschean suspicion that he brought forward in spite of himself. *Being and Time* may indeed fall under the dissecting criticism of the genealogist. But it is a step that must have been taken, without which the phenomenon of a Foucault, or a Derrida, or a "later Heidegger" could not have emerged.

9 Foucault's Analytics of Power

Introduction

Typically Michel Foucault's analytics of power is understood to be a theory that provides a new (or, according to some commentators, not so new) model of power or, at the very least, a methodological tool that can be applied to a variety of fields of study. On the reading to be presented in this chapter, however, the analytics of power is not a model at all, and, if it is a tool, it is a highly specialized one whose primary domain of application is Foucault's own discourse itself, not political struggle in general. In this chapter the analytics will be read as a strategic move in Foucault's campaign to think subjectivity historically, a move designed to undermine some of the obstacles we face when we attempt to think in the absence of transcendental structures. In particular, the analytics of power works to undermine the obstacles presented to historical thinking by the ways in which power typically poses itself for analysis.

In preparation for setting out my alternative reading I will recount briefly the major claims that Foucault's analytics makes or seems to make about power. Then I will sketch the debate that surrounds the analytics in the secondary literature that I have surveyed. Finally, I will offer my reading of Foucault's work, a reading in which the analytics is taken to be a movement of thought rather than a description of a theoretical object.[1]

Foucault's Claims

Foucault's work on power is primarily to be found in *The History of Sexuality*, Volume 1: *An Introduction;*[2] interviews in *Power/Knowledge,* especially "Truth and Power" and "Power and Strategy";[3] and in the afterword to Dreyfus and Rabinow's *Michel Foucault: Beyond Structuralism and Hermeneutics,* entitled "The Subject and Power."[4] I will rely on those sources for the brief account that follows.

Foucault's assertions about power number, roughly, seven:

1. He claims that power is productive, not primarily repressive, as so many theories of power would have it.

2. He claims that power is best understood as relational rather than as a possession that can be held and used, or not used, at the will of a master-subject.

3. Power is best analyzed first at the micro-level; only as events reinforce each other are networks or systems such as ideologies and institutions formed.

4. No one sets up these systems of power from some position outside power networks; we all always already find ourselves within networks that have evolved of their own accord.

5. Hence, there is no outside to power; power is everywhere.

6. Resistance, too, is everywhere. Because power is relational, resistance is always inscribed within it. Since power networks depend at every moment upon the repetition of their sustaining micro-events, they are unstable, so resistances may be able to overcome power networks or at least aspects of them.

7. Finally, Foucault asserts that power itself does not exist; there is no single, unitary, monolithic identity named power that can hold us in its grip.

Characterization of the Debate Surrounding the Analytics

Many, perhaps most, readers of Foucault, as I noted earlier, understand these claims as attempts at description. They understand Foucault to say that other theorists have been wrong about the nature of power; *really* power is thus and so. Some readers have been glad for the alternative. They have begun trying to apply it as an analytical model in fields into which Foucault himself did not venture—feminist theory, for example. But most commentators judge Foucault's work to suffer from grave problems, and they challenge apologists to render some account.

For example, a 1983 article in *Political Theory* criticizes Foucault for failing to define the term *force*. Foucault, the author claims, has defined *power* as an effect of micro-level forces, but he has neglected to explain how we are to distinguish between occurrences of force and other occurrences.[5]

Now, the foregoing may sound like a rather frivolous criticism, one insignificant and wrongheaded enough to be easily dispensed with.[6] But if we take the analytics of power to be a theoretical description, then it does make some sense to expect a careful definition of the phenomenon being described. Given the rules of theoretical work, one perhaps even has a right to demand that a theory give a clear definition of what it is talking about. This critic, just like many of Foucault's defenders, then, has assumed that the analytics of power is in fact simply talking about some real, extradiscursive phenomenon: power. This particular criticism may be clearly misguided, but it is not terribly unlike some more plausible-sounding criticisms and responses on Foucault's behalf. A significant amount of the debate surrounding the analytics concerns clarifications and analyses of terms.

Somewhat more commonly, however, critics and apologists clash over the question of whether Foucault's analytics is politically useful. Some critics claim that on Foucault's analysis we are all reduced to the status of victims, forever trapped in mechanisms of power and unable to extricate ourselves; for Foucault has said that there is no outside to power and that power is everywhere. He offers neither hope nor help in our struggle to escape from power's grip.[7] Foucault's defenders counter with the claim that power is not inherently evil, that there is no reason to long for complete escape, and that resistance to cruel regimes is always possible, as is their eventual defeat. The theory tells us that we can turn network against network, power against power. There is no escape from power per se, but there is escape from particular power structures.

Still other critics have suggested that Foucault leaves us with no basis upon which to evaluate particular power arrangements, no basis upon which to laud or condemn any act or decision on anybody's part. Therefore, even if revolt is technically possible, it can never be justified and so ought not be engaged in. Consequently, if we adopt Foucault's view, no reforms will be undertaken; things will remain as they are. Thus, Foucault is condemned as a thinker who supports the status quo.[8] Defenders of Foucault can reply that this sort of call for transcendental justification of revolt is itself a power formation erected on behalf of the status quo, and all we need to do is undermine it to make possible evaluation and resistance.

However, regardless of the differing viewpoints expressed and varying evaluations defended, this entire debate rests on the assumption that the analytics is to be read simply as a descriptive account of some *thing,* albeit perhaps plural, that we refer to as *power.* None of these commentators or critics entertains the possibility that the analytics is not a theory at all, not an account at all, but rather a strategy, a movement, a deployment of parody. This is the possibility I will entertain.

An Alternative Reading:
The Analytics of Power as Strategy

Instead of approaching Foucault's texts as embodiments of a kind of theory of power, a descriptive account of a static object or repeatable event, I read them as a movement of thinking that works to erode a kind of barrier to its own project. In a 1982 essay Foucault writes, "It is not power, but the subject, which is the general theme of my research."[9] I propose that we read the analytics backward through that statement, that we take that claim seriously in relation to the work on power, that we look at Foucault's texts as attempts to move through and beyond ahistorical conceptions of human being, human subjectivity, the development of human selfhood.

The work of the 1970s, then—that is, the work that seems to display as primary the thematic of the nature of power—will be seen as a development out of the work of the 1960s, rather than as a correction to it. The problematic of power will then appear not as an isolable theory but rather as a dismantling of a kind of barrier that was blocking the movement of historical thinking.

The texts of the 1960s move through questionings that work to destabilize traditional conceptions of truth, knowledge, and rational thought. *Madness and Civilization* attempts (perhaps somewhat unsuccessfully) to think the emergence of madness and rationality as events occurring within and out from historical social arrangements rather than as timeless facts about human being. *The Order of Things* places in question the very notion of "Man" itself as a transcending constant by tracing the functions of "Man" as a historically emergent principle of order and rule. In other words, Foucault's early texts raise the question—move the reader into the question—of how *we* are and came to be; and they move us to expect and to seek non-transcendental grounds for our emergences, our valuations, and our growth. These early texts clearly work toward loosening thinking's dependence upon or adherence to any traditional, transcendental understanding of the nature of human being.

After publication of *The Order of Things* Foucault was labeled a *philosopher of discontinuity*.[10] Many readers understood Foucault to be suggesting that historical causality operates in a disruptive, rather than a linear, fashion. Foucault was often faulted for not specifying more carefully exactly what really was the nature of these disruptive causal forces. But what was at issue, we might say in retrospect, was not the nature of causality; rather, the issue was how to think historical emergence. The question was whether historical emergence could be thought in terms of causality at all.

It was almost inevitable—again in retrospect—that Foucault would come up against the question of power. For it does not seem to be the case that the emergences those early texts described—the birth of the clinical gaze, the advent of the sciences of man—were simply random events. Maybe no one set out to produce these formations, but their emergences do have some of the character of intentional productions; they do seem to serve social and political purposes. Though there is no strategist, strategies seem to have formed and to operate with regard to these events. Therefore, our grammar, our history, our metaphysics lead us to say *something caused* them. We want to say that these events are the effects of power, that power is their a priori, their all-but-hidden ground.

In saying this, however, we can already hear the danger to historical thinking within the traditional thinking of the question of power. The very concept *power* is difficult to think without positing it as an entity transcendent to its effect. We want to say that *power causes,* that power is the machine, the tool, through whose operation events occur. But if we are to think historically, we must constantly remind ourselves, as does Foucault, that power is not to be thought as prior to and separate from events; power is to be thought as immanent in events. Thus Foucault's conceptualization of power functions to disperse the dangerous notion of cause and separable effect.

However, for the project of thinking historical subjectivity the question of power poses an even greater danger. Within the discourses of Western political theory—liberalism, Marxism, radicalisms of various sorts— thinking power typically means thinking some already constituted subjectivity who owns or holds and employs this machine or tool called power over against him- or herself or someone else. Thinking power in these discourses already entails the thought of a subjectivity originally exterior to power, although subsequently imperiled or enriched by its operations. Although within these discourses it is possible to imagine subjectivities changing as they undergo the effects of power and to imagine new kinds of subjectivities forming as a result of these effects, it is not possible to imagine power in the absence of any subjectivity at all. If there were no agency there would be no power; subjectivity is power's a priori in Western political thought.

Therefore, if subjectivity's historicity is what is to be thought, these traditional models of power are useless at best. And, in fact, in the absence of any alternative conceptualization of power, these models not only fail to accommodate; they actually hinder historical thinking in relation to subjectivity. Therefore, if historical thinking is to go on, it must find some strategy for loosening the grip of these traditional views of power on us. It must find a way to bypass the obstacles to the thought of historical occurrence presented by those traditional models of power.

On my reading, that is just what Foucault's analytics of power was designed to do. It is not an alternative theory or model of power at all; it is a strategic deployment whose function is to dismantle conceptualizations that block historical thinking.

The strategy is a familiar one. Its two-step structure is reminiscent of Nietzsche's genealogical works. The first step is to render optional a recalcitrant complex of ideas, such as the assumptions of an undisputed theory or the facts of a canonized historical account. One might do that by presenting an equally plausible alternative theory or account of the same phenomena, as Nietzsche presents an alternative story of the rise of Judeo-Christian morality. But this genealogical dance is a two-step; it does not stop with step one. Next both the recalcitrant theory or account *and* its newly introduced rival are denied truth-status. Both are destabilized as the genealogy works to lay bare, to place in question, and sometimes to cut away their common ground. (Parenthetically, I do not claim that genealogies are actually constructed in this way; but I do think that undergoing genealogical thinking often does occur in just this way—and the "author" of a genealogy probably stands in the same relation to this undergoing that his or her readers do.)

Foucault's first step, then, is to make optional traditional models of power by introducing a plausible alternative, what appears to be a rival model of power. Whereas traditional theories conceive power to be nonrelational, Foucault suggests that power is relational and exists only in its exercise; whereas traditional theories conceive power to be primarily repressive, Foucault suggests that power is primarily productive, and so on. Thus does Foucault produce a "rival theory" of power, a "theory" whose viability and claims are debated in print just as if Foucault had stopped with step one and advanced it as a contender for the status of absolute truth.

But the rival theory's function is not to vanquish its competitors and set itself up as the right way to think about power. Its function is to release thinking to questioning, in particular, to questioning the now-disputed assumptions of the traditional theories. Why must we think of power as the tool of an agent? Why not think of power as nonsubjective? Might it not be useful to think of power as productive instead of as only repressive? And why are these traditional theories so insistent upon protecting their own territory? What are those theories' interests? In what projects, in what outcomes, in what strategies are they invested?

This optionalization and re-examination is the first stage. Next Foucault undermines both his own apparent rival theory and the theories with which it appears to compete. He does this by placing in question their common grounds.

To see Foucault's second move clearly we have to return to the seventh of his apparent theoretical claims. Earlier I noted Foucault's statement, "Power as such does not exist."[11] If we read Foucault's analytics of power as a theory, we might interpret that statement as a pluralizing move or a nominalistic claim. We might understand Foucault to be saying that there is no such thing as a universal, overarching entity, *Power* with a capital *P*; rather there are particular causes, forces, *powers* in the plural and in the lower case.

But on my alternative reading what we hear is not simply a pluralization or a nominalistic claim. Foucault is not just saying that instead of a universal cause, "Power," there are only particular causes, "powers." This second reading asserts that Foucault can be understood literally—*power, as such,* as a cause transcending things, does not exist. There is no *cause* at all *behind* events, no effective nonappearing ground of things. *There are just events.* Insofar as we use the word *power* at all in Foucault's discourse, we are referring to the vitality, the energy, the will-to-be of particular complexes of events. Their power is immanent in them; it does not pre-exist them or transcend them in any sense at all.

Indeed, as we have seen, the analytics of power will hardly allow itself to be read as a set of truth claims about a transcendental object. The harder we try to grasp the nature of some real entity, power, in Foucault's description, the more elusive it all seems to become. In the "description" Foucault gives, power is not some*thing,* not a commodity to be circulated, not a possession that anyone can hold. Power exists only in its exercise; power has no being, but is only occurring. Power is everywhere; power *is in, as, every occurring.* Power networks are occurrings repeating occurrings. Resistances are occurrings of differings occurring. Already, even in this brief restatement of Foucault's words, we can begin to feel that old conceptual entity, power, dissolving and slipping out of our grip. The coup de grace is Foucault's denial of power's very existence. There is no agency behind events, he says; there is no need to posit something pushing history along. Power as such does not exist. Occurrings simply occur.

Whereas the traditional search for a useful or accurate model of power holds us to a commitment to the presence of something beyond events, something transcending historical occurrences, something we actually name with the word *power,* Foucault's conceptualization of power undermines any such commitment. It works against our tendency to think ahistorically. It begins to move us into a thinking in which not transcendentality but historicity is ever affirmed.

Historicity in Foucault's discourse means movements-of-differing-from, plays of valences straying from their origins and even sometimes perhaps perverting, distorting, or destroying the conditions that gave them birth. The thinking of history in Foucault's discourse means that the principles of continual linear development, identity, and logical argument have been and are being decentered, such that nonlinear movements, multiplicities and differences, and speakings that do not seek to prove themselves are allowed to come into play. Once we recognize history at play in Foucault's texts, once we undergo the affirming differing movement of that discourse, we no longer expect to find stable identities maintaining themselves through time. The discourse encourages the expectation that words like *power* that seem to name identities will undercut themselves, disperse themselves, play out the differing movement that moves the discourse on the whole. And that, I am claiming, is what happens with the analytics of power.[12]

Thus what seems at first glance to be a theory about something named *power* turns out, on my reading, to be nothing of the sort. It turns out to be a movement through a complex arrangement of traditional ideas that functioned as an obstacle to historical thought. The analytics of power is a movement of thinking, and it is a strategic movement, a deployment, a destructive device, a ruse, a kind of Trojan horse. It makes no definitive claims. Rather, it moves into the domain of traditional theories of power as transcending cause, and it destabilizes those thought-complexes from within. In doing so, it creates for thinking a new path, a way out of and beyond transcendental discourses that force us to assume the primacy of agency and the ahistoricity of human subjects.

Once the analytics of power has been thought through, we are in a position to conceive of subjectivities as events occurring within matrices of valences. We are in a position to describe the emergence of personalities, identities, normalities and abnormalities, even consciousness or agency itself as sets of historical and passing occurrences. Once Foucault's discussion of power is thought through, the historicity of human being is opened up as a possibility for thinking. On my reading, then, the importance of Foucault's analytics of power lies not in what it talks about, but in what it does, in how it functions strategically to move thinking along in Foucault's texts.

If this strategy is effective, at the end of Foucault's discussions of power we will find ourselves in a discourse where causal priority is not a pressing concern, where individual human identity is taken to be plural and passing within the interplay of nonsubjective events, and where events and actions are allowable and affirmable despite their lack of transcendental grounding. We will be in a discourse where requests for true definitions, demands for timeless justifications, and salvific appeals will not hold very much sway. And all this means that we will most decidedly not remain within the discourses of political theory or of Foucault commentary as they each stand today.

10 The Call of Conscience and the Call of Language: Reflections on a Movement in Heidegger's Thinking

JANE KELLEY RODEHEFFER

Readers of *Being and Time* often find Heidegger's development of the call of conscience *(Ruf des Gewissens)* to be among the least successful discussions in the text. The words that dominate sections 54–60—words like *guilt (Schuld), resoluteness (Entschlossenheit),* and *conscience*—are so fraught with religious and metaphysical meanings that they actually obscure the central issue at work in Dasein's experience of the call. In this chapter I hope to cut through the problems of terminology in Heidegger's discussion of the call of conscience by showing that the clue to understanding these sections is the movement of the call itself; as it emerges, the movement of the call offsets the concepts of conscience, guilt, and resoluteness and marks an opening beyond their exhausted meanings in the tradition. This opening allows the later Heidegger to find in the encounter with the call the beginning of a way of thinking through which we reach the speaking of language.

The view of language as calling to human being to dwell within its speaking is one that dominates Heidegger's later work. When read in light of the language essays, it becomes clear that the experience Dasein undergoes in the call of conscience is primarily an experience with language. Dasein appropriates the call in reticence *(Verschwiegenheit),* which means that it withholds a word for its authentic being from the grasp of *das Man.* Dasein's concealment of a word for its being answers to the withdrawal and concealment that are constitutive of Being's disclosure. In what follows, I will show that it is in Dasein's appropriation of the call in reticence that passage to Heidegger's later thinking occurs. Dasein passes over into the call of language that moves through it, in such a way that language—not human being—becomes the site of the disclosure of Being. I will outline this process in stages, beginning with Heidegger's discussion of conscience in *Being and Time.*

127

The Ordinary Interpretation of Conscience

Heidegger's discussion of the ordinary or vulgar interpretation of conscience provides a point of departure for his suggestion that the phenomenon of conscience has the character of a call *(Ruf)*. The vulgar interpretation of conscience posits two forms of the phenomenon, evil conscience and good, which serve a critical function relative to some deed that has been done or willed.[1] The experience of the evil conscience as pointing backward after the deed is done and reproving, and of the good conscience as pointing forward and warning one with regard to the deed that has been willed, suggests that the voice *(Stimme)* of conscience "is something that turns up [and] has its place in the series of objectively present experiences" (BT 59).

According to Heidegger, this interpretation provides an inadequate understanding of conscience. What is primordial in the concepts of bad and good conscience is not their function of reproving and warning, but their character of pointing backward and forward. When we remove the phenomenon of conscience from its characterization as something present at hand and take it "back into the disclosiveness of Dasein" (BT 54), we find that it has the character not of a voice, but of a call. Heidegger goes on to suggest that "the disclosive character of the call has not been fully determined until we understand it as a calling-back calling-forth" (SZ 280). The calling-back calls forth to not-being "as something to be seized upon in one's own existence" (BT 59). The call is not selective. It does not call back and reprove in one situation and call forward and warn in another. What is primordial but remains unthought in conscience is its character as at once calling-back calling-forth. Dasein is not called to take action, nor is it called to gather the discrete events of its life into a narrative whole. Rather, Dasein is summoned to hearken to the inevitability of its own passing away. As we shall see, it is the calling-back calling-forth of Dasein in and for its deathliness that allows for passage from the call of conscience to the call of language.

The Movement of the Call

If conscience has the character not of a voice but of a call, what is the origin of that call? Who calls Dasein to own its guilt, its not being the ground of its own being? In giving dominance to the call as he thinks about conscience, Heidegger overcomes the traditional view of the phenomenon as originating in either a higher power or a psychic faculty such as understanding or will. He states that "the call without doubt does not come from someone else who is with me in the world. The call comes from me, and yet *over* me" (BT 56). The caller is not an alien presence like God who makes himself known; the caller is not objectively present in any sense. Rather, writes Heidegger, it "remains in a striking indefiniteness" (BT 57). This indefinability "lets us know that the caller uniquely coincides with summoning to..., it wants to be heard only as such" (BT 57). In the essay "Language," Heidegger suggests that the way in which language calls is also marked by a certain indefinability. He writes that "the call does not wrest what it calls away from the remoteness, in which it is kept by calling there. The calling calls into itself and therefore always here and there—here into presence, there into absence."[2] In reading this later passage together with Heidegger's characterization of the call in *Being and Time,* we begin to see how the words *summoning, interrupting,* and *disclosure* work to displace the foundational language of objectivity and subjectivity in interpreting the caller, the calling, and even the one who is called.

To describe the function of the call in *Being and Time,* Heidegger uses the words *interrupt (unterbrechen), breach (Bruch),* and *break (brechen).* He states that "in the tendency toward disclosure of the call lies the factor of a jolt [*stofsen*], of an abrupt arousal [*abgesetzen Aufrütteins*]. The call comes from afar to afar" (BT 55). Neither a who nor a what, the caller and the call occur simultaneously as a to-and-fro movement of abrupt arousal. It comes as no surprise, then, to learn that the origin of the caller lies in the most primordial state of interruptive disclosure, that which Heidegger names uncanniness *(Unheimlichkeit):* "It is Dasein in its uncanniness, primordially thrown being in the world as not at home, the naked 'that' in the nothingness of the world" (BT 57).

Who or what is summoned by the call? Is it not Dasein, the subject who relates to a world? Heidegger writes that "the call passes over what Dasein understands itself as, initially and for the most part in its interpretation in terms of taking care of things" (BT 57). The call does not summon the self to become an object for itself that can then be dissected and analyzed. Heidegger states that "the call passes over [*überspringt*] all this and diffuses it [*zerstreut es*]" (SZ 273). The dominance of a conscience-bearing subject is overcome in Dasein's appropriation of the call as a summons to yield to its own deathliness, to the inevitability of its own passing away. Heidegger's repeated use of the phrase *passes over* in interpreting the call, and his emphasis on its offsetting movement—its calling "to and fro"—suggest that both the phenomenon of conscience and the idea of an identity (Dasein) who is called, are pushed to the edges of thinking so that a new thought can emerge. Dasein passes into a call that moves through it. Free of its moorings in a conscience-bearing subject, the call opens up a region for thinking in Heidegger's discourse, a region in which the question of Being is released from the analytic of Dasein to its occurrence in language.

The Call of Language

From the perspective of Heidegger's later work, it becomes clear that his thinking about the call is already undergoing a process of transformation in *Being and Time,* a process that will eventually lead to the incorporation of the themes of Dasein's call into a different discourse. Dasein's experience of the call is an experience with language. The word for what is called is withheld in order that Dasein may become uncovered to its inmost potentiality. In denying itself, the word is lacking, and Dasein is disclosed to itself as lacking in the ground of its being. Dasein's experience of the call is thus very similar to Heidegger's later characterization of the poet's experience with language. In denying itself to the poet, the word is also said to be lacking, and, through this withholding, language is freed for its own granting occurrence. The release of the call from the realm of subjectivity to that of language carries with it a certain continuity in terms of what thinking is given to think: the themes of silence, reticence, renunciation, and stillness. All of these, which are constitutive of Dasein's call, reemerge as central motifs in Heidegger's articulation of the poet's experience of the call of language. A discussion of these themes can thus serve as a point of passage from the call of conscience to the speaking of language. In hearkening to the call, Dasein gives up the controlling grasp of language that is characteristic of *das Man,* and it is appropriated by the withholding and denial of the word for its being-unto-death. Dasein's reticence answers not to a need for self-fulfillment, but to a need to submit to the withdrawal of Being in language, and to hearken to that withdrawal in the unsaid dimension of language.

In *Being and Time,* Heidegger understands calling not as the speaking of language *(Sprache)* but as a mode of discourse *(Rede).* He states that "every speaking and 'calling out' presupposes discourse" (BT 55), and he defines discourse as an articulation of intelligibility, in which what is communicated "becomes accessible to the *Mitdasein* of others, mostly by way of utterance in language" (BT 56). Yet vocal utterance is not essential to discourse, and hearkening and keeping silent are defined as its most authentic possibilities. The call expresses a primordial possibility of discourse insofar as it speaks "in the uncanny mode of *silence* " (BT 57). The call does not utter anything, it does not come to words. It thus avoids becoming distorted in its character of disclosure insofar as it gives the they-self "nothing to hear that could be passed along and publicly spoken about" (BT 57). In "Das Wesen der Sprache," Heidegger characterizes this denial of the word as the way in which language gives itself as language. This happens "when we cannot find the right word for something that concerns us, carries us away, oppresses or encourages us. Then we leave unspoken what we have in mind and, without rightly giving it thought, undergo moments in which language itself has distantly and fleetingly touched us with its essential being."[3] Yet Dasein's experience is not simply that of being unable to find the right word. It is more like the experience of the poet, for whom "the issue is to put into language something which has never yet been spoken," such that "everything depends on whether language gives or withholds the appropriate word" (WL 59). The call to Dasein to own its mortality, the nonbeing that permeates its existence, is a call to show the difference of Being from Dasein. As an occurrence in which dying is always occurring, Dasein cannot be a wholly integrated being. While the tradition has understood Being as a unity that is both immortal and transcendent, Dasein has been disclosed as fragmented, deathly, and thrown. Words that express identity, foundation, or objective reality thus are inappropriate to describe that to which Dasein is called: an indefiniteness that has never yet been spoken in the grammar of metaphysics.

Although the silence of the call shelters Dasein's indefiniteness, its difference from Being, the notion of silence is not enough to convey the withholding dimension of that disclosure. Heidegger points out early in *Being and Time* that to be able to keep silent, Dasein "must have something to say, i.e. must be in command of an authentic and rich disclosiveness of itself" (BT 34). Thus while the call speaks in the mode of silence, it does not call one to silence but to "the reticence of one's existent potentiality of being" (BT 57). The word *reticent (verschwiegen)* means to conceal, keep secret, withhold, or hide from. In colloquial German one might say, *Ich bin verschwiegen wie ein Grab:* I am as reticent as a grave. This is issued as a kind of promise, that one can be told something and trusted not to reveal it. Dasein is summoned to a withholding of its disclosiveness so that the question of Being may be heard in all of its uncertainty. Like the poet, Dasein does not abdicate the word. Rather, the word withdraws "into the mysterious wonder that makes us wonder" (WL 88). For language to bring to words Dasein's experience of the call would be in some sense to resolve the question of Being. On the other hand, the call does not summon Dasein to silence; what is withheld in reticence speaks and is heard as Dasein is released for its occurrence. Just at the point in Heidegger's discourse where we expect resolution, we find that the word for Being withdraws, and, like the poet, Dasein highlights this withdrawal in experiencing the word as lacking. As it moves through Dasein, the call of language thus passes over the metaphysical temptation to resolve Being into an objectively present identity.

The Saying of Renunciation

What Dasein withholds in hearkening to the call is the articulation of its inmost being guilty, its not being. Like conscience, the world *guilt (Schuld)* is difficult to think without the religious meaning of sin traditionally borne in it. The vulgar sense of guilt as a kind of moral indebtedness, or more generally as "having responsibility for," is overcome when the phenom-enon of guilt is removed from the sphere of moral responsibility and is thought with regard to the disclosiveness of Dasein. Heidegger con-centrates on the quality of the not *(nicht)* that is present in the notion of being guilty. As always already thrown, Dasein can never get "back behind its thrownness"(BT 58). It already stands in one possibility and is *not* other possibilities, having "relinquished [*begeben*] them in its existentiell project" (BT 58). The call summons Dasein to take up its nullity *(Nichtigkeit),* and in hearkening to the call, Dasein is reticent: it withholds a word for the not being that constitutes its inmost potentiality. Such withholding involves a relinquishment of the possibilities of thrownness. Dasein lets such possibilities be lacking. Insofar as it appropriates the call in a nonrelational way (BT 58), Dasein relinquishes or renounces the grasping, self-assured saying of *das Man,* which portrays it as present in one or another possibility of thrownness.

The word *begeben* (SZ 285), which Heidegger uses in *Being and Time* to describe Dasein's relinquishment of the possibilities of ensnarement, is closely affiliated in its meanings with the word *Verzicht,* which is most often translated "renunciation,"[4] but which can also mean to relinquish or give up. In his study of Stefan George's poem "Das Wort," Heidegger states that "renouncing means: to give up the claim to something, to deny oneself something" (WL 142). In George's poem, the poet's renunciation is connected to the breaking off of the word, and Heidegger suggests that, "where something breaks off [*gebricht*], there is a break [*Bruch*], a breaking off. To do harm to something means to take something away from it, to let something be lacking" (WL 141). The lack of the word for the word is said to glance "abruptly at the poet [*blickt den Dichter jäh an*]" (WL 146; US 227), and to have disturbed *(erschütterte)* "the self-assurance of his earlier saying" (WL 148; US 229). This characterization of the breaking off of word as disturbing is important because it echoes Heidegger's description of the call in *Being and Time,* where it was understood as an abrupt arousal that interrupts and breaks Dasein's listening to the everyday saying of *das Man.* The self-renunciation of the poet, like Dasein's renunciation of its they-self, calls to a region in which the word is experienced as oppressively near but at the same time held in reserve. It is the region of language, a dimension in which saying occurs but is not dominated by presence. As Dasein "must have something to say" in order to be disclosive in reticence, so the poet's renunciation is not a "mere lapse into silence. As self-denial, renunciation remains Saying" (WL 147).

Heidegger's development of renunciation serves as a threshold for entering into what he later calls the stillness in language, its "soundless gathering call" (WL 108). In discussing Stefan George's poem "Das Wort," Heidegger suggests that the stillness is to be heard in the line, "where word breaks off no thing may be." In commenting on this line, he writes that "to break up here means that the sounding word returns into soundlessness, back to whence it was granted: into the ringing of stillness. . . . This breaking up of the word is the true step back on the way of thinking" (WL 108). Heidegger's characterization of the call as soundless and as granting all speaking out of its stillness, also has its origins in his discussion of conscience in *Being and Time.* In developing the voice *(Stimme)* of conscience, he suggests that when it is thought in terms of conscience, the *Stimme* is most commonly understood as a *still* small voice. Heidegger plays on the stillness implicit in the notion of voice when he writes that "conscience calls only silently . . . and calls the summoned Dasein back into the stillness [*in die Stille*] of its inmost self, and calls it to become still" (SZ 296). In making such a move, he offsets the problematic association of voice with a calling out or utterance, and allows the calling of language as a stilling to come to thought.

Although Heidegger does not develop the theme of stillness in *Being and Time,* he retains *Stille* as the word that articulates what the call summons. In the essay "Language," he suggests that the voice of language—its speaking—is not an uttering, but stillness. The stillness at the heart of language calls to mortals through the poem, which is the only form of speaking in which a primal calling *(ursprüngliche Rufe)* is any longer to be heard.[5] In his discussion of Georg Trakl's poem "Ein Winterabend," Heidegger states that the verses call the stillness without either thinking it specifically or calling it by name. The stillness is soundless; it is heard as a ringing or pealing between the words and verses of the poem. Just as the call, directed to Dasein's inmost stillness, "speaks" of the difference of Being from fragmented and deathly Dasein, a difference that cannot be named, so the stillness to which the poem calls "speaks" of the difference of language from mortal speech. Like Dasein, mortals who respond to the command of the stillness are *unheimlich,* not at home in everyday language, which Heidegger describes as "a forgotten and therefore used-up poem, from which there hardly resounds a call any longer" (PLT 208).

All of the elements of Dasein's call—its reticent withholding of a name for its disclosiveness; its renunciation of the self-assured, grasping function of the everyday saying of *das Man;* its differencing movement; the hearkening and keeping silent that are revealed as authentic possibilities of discourse; and the stillness to which it calls—are brought together by Heidegger in the essay "Language." Dasein is like the mortal Heidegger speaks of in "Language," who learns to live in the speaking of language by responding to its call. In withholding or reserving its rich disclosiveness from coming to utterance, Dasein becomes still and authentically hearkens to the call. In "Language," Heidegger writes that "every authentic hearing holds back [*hält*] with its own saying. For hearing keeps [*hält*] to itself in the listening by which it remains appropriated to the peal of stillness. All responding is attuned to the restraint that reserves itself" (PLT 209). According to Heidegger, it is through such a hearkening-withholding that human beings respond to the call, since every word of human speech "rests in its relation to the speaking of language" (PLT 208). In walking this way of thinking back into *Being and Time,* we see that it has its beginning in Dasein's reticent appropriation of its inmost stillness.

The movement of Heidegger's thinking suggests that the possibilities of the call do not seek a center in resoluteness or *Entschlossenheit,* the name Heidegger gives to wanting to have a conscience in *Being and Time.* As a static determination to become disclosive, *Entschlossenheit* fails to contain the elements of the call that move through it. Charles Scott recently suggested that translating *Entschlossenheit* as release or openness more accurately conveys the meanings Heidegger intended.[6] The root of *entschlossen* is *schliessen,* which means to close or shut. Heidegger takes the *ent-* of *entschlossen* as privative; the word *Entschlossenheit* thus comes to signify keeping unclosed. "Release" or "open to" would seem a better translation than "resolute." The traditional figurative sense of *entschlossen* is taciturn or reserved, which suggests why Heidegger understands reticence to be constitutive of *Entschlossenheit;* a keeping unclosed or releasing is also a reserving and keeping silent. As Heidegger thought through the authentic disclosiveness of Dasein in the realm of discourse to the originary granting of language that it illumines, the call was released from the dominant structure of subjective resolution in such a way that it could begin to provide a new gathering place for the possibilities it expresses: abrupt arousal, renunciation, the reticent withholding of the word, and stillness.

The narrative of *Being and Time* is broken by the call of language, whose movement serves to undercut the disclosure of Dasein as *entschlossen.* That movement unfolds in Dasein's appropriation of the call in reticence, insofar as its withholding of a word for its inmost possibility answers to the withdrawal and concealment that belong to all disclosure of Being. In his later essays, Heidegger suggests that the experience of the lack of a word for Being is the experience at the heart of poetic saying, which allows what must remain unsaid to withdraw even as it comes to expression. When we trace his incorporation of the possibilities of the call in the quite different context of language, it becomes clear that Dasein's call to the reticence and stillness of its inmost self constitutes an early and important attempt by Heidegger to articulate the way in which language grants the withdrawal of Being.

Part 4

Retrieval of Crises

11 Heidegger and Aristotle: Dasein and the Question of Practical Life

WALTER A. BROGAN

A full assessment of the oft-rumored influence of Aristotle's *Nicomachean Ethics* on Martin Heidegger's Dasein analysis in *Being and Time* will not be possible until the release of Heidegger's 1924–25 lecture course on Plato's *Sophist,* the first part of which is a treatment of Aristotle's *Ethics.* In the meantime, the question of the relation of Heidegger's work to practical human life has assumed a central place in the continuing attempt to come to terms with Heidegger's philosophy. The Aristotelian notions of *phronēsis* and *praxis* and Heidegger's interpretation of these notions are certainly important aspects of this discussion. Yet, one cannot proceed simply by comparing and contrasting Aristotle and Heidegger with regard to their respective understandings of practical life; any such procedure would fail to take into account the hermeneutic impact of Heidegger's interpretation of Aristotle, both with regard to our understanding of Aristotle's philosophy and with regard to our understanding of the issue of practical human life.

In this chapter I argue that Aristotle's *Nicomachean Ethics* is primarily an ontology of human being. Aristotle offers an understanding of human being that suggests a fundamentally non-relational potentiality for being as the human being's way of being wholly itself. Aristotle considers *phronēsis* or practical wisdom to be primarily this kind of self-disclosure, and *praxis* or true human action to be the manifestation of this possibility of being a self in one's situatedness. I attempt to show through an interpretation of the *phronēsis-praxis* structure in the *Ethics* that *praxis* for Aristotle means that way in which the human being factically chooses to be *for its own sake.* I argue further that this apparent retreat from everyday practical involvements back into a concern for one's own being is for neither Aristotle nor Heidegger a form of solipsism but the only genuine basis for human community and for a kind of relating to nonhuman being that can be characterized in terms other than those of the Greek notion of *technē* and modern technology.

Heidegger frequently states that all of Greek ontology is rooted in an overall conception of being as presence. The explication of this conception is guided by the notion of the *ergon*, the work. The work as something present in the mode of having been produced came eventually to be understood through *technē*, the kind of knowledge involved in production. Heidegger claims in his 1931 Aristotle course that the basic concepts of philosophy grew out of and within this understanding of a work-world. Aristotle's notions of form, matter, and end are based on this method of investigation. He says:

> What the Greeks conceived as *epistēmē poiētikē* was of fundamental significance for their own understanding of the world. We have to clarify for ourselves what it signifies that the human being has a relation to the works that he produces. It is for this reason that a certain book called *Being and Time* discusses dealings with equipment.[1]

In this quote, written shortly after the publication of *Being and Time*, Heidegger indicates his awareness of the dependency of his equipment analysis in *Being and Time* on the *technē* model with which he is attempting to come to terms. It may well be that Heidegger's phenomenological commitment to the principle that "no understanding of being is possible that would not root in a comportment toward beings" demands that his starting point be the ways things are historically and for the most part given to us.[2] The slippage in man's relation to beings that began with Aristotle might well be what leads him to begin his own analysis with this *technē* model of the givenness of things. But it would be unsatisfactory if this analysis of equipment were his final word on the subject of human practical life. Not only would this mean that Heidegger's view of beings other than ourselves is seriously limited, but it would also imply a less-than-successful outcome for his analysis of Dasein's being since, as he shows, our very being becomes entangled and caught up in these equipmental structures in a way that is, in Heidegger's terms, fallen and inauthentic.

I will try to show, however, that this is not the case and that Heidegger's account of genuine *phronēsis* and *praxis* are rather to be found in Division 2 of *Being and Time*, where he discusses Dasein's possibility of being-a-whole in terms remarkably parallel to Aristotle's own understanding of *phronēsis* and *praxis* as the way of realizing and articulating the complete life that is characteristic of the happy person. In both the *Ethics* and in *Being and Time*, I want to argue, the possibility of a genuine practical life is based on a drawing back into oneself of one's ownmost potentiality. For Heidegger this takes the form of a movement of retrieval that opens up a world and our ecstatic situatedness in the midst of other beings. For Aristotle, this drawing back into oneself of potentiality is made explicit in his discussion of friendship, as I will show later. For both, it is our way of being open to the truth of beings or what Aristotle calls *theōria.*[3]

Before turning to Aristotle's *Ethics* I want to bring into the discussion a few passages from Heidegger's 1931 lecture course on Aristotle that bear on the problem. Heidegger deals in this text with Aristotle's attempt to explicate *dynamis* and *energeia* as one of manifold ways in which being is expressed. Of particular interest to us is the second half of the text, where Heidegger considers Aristotle's division of beings on the basis of two different kinds of *dynamis* or potentiality. Those beings that have logos are differentiated from those without logos. The *dynamis* that belongs to human beings is *"meta logou."*

On Heidegger's reading of Aristotle's definition of the human being as *"zoon logon echon"*—the living being whose being is essentially determined by the potentiality for discourse—logos constitutes Dasein's way of being, its way of holding itself in relation to itself. Heidegger says that Aristotle's phrase *dynamis meta logou* means to exist in the sense of the "ecstasis" of Dasein. The human being is always already beyond itself. Existing in the mode of *dynamis,* we do not have our being as something we possess. Rather, through the force and command of language (logos) we are able to rescue ourselves from the everyday "they" and say who we are. But the human being never becomes a work in the sense of a finished product. For Aristotle and Heidegger we have our being in a different way. Our self-realization involves holding ourselves in relation to not being ourselves and thus to what is other than ourselves. With logos there is a dwelling in the midst of others as well as an openness to what can be.

Although Aristotle devotes the first two chapters of Book 9 of the *Metaphysics* to the explication of this human potentiality (which Heidegger calls *worldliness)* in terms of our capacity to produce beings, he takes up the question in another way in the third chapter. Here Aristotle is responding to the Megarians who charge that since to be is to be actual, no potentiality can exist except when it is actively being realized. So, for example, the builder is only a builder when he is building. But Aristotle accuses the Megarians of misunderstanding the way in which the *dynamis* is present in the human being. His point is that it is precisely when one is not engaged in the performance of a skill that one "has" the skill. Aristotle gives the example of learning. When one is learning to build and practicing how to build, one is not yet a builder. It is when one is no longer practicing that one is practiced and that the realization of the skill is most present in the person. In another example, when one is not yet running but fully concentrated and gathered into oneself at the start of a race, one's capacity to run is most fully present. So one's capability is fully present when it is drawn back into oneself and held in readiness. This is the *energeia,* the being-fully-engaged of *dynamis* as *dynamis,* the full realization and fulfillment of movement as such. To be gathered into oneself in this way is to have a way of being that embodies the temporal ecstases of always already having been within and being-toward the realm of one's involvements.

But what I would like particularly to emphasize here is that this openness or worldliness is first of all what makes possible specific human activities, such as building, and that it is precisely when one is not specifically engaged in this or that way that our involvement is most truly and fully our own. Likewise, there is a sense in which this drawing back into ourselves of our potentiality to be is necessary in order not to take over the being of others. For example, in the case of the builder, it is when the builder finishes building and withdraws from skillful activity that the building is able to be on its own. In an example that does not rely on *technē* but on *aisthēsis* or perception, Aristotle says that when perception withdraws into itself and is no longer actually being exercised, the perceivable being is given back to itself and does not just disappear. Holding oneself back toward oneself is not a disowning of one's concrete relationship to other beings but is a way of granting to other beings a being of their own.

In the beginning of the *Ethics,* Aristotle argues that logos is the *ergon* or work of man in the sense that through logos our being is most fully realized. Yet, his attention is first drawn to a discussion of the formation of character and the inculcation of virtues. Virtues are dispositions toward acting and feeling in a certain way, namely, in an excellent way. They constitute the general way in which we comport ourselves rather than determine particular or specific actions or feelings. In one sense, virtuous dispositions protect us from having our feelings and emotions determined by outside forces. So here already Aristotle is taking a step in the direction of retrieving the person from an inauthentic involvement with beings. We have feelings because we are capable of feeling. We are afraid because being fearful is a way of being for us, a possibility that is open to us. The formation of virtues is a process of taking charge of those capacities for ourselves. We can notice that having emotions—anger, fear, joy and the others Aristotle lists—indicates that we already stand in relation to the world around us. Anger and fear are responses to our situatedness and involvement with others. These emotions arise because we are capable of being affected. Being virtuous does not exclude being affected by these outside forces. It is rather a question of whether we take charge of these capacities, make them our own, concretize them in some fashion that allows us to stand out in relation to our involvements rather than merely being there as part of them. Virtues open up a relationship to oneself, to one's capacities as a source for directing one's emotions and actions. I am afraid because I can be afraid, but I can also not be afraid. What I want to point out here is that the movement is from an actual entanglement with one's surroundings to a return to oneself, and that this distancing of oneself from the immediacy of one's involvement opens up a horizon of possibilities for being oneself in that situation.

Aristotle's discussion of the mean in relation to virtue indicates again the broader context for an understanding of human *praxis* toward which Aristotle is aiming. The virtuous person is able to see the parameters of the situation, the excess and deficiency, and choose what to do within this broader context of understanding; thus, our natural tendencies and leanings are not allowed to distort our judgments or decisions about what to do in a given situation. For Aristotle, to be virtuous is to find pleasure in what is most worthy of being pursued. This in turn requires openness to options, a lack of immediate compulsion, a certain distance from the moment, which for the good person heightens rather than weakens the intensity of the moment. Virtue requires forethought and decision about what can be done.

Let us look briefly at the virtue of courage as an example of the way Aristotle directs the question of practical living toward the question of human being. Courage allows us to be well-disposed toward what is fearful, primarily toward what is most terrifying *(deinon):* death. The courageous person endures the end nobly. To be courageous is to stand resolutely in the face of the possibility of no longer being, in particular, Aristotle says, where not some specific aspect of our life is at issue but the whole of our life. Fearlessness in other matters, Aristotle says, resembles courage but is not the same. Thus the citizen soldier who endures danger for honor and for the sake of the law is not strictly speaking courageous. He does not face death for its own sake, for the nobility or intrinsic worth of acting in this way. Aristotle goes on to say that the courageous person can fear what is fearful but endures it in an appropriate way, according to the situation, as logos directs. The point I would want to emphasize here is that courage is first of all a disposition toward one's own being and concomitantly a way of relating ourselves to others.

In a similar fashion, *megalopsychia,* greatsouledness, is the gift-giving virtue of one who knows his or her superiority by virtue of knowing his or her limits. Such a person, Aristotle says, would rather give than receive, so exuberant and full of life is the soul. Such a person is said to be open in hate and love, neither resentful nor gossipy. Here, as in the case of the complementary virtue of *sōphrosunē,* which is described as a capacity to hold oneself back in the situation, the virtue is primarily a way of being and thereby a way of being with others.

But even if this is true and Aristotle continues to concern himself primarily with the ontology of human being and continues to draw the discussion away from the specificity of practical life, as I believe he does, I do not think this contradicts his claim to be concerned with the question of political life; rather, I think he is trying to win the proper foundation for such an inquiry. This emerges quite clearly in his discussion of justice, the paramount political virtue.

Aristotle names justice as the whole of virtue. This is because the healthy, excellent person achieves self-rule, a certain harmony between logos and *alogos.* Aristotle says that to be in command of oneself is also to both follow and listen. The model of the good citizen is to be able to be both a ruler and ruled in turn. To have command of logos is to be able to say who one is in relation to others, and thereby to face others as the kind of being who takes charge of one's being and is responsible for one's being. Thus to be fully just is to be law-abiding, to dwell amidst others in accord with logos. This requires knowing one's being as well as what is appropriate to one's being in given situations.

Partial justice involves having a sense of how to measure oneself in relation to others, how to differentiate oneself from others—how to determine the *isos,* what is equal to one's being, what is one's own. To do so, as Aristotle points out, requires more than a virtuous disposition. The *dianomē* or distribution that justice requires demands not only a knowledge of oneself but of what does not belong to oneself but to others. Justice is proportionate, *ana-logos.* It knows what is and is not suitable to one's being.

Aristotle says that inasmuch as moral virtues *(aretē)* are habitual *(hexis),* they are not open to that which is other than themselves. But, like the doctor who must have knowledge of health and sickness, the distributor of justice must not only know what belongs properly to the person but also what does not. Thus justice is the link between intellectual virtue and moral virtue. All of the virtues are through justice disposed to listen to logos and can therefore stand in relationship to what they are not. Justice as the highest virtue gathers the human being into a whole but also concretely articulates and specifies what belongs to and does not belong to each human being. At this level, justice is akin to deliberation as the activity of articulating what is to be done in the realm of *praxis.* The point that I would like to draw from this discussion is that it is precisely because the human being has come to recognize his or her own limit and can see in some sense who he or she is in the whole of his or her being that the possibility of political life has emerged.

Aristotle says the work of the intellect is *alētheia*. He begins his discussion in Book 6 with a twofold division of logos, a division made on the basis of the way of disclosure or truth, on the one hand theoretical and on the other practical. I want to address my remarks here only to the latter kind of disclosure and discuss only the kind of practical revealing that Aristotle calls *phronēsis* or practical wisdom. He defines *phronēsis* as a truthful disposition to act with logos in matters involving choice between good and bad in such a way that the person chooses and acts for the sake of the end, the good life as a whole, toward which he or she is directed. He says that *phronēsis* is not politics because *phronēsis* is concerned more with one's own *eidos*, with the aspect in which one's own being comes to be shaped, although politics and practical wisdom do not exclude each other.

At the risk of being too schematic, I would like to suggest that in delineating the relationship between *phronēsis* and *praxis* Aristotle thinks through how the situated, finite human being can act in such a way that each action affirms his or her being as a whole and allows the person to be fully present as a concrete individual. Action, deliberation, choice, desire, and *nous* (the simple saying of one's being that accompanies action and the good life) are the main ingredients that come together in Aristotle's notion of practical wisdom.

Aristotle indicates by his notion of *orexis*, desireful striving, that our way of being related to our end, our way of having our end, is in the mode of being-toward. The end is the good life *(euzen);* this is the end that Aristotle calls *aplōs*, in itself simple and unqualified and never a means to something else. Deliberation, Aristotle says, considers what is *pros to telos*, the means in the sense of what is in relation to or in accordance with the end and intrinsic to it. Through deliberation the end is articulated and specified and made actual for action. Human action is not like *poiēsis*, with its means-end formula. *Praxis* has to arise out of oneself and be done for its own sake because of its intrinsic nobility. The goodness of the agent determines the quality of an action. What counts for Aristotle is that the action manifests the excellence of the person. So the end of human action is not outside the human person who acts, except inasmuch as the excellent person is outside himself or herself. To sum up: In advance of acting, we are to single out, to choose what is to be done on the basis of a view toward what is involved, which is disclosed in a deliberation based on a fore-grasp of the good that is the ultimate end for which we act. So action requires a lot of advance activity. As Aristotle says frequently, deliberation takes time.

So where, then, in Aristotle's *Ethics* do we find the link between the ontology of human being and that being's practical life? I would respond that in one sense the link is there already in that the question presupposes a division between something like a theoretical life and a practical life. But Aristotle does not assume such a division. One indication of this is that his first mention of *theōria* after Book 6 comes in his discussion of friendship. He says that we can observe or witness *(theōria)* our neighbor's actions better than our own. We come to be aware of the being of our friend because, Aristotle says, we perceive, on the basis of our experience of ourselves, that human life is reflective and goes beyond itself and that life is intrinsically good and pleasant, especially for the good person. The being of another is like our own. Our awareness of our being implies awareness of being and thus the being of others. The being of another is pleasant and desirable to us. In perceiving ourselves, we perceive at the same time others like ourselves.

Aristotle says that all knowledge presupposes a certain kinship between the knower and what is known. Aristotle calls this kinship *truth. Theōria* is the activity of knowing the being of that which is other than ourselves. It implies a kind of thinking that transcends mere thinking and opens up a kinship between thinking and being. If *theōria* involves a kinship that allows the truth of beings as such to be uncovered, and if *theōria* is a characteristic of friendship, then presumably it is a kind of apprehending that mutually and reciprocally reveals the beings involved. Friendship goes beyond justice in that it takes up in a positive manner the capacity of the just person to know the difference between what is his own and what belongs to others.

I suggested earlier that the full treatment of the question of practical wisdom and action in Heidegger's *Being and Time* is not to be found in the first division of that work. The concern there is with the retrieval of human being from an inauthentic involvement with other beings. If we read Heidegger's discussion of equipmentality as his final word on Dasein's involvement with things, we will miss the import of what Heidegger has to offer vis-à-vis human practical life. Reading *Being and Time* backwards, we need to understand this analysis in the light of Division 2 of the work where Heidegger speaks of Dasein's potentiality for being a whole. Similarly, Aristotle's discussion of *phronēsis* and *nous praktikos,* as well as his discussion of friendship and happiness in the later books of the *Ethics,* are the appropriate context within which to understand his earlier discussion of habit and virtuous behavior.

Aristotle says that happiness as the end of human life requires self-sufficiency and a complete life. In his discussion of *phronēsis* he says that this end can never be chosen because it is always already there as that toward which action is ultimately directed. Aristotle wonders whether happiness can be attained before death and answers that being in one's end in this way is possible as an *energeia,* a being at work, that in its choices and actions chooses to choose itself and thus to disclose itself as fully and humanly present in its situation. Aristotle says: "What is always chosen as an end in itself and never as a means to something else is called final in an unqualified sense. This description seems to apply to happiness above all else" (1097a35). Happiness is not a good among others that we can choose. Happiness is that kind of human action that takes up for itself its own end as a possibility for being. In happy actions, we choose ourselves. In his discussion of practical wisdom Aristotle says: "When a person becomes corrupted by pleasure or pain, the end no longer appears as a motivating principle. The person no longer sees that he or she should choose and act in every case for the sake of and because of this end" (1140b17–20). Practical wisdom is the capacity to hear the call of our end as the source of human action and the capacity to call ourselves back resolutely to stand by this guiding force. Aristotle contrasts such a person with the morally weak person who cannot abide by the choice he or she has made.

In speaking of conscience, Heidegger says: "When our understanding of the appeal is interpreted existentially as resoluteness, the conscience is revealed as that kind of being—included in the very basis of Dasein—in which Dasein makes possible for itself its factical existence, thus attesting to its ownmost potentiality-for-being."[4] In one of his earlier lecture courses on Aristotle, Heidegger translates *phronēsis* as *Gewissen* or conscience. The translation seems to me to be rooted in a meditation on Aristotle's *phronēsis* in the context of his discussion of moral weakness, a discussion on Aristotle's part that is comparable to Heidegger's discussion of losing oneself in the publicness and idle talk of the "they" and thus failing to hear one's ownmost self while listening to the they-self. In this regard, I see a close connection between Aristotle's notion of *orexis* or striving in his description of the *phronēsis-praxis* structure and Heidegger's discussion of "wanting to have a conscience." In his 1931 Aristotle lecture course, Heidegger translates *phronēsis* as *Umsicht* or circumspection, a notion akin to Aristotle's description of deliberation. He says that *phronēsis* is the *Selbstbesinnung* of the human being, our human way of being authentically in a situation.

In conclusion, I would like to quote a passage from Division 2 of *Being and Time* that specifically indicates that resoluteness in the face of one's own being is for Heidegger the basis of a free relationship with beings other than ourselves, a position that, as I have attempted to argue, is thoroughly Aristotelian:

> Resoluteness, as *authentic being-one's-self,* does not detach Dasein from its world, nor does it isolate it so that it becomes a free-floating "I". And how should it when resoluteness, as authentic disclosedness, is *authentically* nothing else than *being-in-the-world?* Resoluteness brings the self right into its current concernful being-alongside what is ready-to-hand and pushes it into solicitous being with others.
>
> In the light of the "for sake of which" of one's self-chosen

potentiality-for-being, resolute Dasein frees itself for its world. Dasein's resoluteness towards itself is what first makes it possible to let *others* who are with it 'be' in their ownmost potentiality-for-being and to co-disclose this potentiality in the solicitude that leaps forth and liberates. When Dasein is resolute, it can become the "conscience" of others. Only by authentically being-their-selves in resoluteness can people authentically be with one another.[5]

12 Economies of Production: Heidegger and Aristotle on *Physis* and *Technē*

DENNIS J. SCHMIDT

"Wo Welt—da Werk, und umgekehrt."[1] So says Heidegger, at least in his 1931 lecture course on Aristotle's *Metaphysics*. That is a remark found in the context of a discussion of the meaning of production and work, a discussion that problematizes both while setting aside the notion of "world"—although after *Being and Time* such a "setting aside" should be recognized as only provisional and ultimately illegitimate. The significance of that problematic gets thrown into sharper relief by a previous passage, in which Heidegger says that we must recognize that "the Greeks, Plato and Aristotle, not only worked through the interpretation of this phenomenon of production, but [also that] the fundamental concepts of philosophy [*Grundbegriffe*] grew in and out of this interpretation."[2] And that call for a return to the Greeks as a means of confronting and overcoming the immobility of thinking characteristic of metaphysics echoes the passage in his 1939 text on Aristotle's *Physics* in which Heidegger calls that book "the hidden, yet inadequately thought, cornerstone [*Grundbuch*] of Western philosophy"[3]—inadequately thought because the measure it sets up in the analogy and set of exchanges between *physis* and *technē* has yet to be questioned.[4]

Heidegger's own efforts to think through and dislodge such traditional "grounds" of thinking repeatedly led him back to Aristotle's texts, particularly to the *Physics* and the *Metaphysics*. This is the case from the early lecture courses through *Being and Time* (1927), which aborts its self-rewriting project when that project tries to inscribe the Western tradition, read as culminating in Hegel's identification of nature and spirit, within a certain reading of Aristotle's reflections on *physis;* this is also the case through the "Origin of the Work of Art" (1935), with its effort to recapture the truth of art from the category of the beautiful, showing

147

instead that the truth of art is found in its capacity to open and expose the folds and fissures that articulate the struggle of *physis* and *technē,* which is witnessed as the *polēmos* of earth and world.[5] But this concern with Aristotle continues through the *Nietzsche* volumes (1936–1941) as well, where Nietzsche's reading of the Greeks is criticized for not recognizing the advance that Aristotle makes by taking a step back into the pre-Socratic thinking of *physis* (that insofar as Aristotle thinks being as *entelechia),*[6] and of course through *The Question of Technology* (1953), where making, technique, production, and reproduction in the contemporary world are all measured against their measureless possibilities as they are thought in Aristotle's discussions of *physis* and *technē.* The list of relevant texts in Heidegger's work could be extended, of course.

Heidegger's persistent claim is that there is a calcified core of the Western tradition, one that is the effective historical legacy of certain Greek texts, including those texts of Aristotle, and that this congealed legacy has held thinking through Marx and Husserl in a tight and restrictive grip and so needs to be called into question. Furthermore, the same hardened core of presumptions that has sedimented out of that Greek legacy is most visible when it is seen as rotating around a set of oppositions that bounce off the concept of nature—the analogical relay of nature/art, nature/spirit, nature/history—and a set of assumptions spun off of those oppositions— the assumption, for instance, of a producing subject laboring in an objective world, struggling to overcome the alienation of both world and labor by humanizing nature and naturalizing humanity (a spin that leads unswervingly to a constellation of world and subject viewed techno- logically, a world defined by congealed subjectivity). Since those corner- stone Greek texts compose a "core" and articulate a "ground"—not insofar as they name any consensus, but insofar as they define the sites and frames (the *topoi)* for thinking—the call to displace those seemingly irreducible oppositions must be heard as a call for a topological shift. It is equally well described as an economic shift—that is, as a shift not only of sites and frames, but of the mediating laws and measures of transfer and translation between those places. This is the meaning of the epochal shift, the "step back," the return to the Greeks that Heidegger wants to effect.[7] It is a return to the Greeks that throws them out of "the" so-called Western tradition they are said to found, a return that gives them what Holderlin character- ized as their "Oriental vitality," a return that belongs to the project of blasting the borders of the Western world that takes itself to be heir to "the Greeks."

In taking this step it is helpful to acknowledge the dual role of Aristotle as both founding the effective history of metaphysics and harboring the critical seeds for the overcoming of metaphysics. For Heidegger, then, Aristotle marks a double place, one of foreclosure and disclosure alike:

first, inaugurating and engraving the fundamental shape of metaphysics, the sites of its future perfections; and second, with the possibility of the death of metaphysics—its original destination disclosed—providing the measure of its own failure.[8] This doubled place that Aristotle marks is inverted in the "last Greek," Hegel, who shadows every effort by Heidegger to enact that return to the Greeks.

On the Scope of the Question

My purpose in reminding you of the persistence and importance of Aristotle in Heidegger's thinking is to draw attention to the recurring matrix of topics that holds Heidegger's attention on Aristotle: the matrix named by the words *physis-technē-poiēsis*. And it is that matrix, and in particular how the filial lines linking those notions are best understood as mimetic lines, that I would like to address. More precisely, I would like to look at Heidegger's treatment of the *physis-technē* relation in Aristotle and do so with special attention to the notions of production and work as they can be thought freed from the economy of the producing and working subject and as they can be thought in a way that firmly rejects the idea that mimetic activities, such as they are, can be understood as matters of representation and imitation.[9] My thesis is that production *(Herstellung)* is best thought freed from the claims of representation *(Vorstellung)*, claims that tame the mimetic impulse by limiting it to tagging along behind its own reification. From the point of view I would like to move toward, one would finally say that Heidegger does not push the point hard enough when he says that "the anticipatory re-presentation of the ergon in its *eidos* is the true beginning of production."[10]

I choose these particular themes not simply because I believe they lie at the center of Heidegger's reflections on Aristotle, but also because I believe that they offer the clearest avenue for politicizing Heidegger's own thought—pulling it away from Heidegger's tendency to depoliticize questions and aestheticize politics; pulling it away from the onto-technological political economy of metaphysics and its struggles with domination and alienation, away from the discourse that Jean Baudrillard has analyzed as operating under the political economy of the sign; pulling it toward another economy, one that is not simply a simulacrum and liberalizing reform of the past, an economy outside the economy of exchange and the laws of identity and retribution that such exchange makes thinkable. In the end, rethinking *physis* brings in its wake a new understanding of the *nomoi* which it is our *physis* to institute; refiguring *topoi*—the essence of every polis—is an essentially political gesture that sets the margins of the polis in motion.

At the outset, it is worth noting that these issues of the opposition between *physis* and *technē*, and of the decision about the nature of the production at work in both domains (taken ultimately as a political decision), should not be viewed solely as a dialogue between Heidegger and Aristotle. In the end, already acknowledging the limitations of my own remarks that follow, I would say that the field of their discussions is simply not wide enough to pry the matter open, and that Heidegger alone might not offer the resources to reply to the very set of questions that he makes unavoidable today. Among the names of the more obvious contributors to that discussion belonging here are Marx and Hegel, who speak to the very thought of the dialectic of such oppositions (such as nature and spirit) as leading to the principle of their reconciliation, as well as Walter Benjamin, given his concern with the ways in which technological reproduction has altered and reopened the question of production. One might well argue that Benjamin goes farther than Heidegger toward stripping *mimēsis* of every claim of representation thought metaphysically insofar as he pulls mimetic activity away from its auratic attachments. But, of course, there are others as well and this is another list that could be extended.

Yet I would suggest that the crucial missing figure—the one who cannot be avoided—is Kant (something that Heidegger strangely never acknowledges; in fact, in one of his very few references to the third critique Heidegger goes so far as to reduce Kant to being a prime example of the modern effort to think nature as a technique).[11] But even if Kant himself mistakenly took the third critique to be oscillating within those traditional oppositions of nature and art that Heidegger is calling into question— oppositions Kant takes as so self-evident that the whole of judgment divides into the aesthetic and teleological along the fault lines of their differences—even if that is the case, Kant, as much as Heidegger, undeniably shows those oppositions to be misleading and untenable. Kant makes that point quite clear when he says that "we say far too little if we call [nature] an analogue of art."[12] But there are other points on which Kant is not to be avoided. In the notion of the genius, Kant, as much as Heidegger, breaks through the horizon of production determined by the subjectivity of the producing subject. Most important, though, is that, besides rivalling Heidegger in the radicality of his challenge to the tradition, Kant's efforts to think outside that frame have, as Hannah Arendt knew, a more overtly political cast than one finds in Heidegger.[13] Nonetheless Kant is thoroughly Aristotelian in the orthodox sense when he writes, "*Art* is distinguished from *nature* as doing is from acting....and the product...of art is distinguished from that of nature, the first being a work, the second an effect."[14] On the side of nature is mechanical necessity; on the side of art, the play of freedom. Between the two we witness the site of judgment and the conflict housed in every teleology. It is a distinction that leads directly to the antimony of reason itself; a distinction that judgment must bridge because every possible series of middle terms fails to close the abyss disclosed in that antimony. Aristotle's distinction, you will recall—the one that resonates in Kant and that Heidegger finds decisive—reads: "Some things are due to *physis;* for others there are other causes" (192b8). This is the sentence at issue, and so a brief rehearsal of its context is in order.

Aristotle on *Physis* and *Technē*

Aristotle's intention in distinguishing between these two causal domains is to restore the independence and integrity of *physis,* which he argues is missed by his predecessors, especially by Plato. In Plato *physis* in itself is incoherent, unintelligible, and without purpose or "good." Intelligibility, form, and purpose are not intrinsic to *physis* but must be introduced into it. That is why Plato says in the *Timaeus* that *physis* itself is the product of a divine artifice, and that without the intervention of a god it "lacks a logos" (53b), that is, it lacks all reason, meaning, and measure. Although *physis* is not necessarily hostile to reason and truth, it nevertheless teaches us nothing about either, and in the end it awaits the impress of both from elsewhere.

Against Plato, Aristotle rejects the explanation that the knowability of *physis* is introduced *ab extra*. Rather, Aristotle's sentence says that if *physis* is to be understood, then it must *not* be understood as a product of *technē*; that is, it must not be understood technomorphically, not even autotechnomorphically, but according to some other set of reasons that explain its coming into appearance. Though there are a number of differences between that which is a product of *technē* and the beings of *physis,* the most crucial and never-problematized difference is the *origin* of the movements that bring each into being: in things made, that source is outside the thing in the maker (the *archetekton*), whereas in "natural" things, that source is in the thing itself. Thus the materials and shape of the house are determined by the reasoning of the architect, whereas left to itself the rose "knows" no external reasons. The individuality of the being of nature lies in its capacity to draw itself out of itself. In the words of Meister Eckhart, so frequently cited by Heidegger: "The rose knows no why; it blooms simply because it blooms." Or in Aristotle's words: "A man is born of a man, but not a bed from a bed" (193b9). Nature is this "drawing out" of itself; nature simply produces what produces—that is the meaning of its self-sameness and transience alike, and this is the point where something non-artefactual first glimmers in nature.

But significantly, despite this and other differences between that which is a product of *technē* and that which comes to be "by nature," and although their relation is a relation of otherness, Aristotle argues that *physis* works analogously to *technē*, and he even pushes this parallel to the point of a real identity. Thus he writes that "if a house were one of the things which came to be by nature, it would come to be just as it does now by art; and if the things which are by nature came to be not only by nature, they would come to be just as they are by nature" (199a12–14). In short, houses might grow like mushrooms, while mushrooms might, in turn, be engineered like houses. It is important to note, though, that the identification here is not concerned with the respective products of *physis* and *technē* but with the two productions. The point concerns engineering and growth, not houses and mushrooms.

Consequently, despite his intention to clearly distinguish the horizon and integrity of *physis* from that of *technē*, Aristotle also holds on to a sense of their profound intimacy, and in speaking of this relation it sometimes seems that he gives *technē* the hermeneutically upper hand; that is, *physis* is interpreted according to the model of *technē*, which, for Aristotle, is more easily known. The critical assumption is that the "forehaving" at work in making things that we "have in mind" (the *eidos prohaireton*) and our "know-how" *(technē)* is a process like the processes found in nature, but a process that, because it is assumed to be initiated by us, is assumed to be more transparent to us than the initially quite opaque processes of nature. According to Heidegger, the interpretive priority that Aristotle accords *technē* in this relation eventually gives way to the essential technologization of every metaphysics of nature. The high point of this process is found in the modern world when Galilean mechanics and the Cartesian abolition of final cause in nature eventually led, in Hobbes, to the final disruption of the uneasy ontological parity between nature and *technē* found in Aristotle. Nature becomes artifice par excellence; ontology gradually becomes an invitation to technology.

Aristotle on *Physis* and Repetition

When discussing the movement peculiar to the life of nature Aristotle emphasizes the perpetually unfinished quality of all that comes to be "by nature." Whereas the products of *technē* either succeed by coming into their telos or do not succeed, the beings of nature, marked as they are by undying *energeia* and *kinēsis,* can never be said to be finished, but must be understood as *entelechia* and so *energeia ateles.* A product of *technē* cannot be said to be unfinished in the same way as a being of nature: an unfinished house is not yet finished in a very different way from the way in which a seedling is not yet the tree that, barring intervention, it is on the way to being. Of course, every homeowner will object that work on a house is never finished. But such being-unfinished is to be distinguished from that self-sustenance exhibited by the tree: we call the required work on a house *up-keep* or *maintenance,* that is, the work required to preserve the house as a product of *techne*. If we cease such maintenance, the house eventually decays until it ceases being recognizable as a product of *techne,* and it ultimately returns to the *physis* out of which it was fabricated. Nature, on the other hand, is always on the way to more of itself; *physis* is always *"hodos physeos eis physin"* (193b12), it is always repeating itself, doubling itself as *energeia*. Nature folds back upon itself and, in that sense, is to be thought in terms of that repetition.

This redoubling of nature is its specialty and, in Aristotle's view, the reflexivity of human thought is the best example of nature's relation to itself: that is what Aristotle means when he says that nature is like a "doctor doctoring herself" (199b29–30). The mind is at its best, its most natural moment, in recognizing itself, in following its homing instinct, retracing its steps, circling back to itself. That alone is thought which is able to hear itself call to itself. At its best, hearing and heeding that call, thinking is nature's best reflection of itself. At the conclusion of the *Physics* Aristotle says that "there is, in nature, a motion ever-enduring, uniform and uninterrupted, and its nature is that of rotation in a circle" (261b27). At the moment it is most itself, at the summit of its freedom, thinking follows the circle as well. Of course, at this point one can already feel the approach of Heidegger's description of the circle as "the feast of thinking."[15]

But the important point to note is that in this discussion of the repetition at work in nature, its identity and difference with *techne* emerges most clearly in looking at the different ways in which the products of each decay. Nature is an incompletable incompletion, and it continually renews itself as such insofar as its production is the productive motion itself, insofar as it produces what produces. Artifacts, on the other hand, separated from their own productive source, are completable and do not renew themselves. For example, a forest continually replants and renews itself out of the fragments of its own death; the evidence of its own decay becomes the seed of its repetition and renewal. The Acropolis, on the other hand, continues to erode as a result of both the elements and pollutants, and no *techne* has yet been able to halt that decay, let alone renew the Acropolis; the evidence of its decay testifies to its removal from its own originative and productive source. That which owes itself to *techne* is removed from this motion of productive repetition, this movement of time, becoming instead a matter of a reproductive restoration. The return in *techne* is restoration; the return in *physis* is repetition. Heidegger accounts for this difference by saying that the *"eidos* of an *ergon* is *telos*. . . . To produce something. . . is to bring it into its limit."[16] Because nature has its telos and labile limits in itself, because nature produces what produces and so is *entelechia,* it always lives at its limits and as such lives as a perpetual renewal that thrives because it always is at its end and yet is never finished.[17] As such, nature has an essential—that is, living—relation to death that is different from the relation to mere decay found in the horizon of *techne* as Aristotle thinks it. Again, Heidegger: "Every living thing begins to die as soon as it begins to live and vice versa. . .*physis* is the self-producing removal [*Wegstellen*] of itself."[18] It is this reciprocity between its life and death that defines the repetition that is *physis*. And it is this struggle that defines *physis* as that with the capacity to throw itself ever anew into darkness.

The key here is that to the being of *physis* there thus belongs an ineluctable lack, a *steresis*, which shows itself simultaneously in the dual modes of a not-yet-attained goal and of the perishing of a present state in favor of a coming one. Movement itself is the telos of nature, and the bidirectionality of this movement toward both novelty and loss is the source of the eternal character of all that has to do with *physis*. That is why Heidegger says, "The essence of *physis* reveals itself in *steresis*."[19] And that is why Aristotle says, *"Steresis* is a kind of *eidos"* (193b19). With this in mind Heidegger says that *"steresis* certainly refers to an 'away,' but always and above all it means that something falls away, has gone away, remains away, becomes absent. If we bear in mind that *ousia,* beingness, means presencing, then we do not need a long explanation to show where *steresis* as perishing belongs."[20] The point is not simply to oppose *steresis* as perishing to *ousia* as presencing, but to recognize the twofold character and repetition at work in *physis* as a movement that is both perishing and presencing. Understanding the *steresis*-character of *physis* is requisite for an understanding of Aristotle's non-technomorphic account of nature as having its end in itself, as being *entelechia,* a sense of the being of nature that is voiced in the Heraclitean fragment that says, *"Physis kryptesthai philei. "*[21] This self-encrypting motion of *physis* is the secret of its repetition and life.

The generation of nature is always equally a degeneration; its work always makes room for its own unworking—a movement that is incalculable, uncontrollable, and as such always at odds with the modern, Baconian urge toward calculation and control. Eternally productive and as such mortal, nature is a domain of self-sacrifice that disavows every integrative and totalizing claim. This self-sacrifice and enormity is what Kant addresses when he speaks of the judgment of the sublime.[22] Put in other words, its truth is truing, a disintegrative truth. This is why Theodor Adorno was able to suggest that it is best to think nature as a fragment—"a work tampered by death"—rather than as an organic unity; and this is why the romantic movement in literature, one defined by its effort to meditate upon the meaning of poetic production itself and to think nature as auto-poetic, is so taken with the idea and possibilities of fragment. The full task of rethinking the being of nature as eternally transient, as what Schelling called the *Unvordenklich* (the unrethinkable), begins with the relation of this *kryptesthai* and *sterēsis*—a mobile relation of mobility that Heidegger described as the aletheic movement.

Heidegger's Repetition of Aristotle's Notion of *Physis*

My purpose thus far has been to unfold some of the issues that Heidegger sees at work in Aristotle's analogy between *physis* and *technē* in order to raise some questions about Heidegger's efforts to rethink that founding relation. Rethinking this relation is a task that turns the basic analogy upon which it is built back upon itself; in the return that he wants to effect, Heidegger finds the first move toward a rethinking of thinking that too long has been taken as a *technē* in the service of an ill-conceived model of production, a *technē* itself in servitude to an image of the subject modeled after the ideal of an infinite and omnipresent mind. The analogy between *physis* and *technē* determines far more than the terms that determine it, since, in the end, it articulates an economy of producing subjects laboring in a world conceived according to onto-theological presumptions. So Heidegger's claim is that calling the analogy and all of its attendant relays into question puts far more than its own terms in jeopardy. That is why questioning the *physis-technē* relation is fundamental to the project of overcoming metaphysics.

But, when asking about Heidegger's challenge to the assumptions that underpin the distinction upon which this founding analogy is built, it is important to ask how far Heidegger thinks within this analogical frame. To what extent is Heidegger's effort to repeat and reverse the analogy, to fold it back upon itself in the return that it calls for, merely shifting the sense of *technē* by splitting a hair—a split that Derrida claims has a fundamentally mercenary concern[23]—splitting *technē* into art and artifice, taking "great" or "fine" art as the model for the aletheic movement of *physis,* rejecting craft and practical artifice (perhaps unwittingly on the grounds of its relation to wages)? The economy that Heidegger is trying to open is still defined only negatively; that is, as non-representational and as not bound to the notion of the producing subject. But one must ask how far his own analysis of *technē* remains captivated by those very notions. In this regard, Benjamin's analysis of the work of art in the epoch of its technical reproducibility provides an illuminating backdrop against which one might push this concern. Then one would do well to ask about the extent to which Heidegger remains bound to an auratic conception of the work of art, for insofar as it is bound to such a conception one must acknowledge that Heidegger's own sense of *mimēsis* as repetition is still tied to a concern with art that bears a significant resemblance to the very sense of representation against which it is directed.

Heidegger's critique, leveled more against Aristotle's legacy than Aristotle himself, is that this analogy is problematic on two counts: the discussion of the origin and the nature of the movement characteristic of both *physis* and *technē*. First, against Aristotle, Heidegger argues that the process of *technē* is not more easily known than the process of *physis* simply because *technē* seems to originate in the governing *prohaireton eidos* of the maker. (This is the point at which Kant's concept of the genius helps advance Heidegger's point. The genius is the one who is at one with nature, taking its dictation, making rules without following them, reproducing; the genius is the one following the *eidos* of production [*poiēsis*] itself, repeating nature in its productive moment, but breaking with mimesis understood as an imitation of what is, as replication. In short, the genius is the one who works with *physis* as "*poiēsis* in the highest sense."[24] In the genius we witness production not as a matter of a subject, since the genius is the one whose subject-being is effaced, and we equally witness the inimitable truth of all imitation.) Second, against Aristotle, Heidegger does not regard the products of *technē* as outside of the twofold, generating-degenerating movement of perishing and presencing. Against Aristotle's claim that the work of *technē* must be thought of as freed from an essential relation to death, Heidegger argues that no work of *technē* has a life outside of the self-surpassing motion of history and the renewing power of tradition that is animated by such works themselves. The work of art does not stand apart from time or history. This is especially clear in the case of art works and the way in which they can be said to found a world. From the vantage point of the possible death of art, of its break with its own tradition held together by its adoration of beauty and the vision of an integrated life, we see that art finds its center of gravity in history, not in the subject. From that vantage point, we can see the essential relation between art and death insofar as history becomes visible as the real content of art works.[25]

Toward Another Economy of Production

Heidegger's claim is that, taken as a matter of the production of a subject, *technē* disenfranchises itself from its historical truth, becoming instead either aesthetics or technology, both of which are frozen modalities of subjectivity severed from their living source. This is why Heidegger begins the essay "Origin of the Work of Art" by disavowing the thought that art can be thought as originating in the artist; and this is why he begins "The Question concerning Technology" by rejecting the anthropological interpretation of technology that takes technology and technofacts to be results of our *prohaireton eidos* and consequently at our disposal.

Heidegger's claim is that the trajectory of philosophy as metaphysics that Aristotle inaugurates points precisely to the view that Heidegger wants to dislodge—a trajectory that ultimately discloses the hidden truth of metaphysics in the links that bind it to modern technology and to the thinking that characterizes such a world view—a world view that, in Heidegger's opinion, finally takes work to be the ultimate self-relation, not a relation of otherness. In this traditional view *technē* is understood to be reproduction ruled by identity. In Heidegger's view, it is repetition marked by difference. So, for Heidegger, the metaphysical view is a narcissistic view, one that Hegel brings to perfection when he describes the warrior, the one who annihilates the other, as carrying out the highest work of the production and reproduction of self-identity.

Of course, between Hegel and Aristotle we find the full genesis of the notion of the subject that becomes substance in Hegel. Heidegger is obviously not trying to cram the subject into Aristotle's model of *technē*. But he is trying to argue that that model is bound too tightly to the structure and economy of representation, and that, thanks in large measure to misconceiving the origin and nature that distinguishes *technē* from *physis*.

Aristotle believes that the real difficulty faced in considering the *physis-technē* relation is found in the need to account for the movement of *physis*. Eventually playing off its identities and differences with what is taken to be the movement of poetic production, Aristotle arrives at the decision that nature's motion is *repetition,* the free folding and unfolding of itself into itself, a motion that Aristotle finds most clearly evident in the generation of sexual difference, sexual reproduction, and the periodicity of seasons and stars. This movement of repetition is marked by *sterēsis,* and as such it is a movement of presence and absence, a surpassing that cannot overcome itself because it lives at its limits. But while Aristotle lets a preliminary sense of the production of *technē* inform his analysis of *physis,* he does not reverse the analogy fully in order to ask if their likenesses extend to the point at which one finds the productive, circular repetition at work in *technē*. The anticipatory structure that guides the establishment of the analogy itself resembles the movement that Aristotle describes as belonging to *technē*, not the repetitive movement of *physis,* not the movement of thought at its best. Instead of making that move he stays with a notion of *technē* that works along the lines of representation and reproduction—and a sense of *mimēsis* as ontologically inferior.

Heidegger's purpose is to complete the Aristotelian move, to work within a refunctioned frame of the *physis-technē* relation, to work back and forth along that relay, seeing the structure of repetition at work in *technē*, finding the folds of mimesis—freed from its link with representation—at the site of the (re)flexion of *physis*.[26] This is a possibility that would make sense of Aristotle's otherwise puzzling remark that *technē* completes what *physis* cannot, and that it imitates *physis* as well. It also helps us make sense of Heidegger's own otherwise perplexing claim that "the work of art is a work not primarily because it is produced or made, but because it brings about being in a being; here to 'bring about' means to set to work and bring about the phenomenon as that in which the emerging power, *physis,* comes to shine."[27] The movements of repetition at work in *physis* and in the work of art set each other in motion, call one another forth.

Rethinking *technē*, and rethinking, shifting the topos of its relation to *physis* (a relation that names one of the fundamental ways in which we are in the world)—means coming to see art not as the product of a subject, not as a product embedded in history, but as the making of history itself. That is what Adorno means when he says that "what is historical in art is not artefactual: thus it is through history that art is freed from being a product of mere invention. Truth content is the crystallization, in art works, of history."[28] And that is also what Heidegger is driving at when he says that "whenever art happens, that is, whenever a beginning is, a shock happens in history, then history begins for the first time or again.... Art is historical and as historical it is the creative presentation of truth in work."[29]

Of course, more remains to be said. I have already indicated that I believe Kant would be particularly helpful in furthering this move away from a conception of art that binds itself to a restrictive notion of the subject. The concept of mimesis that works in the discussion of genius, where genius is identified with the production of production itself, and the sense of mimesis disclosed in our disappointment before reproductions of nature (you recall the story of the imitation of the bird calls),[30] outline a movement that forbids taking production to be imitative reproduction or replication, and thus draws mimesis, the truly productive moment, closer to nature's own repetitions.[31]

Furthermore, I believe it must be asked whether Heidegger unduly restricts the possibilities of *technē* whenever—as, for instance, in "Origin of the Work of Art"—he restricts it to "great" or "fine" art.[32] But then Heidegger's own ambivalence about the "death" of art plays into this point: "the decision about Hegel's proclamation [on the pastness of art] is not yet made";[33] the demise of "fine" art is the end of the link that binds art to the wholesome wholeness of beauty's claim.[34] Heidegger's hesitation before this decision is justified and once again makes Kant pertinent, this time with regard to the universality and communicability of such a claim. But it might well be the case that Heidegger has not yet fully confronted the thinking of *technē* as reproduction and representation with the thinking of *technē* that takes *technē* as a matter of repetition. Perhaps the most promising route for that confrontation in Heidegger's own work would be through his reflections on language that is defined by its repetition, density, and concentration—namely, language in the poem.

But the final point, the real question to which all this concern with the *physis-technē* relation leads, is to ask about the new economy to which this shifted and refunctioned relation points. It is clear that Heidegger's move is away from the economy of representation and reproduction—an economy of exchange, identity, and promissory notes, an economy ultimately of retribution. This is the economy Heidegger describes in 1946 in a text written at a politically charged moment in his life, one written along with the "Letter on Humanism," the final text of the essays among the *Holzwege* that opens with the "Origin of the Work of Art," namely, in "Anaximander's Saying," where he speaks of "a kind of barter system in nature's immutable economy"[35] and the inadequacy of our grasp of this economy when the *adikia* it articulates is characterized as "penalty." Heidegger's rethinking of the Anaximander fragment, his effort to pull that meditation on what has been translated and so thought as "injustice" and its relation to "time" into a new route of thinking, belong to this economic turn. Likewise, if Heidegger's project in this regard is to return to itself, taking seriously its own claims to repetition, then it must break away from an economy attentive only to the forces of production. It must link with an effort to outline a general economy, one of consumption and expenditure as well as production and excess.[36] One day we must ask about this new economy sheared free of retribution. We need to ask about this economy that is historical, repetitive, mimetic, one of truly productive forces, one aware of its own consumptive demands.

13 The *Deinon* of Yielding at the End of Metaphysics

THOMAS A. DAVIS

To further a path of thought, it must already be attuned to new possibilities; yet only in the last several years has commentary on Heidegger's later thought confronted the question of determining the fundamental attunement, or *Grundstimmung,* of thought at the end of metaphysics.[1] To develop this problematic I want to examine the notion that the opening of "another thinking" takes place through a correspondence between the fundamental attunements of thought at the origin and end of the metaphysical tradition.[2] The hint I will follow to establish this correspondence will be to show how *Gelassenheit* is rooted in the *"deinon* of yielding"—the uncanniness of giving way to the claim of another—that is at work in the downfall of Creon in *Antigone.* To begin to follow out this hint, we first need to get a better sense for why a correspondence between attunements of origin and end is called for today.

In his 1939 lectures on Nietzsche, Heidegger claims that the peculiar greatness of the consummation of the commencement of Western thought in Aristotle resides in "the immediacy and purity of the original envisaging of the essential configurations of being" (N 113). He then goes on to assert that

> if a more original consideration of Being [than Aristotle's] should become necessary because of a real historical need of Western man, such thinking can only occur in confrontation with the first beginnings of Western thought. This confrontation will not succeed, will remain inaccessible in its essence and necessity, as long as the greatness, that is, simplicity and purity of the corresponding fundamental attunement of thinking and the power of the appropriate saying, are denied us. (N 113)

In other words, if we need now to open the possibility of another kind of thinking, we can do so only by confronting the origin of our thought; but we can gain access to that confrontation only by overcoming the way the fundamental attunement of that origin is denied us. How, then, can we overcome such denial?

The notion of "overcoming" here can make sense only if a correspondence between the fundamental attunements of the origin and end of the metaphysical tradition is possible. If, however, "modern" thought is "out of tune" with its origin, a confrontation with the Greeks is not possible. Indeed, Heidegger goes on to assert that although "Nietzsche in an immediate way comes closer to the essence of the Greeks than any metaphysical thinker before him," "a confrontation does not take place" (N 113). And although Heidegger does not explicitly mention the attunement of Nietzsche's thought, we can surmise that a genuine confrontation with the Greeks does not take place because Nietzsche "thinks in a *modern* way, thoroughly and with the hardest stringency," and the attunement of this way of thinking closes off the fundamental attunement of the origin of the metaphysical tradition (N 113). Yet for Heidegger it is precisely Nietzsche's thought that initiates the end of the metaphysical tradition. Thus if thought today is attuned by that ending, it seems clear that it, like Nietzsche's, will be "out of tune" with the possibility of a confrontation with the "essence of the Greeks."

But perhaps the way that thought today is "out of tune" with its origins is even more radical. Perhaps the *Grundstimmung* of thought at the end of metaphysics is denied us altogether, so that, unlike Nietzsche, a "confrontation" with the "essence of the Greeks" would not even make sense metaphysically. Can this be true? Surely not, for I take it that we assume we can name the *Grundstimmung* supposedly denied us, *Gelassenheit*.

Such an assumption, however, neglects the complication that in 1955 Heidegger gave two lectures that seem to present quite different possibilities concerning our access to the fundamental attunement of thought today—and thereby our access to a confrontation with the Greeks. In "What Is Philosophy?" Heidegger asks whether the end of modern thinking is determined by another attunement, and then continues:

> It looks as though we are only posing historical questions. But, in truth, we are pondering [*bedenken*] the future essence of philosophy. We are trying to listen to the voice of Being. Into which attunement does this bring today's thinking? The question hardly has an unambiguous answer. Presumably a fundamental attunement holds sway. But it still remains concealed from us. This would be a sign that our thinking today has still not found its unambiguous path. What we

encounter is only this: variously different attunements of thinking [*verschiedenartige Stimmungen des Denkens*]. (WP 89)

Yet in his "Memorial Address" Heidegger commends us to the possibility of commemorative thinking in terms of *"Gelassenheit* toward things" and "openness to the mystery."[3] Thus it would seem that in the space of a single year Heidegger both affirmed that the fundamental attunement of thought today remains concealed from us and pointed to what that attunement must be for commemorative thinking to be possible. How can he do both? More specifically, if it is the dispersion of various attunements of thinking that "conceals" the *Grundstimmung* that "presumably" prevails, then what is the relation between the concealment at work in such dispersion and the (presumed) opening at work in *Gelassenheit?*[4]

The difficulty here is understanding the kind of correspondence that could exist between dispersion and *Gelassenheit.* To begin to understand the nature of this correspondence we need to turn back to the notion of "denial." If we are aware that we are denied access to something, then we must already have *some* access to it, or the notion of "denial" would not make sense. Yet if we *are* denied access, how can we follow out the kind of hint that such denial could itself present? We could do so only if the way such a hint is a part of the dynamic of the denial would open the possibility, through following out the hint, of overcoming the denial. If the dispersion of attunements at the end of metaphysics carries within itself a hint to its own self-overcoming, that hint is called *Gelassenheit.* But this means that the possibility of a correspondence between the concealment at work in dispersion and the opening presumably at work in *Gelassenheit* is rooted in the way the dynamic of dispersion can overcome itself through the dynamic of *Gelassenheit.* To further clarify what is at work at this juncture, we need to consider again the fundamental difference Heidegger sees between Aristotle and Nietzsche.

In contrast to Nietzsche's consummately "modern" thinking, Aristotle's thought "lack[s] . . . any need to go *back behind* its own positing. The Greek thinkers 'only' show the first steps *forward"* (N 113). That is, the greatness of Aristotle's thought is the "simplicity and purity" by which it is attuned to think forward from out of the "unsaid" dimension of Being, in contrast to the attunement of modern thought that suffers the need to go back behind itself so as to think about itself. What is this "unsaid dimension" of the origin that Aristotle simply and purely thinks *from* but does not think *about?*[5] Heidegger names it in this poetic "hint":

> The oldest of the old follows behind
> us in our thinking and yet it
> comes to meet us.

That is why thinking holds to the
coming of what has been, and
is remembrance.[6]

It is the "unsaid dimension" of the *Grundstimmung* of the origin of
thinking in the Greeks that "comes to meet us" today in the correspondence
between dispersion and *Gelassenheit;* and it is the disposition of this
correspondence that is our access to the "unsaid dimension" that originally
destined it. The circular *co-respondence* at work here is the site of the
confrontation with the Greeks through which "another thinking" might be
possible. How, then, are we to find the right way to enter *this* circle? By
following out the right hint.

From the course of our reflection thus far, we should now be in a
position to say that *if Gelassenheit* contains within itself a hint to the way
the denial at work in dispersion can provide for its own self-overcoming
and *if* it is the unsaid dimension of the originary Greek *Grundstimmung*
that has destined the dynamic of such dispersion, including the possibility
of its self-overcoming, then the hint we must follow is the way *Gelassenheit*
is rooted in the unsaid dimension of that originary *Grundstimmung.*
Heidegger, however, never provides us with a direct way of determining the
"unsaid dimension" of the fundamental attunement of Greek thought;
rather, he raises the problem of such an "unsaid dimension" indirectly
through the question of the relation between philosophy and poetry. For
the source of the consummation of the commencement of Western thought
in Aristotle is the "poetic thinking" of Anaximander, Heraclitus, and
Parmenides. This "poetic thinking" took place in essential relation to the
way the "essence of the Greeks" was presented in tragic poetry.[7] Thus, to
help articulate the meaning of *to gar auto noein estin te kai einai,* the saying
from Parmenides in which "the decisive determination of being-human
first takes place," Heidegger turns in his *Introduction to Metaphysics* to the
second chorus of Sophocles' *Antigone* (IM 123). With this turn we seem to
have arrived at the text with which to follow out our clue. But if Heidegger
only considers Sophocles' notion of *deinon* in the second chorus, why is it
necessary to go beyond that chorus to consider the role *deinon* plays in
Creon's downfall?

To return to the 1939 Nietzsche lectures, we find that Heidegger locates
the end of the metaphysical tradition via the advent of Zarathustra in
Nietzsche's thought. This end is the limit that both carries metaphysical
thinking to its extreme and opens the possibility of another thinking. The
double edge of this situation is located by the phrase *Incipit Zarathustra.*
Heidegger says of this phrase that "one must *act by way of thinking* with the
'Incipit,'" which itself "assumes another name: *'Incipit tragoedia'*"(N 135).
The implication is that thought now has to confront this inception; and

Heidegger goes on to say that the obscurity that might threaten at this juncture cannot be thought through as long as "we do not comprehend and ponder the fact *that* tragedy always *begins* with the *'going under'* of the hero, and *why* it does so" (N 135). In this way Heidegger asserts that at the limit of philosophy understood as metaphysics there is the return of a question concerning the essence of tragedy—and specifically the question of why tragedy begins with the "going under" of the tragic hero. My claim in what follows is that Creon's refusal to yield, which brings him to confront the *deinon* of yielding itself, articulates Sophocles' answer to this question. What we need to do now is establish the co-respondence between Sophocles' answer and *Gelassenheit*. To do this we need to determine what Heidegger thinks *deinon* means in the second chorus of *Antigone,* and then see what role it plays in Creon's downfall. The key to understanding Heidegger's interpretation of *deinon* in *Introduction to Metaphysics,* however, is to be found in the way that interpretation is governed by a particular tension it inherits from Heidegger's *Rektoratsrede* of two years earlier. We need to briefly consider this tension before turning directly to Heidegger's comments on *deinon* in the second chorus of *Antigone.*

Heidegger's Understanding of *Deinon*

For all the current interest in Heidegger's rectorial address, insufficient attention has been paid to the conflict between the different attunements at work in it. Yet even a cursory reading reveals that its call for a sensibility attuned to "battle," to a kind of *polēmos,* is not univocal. For one is immediately struck by the tension that arises between the violence of the call for a resolution that would enact a passion for knowledge, and the sense of that same resolve being abandoned before the overwhelming force of a kind of destiny. The *pathos* of the rectorial address is found in the decision to be resolute within or before such abandonment. To will that decision is, in Heidegger's eyes, to determine the destiny of the German people. Thus his address is a call to action. But the sense of that call is attuned to the inevitability of abandonment. *Wissenschaft* runs up against a fundamental limit in that abandonment, and the mood of that abandonment is dread. Let us see how Heidegger came to consider the tension here between resolute action and anxious abandonment.

When Heidegger in his 1945 essay, "The Rectorate 1933–34: Facts and Thoughts," sought to "justify" his rectorship, he put his decision to assume it in terms of a "renunciation" of the "most proper" vocation of a thinker (R 498). He undertook this renunciation in response to the need he had perceived for intellectual leadership of the Nazi movement. He had thought he could make an essential difference. The extent of his failure, however, was complete. His call was spoken, as he says, "into the wind" (R 493).[8] And he in turn underwent the abandonment of his calling as a teacher and a thinker. In 1945 he saw such abandonment as a consequence of "the consummation of nihilism" (R 498). But in 1933 he was caught in the "unsaid" irony of a call to action that could come to understand itself only through the necessity of its enacting a tension between resolute action and anxious abandonment that it could not resolve but *only* abandon itself to. The dynamic at work in this tension governs Heidegger's interpretation of Sophocles' *deinon* in *Introduction to Metaphysics.*[9]

The opening line of the second chorus of *Antigone* reads: *polla ta deina kouden anthropon deinoteron pelei.* Heidegger translates: "There is much that is strange [*Unheimliche*], but nothing that surpasses man in strangeness" (EM 114/IM 125). And he goes on to say that for the Greeks, "man, in one word, is *to deinotaton,* the strangest [*Unheimlichste*]. This one word encompasses the extreme limits and abrupt abysses of his being" (EM 114/IM 125). But if being human is encompassed in this single word, the word itself traditionally has three meanings: awe or wonder, terror, and cleverness. Of this multiplicity Heidegger says:

> Das griechische Wort *deinon* ist in jener unheimlichen Zweideutigkeit zweideutig, mit der das Sagen der Griechen die gegenwendigen Auseinander-setzungen des Seins durchmisst. (EM114/IM 126)

> The Greek word *deinon* has that strange ambiguous ambiguity with which the Saying of the Greeks measures out the counterturning confrontations of Being.

Aus-einander-setzung names a confrontation in which that which is set apart is allowed to come into its own. *Gegenwendig* indicates that such confrontation takes place in a movement of turn-counterturn. *Die gegenwendigen Aus-einander-setzungen des Seins* means that Being takes place through such counterturning confrontations; and *deinon* shows the way this movement of Being is measured out in Greek. We can see a clue to this movement in the way Heidegger distributes the three traditional meanings of *deinon* into a confrontational economy of two senses:

> On one hand . . . *deinon* is the terrible in the sense of the overpowering power [*des überwältigenden Waltens*] that in a like manner exacts panicky horror, true dread, as well as the collected, reticent awe that vibrates in itself. The powerful, the overpowering [*Das Gewaltige, das Überwältigende*] is the essential character of power itself. Where this befalls it *can* keep its overpowering power [*überwältigende Macht*] to itself. Yet in that way it does not become harmless, but only *still* more terrible and remote.

But on the other hand, *deinon* means the powerful [*das Gewaltige*] in the sense of one who uses power [*Gewalt*], who not only disposes [*verfügt*] of power, but is violent [*gewalt-tätig*] insofar as the use of power [*Gewaltbrauchen*] is not only the basic trait of his action but also of his *Dasein*. (EM 114–15/IM 126)

In Heidegger's twofold reading of *deinon,* its traditional meanings of "terror" and "awe" are incorporated into his first sense of *deinon* as the overpowering power, which he will further develop in terms of his reading of *dikē* as the "overwhelming enjoining order" [*der überwältigende Fug*] (EM 126/IM 139). This sense translates awe into a specific form of the terrible: the self-collectedness by which the overpowering keeps its power to itself commands a reticent awe that is itself terrifying. And the second sense of *deinon* as the violence essential to *Dasein* incorporates the traditional meaning of "cleverness" in Heidegger's reading of *technē* as the "violence of knowing" [*die Gewalt-tätigkeit des Wissens*] (EM 126/IM 139). The key to Heidegger's twofold reading of *deinon,* however, is not this distribution of traditional meanings into *dikē* and *technē,* but the insight that establishes the confrontational relation between *dikē* and *technē* as the heart of the dynamic at work in *deinon:* "The *deinotaton* of *deinon,* the strangest of the strange, lies in the counter-turning relation [*gegenwendigen Bezug*] between *dike* and *techne*" (EM 124/IM 136). The turn-counterturn of this relation is defined by a double-edged violence: "Thus the *deinon* as the overpowering [*das Überwältigende*] *(dike)* and the *deinon* as the violent [*das Gewalt-tätige*] *(techne)* confront one another. . . . In this confrontation *techne* bursts forth against *dike,* which in turn, as the enjoining order [*Fug*], disposes [*verfügt*] of all *techne*" (EM 123/IM 135).

To see the insight that rules this violent confrontation we need to note that the distribution of the three traditional meanings into a twofold economy is governed by Heidegger's use of a nexus of words rooted in the verb *walten.* But translating *Gewalt* as power, *Gewaltige* as the powerful, and *Überwältigende* as the overpowering power fails to articulate the essential sense of *walten* at work in these words. *Walten* means holding sway in the sense of a power that rules or governs, that is, the ruling force of a governing order. Thus *Überwältigende* means the "overwhelming force" of that which holds sway. And while *Gewalt-tätige* does mean that which is violent, Heidegger hyphenates the word to help *tätig* bring out the active character of *Gewalt* as a kind of force. *Gewalt-tätige* is the violence of force that *must* overwhelm any limits placed on it in order to be force.

This brief examination of *walten* should help us see that for Heidegger that confrontation between *dikē* and *technē* is governed by a particular insight into the "unsaid" relation between the power of enjoining order and the downfall into ruin demanded by *phusis:*

The conflict [*Gegenwendigkeit*] between the overwhelming presence of beings as a whole [*überwältigenden Seiende in Ganzen*] and man's violent *Dasein* creates the possibility of downfall [*Absturz*] into the issueless [*Ausweglose*] and placeless: ruin [*der Verderb*]. But ruin and the possibility of ruin do not occur only at the end, when a single act of power fails...; no, this disaster is fundamental, it governs and waits in the conflict between violence and the overwhelming. Violence against the overwhelming force of Being [*Übergewalt des Seins*] *must* shatter against Being, if Being rules in its essence, as *phusis,* as emerging-holding-sway [*aufgehendes Walten*]. (EM 124/IM 136)

It is this insight into a need *(Not)* created by *phusis* as *aufgehendes Walten,* as the force of that which holds sway through emerging presence, that governs Heidegger's reading of *deinon*. Man is essentially *unheimlich* because Being as *phusis* needs man "in order to appear in its power, *requires* a place, a scene of disclosure" (EM 124/IM 136–37). This insight attunes the dimension of awe to the tenor of a dreadful shattering, a shattering by which the venture *(tolma)* of *Da-sein* is governed by a counterturning movement that breaks the familiar:

> The strangest (man) is what it is because, fundamentally, it ventures and protects the familiar [*das Einheimische*], only in order to break out of it and to let what overpowers it break in. Being itself throws man into this breaking-away, that forces him beyond himself to set forth toward Being, to set it up in the work, and thereby hold open beings as a whole. (EM 125/IM 137)

To deinotaton names man as the strangely violent one, who *must* set forth against the order that *will* dispose of him through the way he creates works that reveal beings as a whole.

This violent disposition of the correspondence between Being and human being marks Heidegger's inheritance of the tension at work in the *Rektoratsrede.* It is a disposition fulfilled for Heidegger by the advent of the "creative one" *(der Schaffende)* to whom "down-going [*der Untergang*] is the deepest and broadest 'Yes' to the overpowering. In the shattering of the wrought work, in the knowledge that it is mischief [*Unfug*] and *sarma* (a dunghill), he leaves the overpowering to its order [*überlässt er das Überwältigende seinem Fug*]" (EM 125/IM 137). That is, the creative one abandons his work to the claim of the overpowering even as the overpowering disposes of it. In this he confronts the limit that is hidden in the heart of *deinon:*

All violence shatters against *one* thing. That is death. It is an end beyond all completion [*Vollendung*], a limit beyond all limits. Here there is no breaking-out or breaking-up.... But this strange and alien thing that banishes us once and for all from everything in which we are at home....It is not only when he comes to die, but always and essentially that man is without issue [*Ausweg*] in the face of death. Insofar as man *is,* he stands in the issuelessness of death. Thus his *Da-sein* is itself the happening of strangeness. (EM 121/IM 133)

For Heidegger, the "counter-turning confrontations of Being" measured out by *deinon* take place by way of the creative violence of a release that is also an abandonment before death. Such release-abandonment determines Heidegger's translation of the dimension of awe through the contending dimension of terror; for it is the terrifying dread of death that establishes the site of that creatively violent *polēmos* that defines the limit and essence of being human.

At this juncture we can make explicit one clue to the origin of *Gelassenheit;* for if we turn to different verbs rooted in *lassen,* we find a playing back and forth between the restraint that leaves something alone and the relinquishment that abandons it, so that the sense of allowance that predominates in *einlassen* is countered by the sense of being forsaken that predominates in *verlassen.* These words form a nexus within which the usual senses of *Gelassenheit*—calmness, collectedness, patience, and deliberation—are modified by a tension that would at the same time seek to leave something to itself and thereby preserve it, allow it to be the thing it is, and yet in that way precisely abandon it to its destiny as the thing it is.[10] Such a destiny Heidegger in the year following his rectorship identified with that of the resolve of the "creative man" to release-abandon his work to the "issuelessness of death," and thereby leave the "overpowering to its order."

With this brief review of Heidegger's reading of *deinon* in the second chorus of *Antigone,* we should be ready now to turn to Creon's downfall. For if in following Heidegger's insight into the essence of the tragic we have found terrifying dread to be the dominant key to the attunement of *deinon,* the question remains open whether Heidegger's own disposition of the traditional meanings of awe and cleverness will be maintained in the event of Creon's *Untergang.* We need to follow out the play of *deinon* in the dynamic of that downfall to see how the *Aus-einander-setzung* at work in *deinon* turns out in *Antigone.* Along this way we will see what the turns and counterturns of *deinon* can show us about the origin of *Gelassenheit.*

The *Deinon* of Yielding in Creon's *Untergang*

Creon's *Untergang* begins with Antigone's last comment on the conflict between them. She says that Creon has judged what she has done to be *"deina tolman,"* a terrible venture.[11] She says this having just offered her justification for burying Polyneices, the action she undertook so that her *ethos* could endure. For Creon both act and justification are *deina tolman,* since they fundamentally violate the *ethos* from which he has condemned her to death. Thus the force of Antigone's use of *deina* here is to acknowledge (as she has done earlier) that she and Creon are each claimed by a different *ethos,* the enactments of which are experienced as terrible to the other. But not just "terrible," for *tolma* means the violence of a venture that is "daring" and "reckless." The courage of such daring is to be marveled at as much as its recklessness is terrifying for the *polēmos* it reveals: that the continuing existence of the *ethos* in which each is at home cannot abide the other, and yet nonetheless is claimed by it. This *Auseinandersetzung* shows to each the limit and essence of the *ethos* that each claims as his or her own, but only by having that same *ethos* first risked and then destroyed in the very violence by which it is revealed and maintained.

Within such conflict, the human encounters the divine as daimonic, as the overpowering other; through such conflict, the daimonic sustains the mortal as mortal, as being bound to death. It is at the place of this *polēmos* that Antigone releases herself to that encounter with the daimonic in which her life is abandoned; having commented on Creon's judgment, she turns to her final lament. In the singing of that lament she abandons herself to her destiny, her going under.

The next occurrence of *deinon* happens in the chorus that immediately follows Antigone's exit to her being buried alive. It is a simple gnomic saying that briefly comments on her death: *"all ha moiridia tis dunasis deina"*: but the power of destiny is *deina* (line 951). The force of the comment turns on the quality of Antigone's abandonment. The abandonment is clearly destined, and the relation between *moira* and being mortal is made manifest in it. For Antigone has seemingly done the will of the gods, and yet at the moment of her facing an unholy death, there is the simple fact of their leaving her to face it alone. To that fact she responds with the release that acknowledges her abandonment; she abides a sign from the gods that does not come, she sings her lament. *Moira* here sustains the difference, or call it the dissonance, between mortal and divine. The power of such *moira* is *deina,* terrible and wonderful. With this saying the play comes to a kind of hinge by which the dynamic of the unfolding of *moira* now turns to Creon with the ending of this chorus and the arrival of Teiresias.

Deinon appears next as part of Creon's response to Teiresias's locating him on "the razor's edge of fate" with a warning that he must yield to avoid the *moira* that awaits him. To this Creon replies in a rage that ends with his mocking Teiresias's *"deinoi,"* his cleverness, that is bound to fall to ruin in the treachery of its using fair words for foul profit (line 1047). This occurrence of "cleverness" for *deinon* happens in the context of Creon's fundamental misreading of Teiresias's message. In the violence of that misinterpretation, Creon sets the stage for his own down-going. Creon's violence here echoes his earlier confrontation with his son Haemon. In each encounter the attempt by the other to persuade Creon to yield fails, and in each the issue from Creon's perspective becomes one of the power of different kinds of profit to corrupt the rightful order. Creon judges the other within an *ethos* that can be maintained only through his insistence on the unquestionability of his own power. The dearest name Creon has given to that power is "judgment," or better, simply *to phronein,* the power of thought itself. To yield his grasp of that power would mean the end of his world. His response to Teiresias now secures that same ending.

With Teiresias's departure Creon is suddenly confronted with the chorus leader's reminder that Teiresias has never been wrong, and thus that his prediction of Creon's fall must certainly come true. In this context we have the final two occurrences of *deinon* in *Antigone,* both in the same speech by which Creon reenacts the beginning of his downfall:

egnōka kautos kai tarassomai phrenas;
to t' eikathein gar deinon, antistanta de
ate pataxai thumon en deino para.

I myself know it and my mind is torn in confusion;
for to yield is *deinon,* but to resist? and thereby be struck in my own
heart with raging blindness? that too is *deinon.* (lines 1095–97)

Creon's response seemingly acknowledges the inevitability of Teiresias's words. Then everything turns on his power to interpret those words, yet that has already been shown to be guided by the violent insistence on the sufficiency of his own understanding. Thus he says that his mind is torn. That is, he finds himself in confusion, not knowing which way to turn. The tear he is experiencing is the recoil of a demand the consequences of which have already been set in motion. The name of that tearing of his own mind is the repetition of the demand to yield.

We have seen *deinon* focus the power of *moira.* In the aftermath of Creon's response to Teiresias, he seems to acknowledge the power of yielding: he says it is *deinon.* With this seeming acknowledgement is an echoing of the opening sentence of the second chorus, where *deinon* names the essence of being human. Creon is poised at the end of the dynamic that has unfolded from the beginning of the play. He has been brought to the limit of the *ethos* that defines his life. And as with Antigone his placement at that limit is marked by the confrontation with the daimonic that occurs as the risking of the *ethos* that is his own. "Yielding" demands the abandonment of that *ethos* for the sake of acknowledging the claim of another. When Creon utters his speech here, he faces—and refuses—the suspension of that abandonment. He comes to the edge of understanding what he has been called on to do, then refuses to carry through that understanding. Thus he says that "to yield is *deinon,*" then immediately goes on to consider his options: "But to resist? and thereby be struck in my own heart with raging blindness?"

The turn to consider resistance is the sign that Creon cannot carry through the opportunity his initial insight might have offered.[12] "Resistance" for Creon means to continue to set himself against that which makes a claim on him. But now Creon has realized that his opposition is not simply to the difference of this woman with her perverse commitment to loving the dead and the *nomos* of the dead, but rather that he has set himself against the difference that defines what it means to be mortal. In setting oneself opposed to such a difference one tacitly claims its transcendence. This is the *hubris* that summons the raging blindness, the *atē* that summons the *nemesis* of one's own destruction. This too is *deinon:* terrible in the sense of the dread that suddenly reveals our abandonment as merely human, and astonishing in the sense of the wonder whose violence releases us at the limit of the human to yield to the claim of the daimonic. The question that determines our situation as human is whether we can abide the *deinon* of such a yielding.

Thus Creon's speech marks the site of his abandonment. It is not a place he can abide. For he cannot sustain his own repetition of *"deinon,"* so he translates the *deinon* of yielding into another variation of his own repetition of the power of *to phronein,* of his own thinking. He accepts the necessity to give in, but understands this to mean abandoning himself to the advice of the chorus, hoping in that way to release himself from the judgment of the gods. So he decides to take their advice while still maintaining that he is in control: he has bound Antigone, he shall set her free. So he decides, inexplicably, to bury Polyneices first, though Teiresias had told him to first take care of Antigone, and thereby gives her the time she needs to hang herself. So he undoes the world he holds dear. What can we learn here about the origin of *Gelassenheit?*

The Origin of *Gelassenheit* in *Antigone*

Remember the motivation for Heidegger's question, Why does tragedy begin with the going under of the tragic hero? If we indeed have to undergo the *incipit tragoedia* to locate the situation of thinking today, then what of Creon? If Creon begins to "go under" in his refusal to yield, then what clue does the dynamic of that refusal give us for understanding the origin of the fundamental attunement of thought today?

The clue is in the relation between two different senses of *to phronein* and the *deinon* of yielding. We have seen one sense of "thinking" at work in the refusal by which Creon steps into the tragic; another sense is revealed in the final chorus of the play. This chorus comments on Creon's "going under" with the opening words: *"pollo to phronein eudaimonias proton huparchei"*: *to phronein* is *the* original source of *eudaimonias* (line 1349; my translation). If we translate *eudaimonia* as "well-being," what sense of *to phronein* is *the* original source of human well-being? To answer this question, let us first consider the contrast that sets the context for the chorus's invocation of "thinking." What precisely does *to phronein* mean for Creon?

Creon is a man of decision *(phronēsis)* whose decisiveness is not attentive to the otherness that situates it. Thus in each of his encounters with the necessity to yield, he refuses to pause, to stop and be still, out of an insistent reliance on the self-sufficiency of his power to discriminate the right course of action. But being able to stop and be still is essential for the careful mindfulness at the root of *to phronein*. And in turn, the root of the capacity to stop is being available for the claim of the kind of opening occasioned by the advent of astonishment or dread. That is, in awe, wonder, or astonishment, and in dread there is the same enactment of suddenly stopping and becoming still that opens the possibility of attending to that which addresses us. We have seen how such stopping and becoming still is necessary for the movement of yielding to take place, and in the movement of yielding one sense of decisiveness is displaced by another. The self-authorization inherent in one attunement of *to phronein* is displaced by a self-suspension that abides at the limit it encounters, the place that is opened when the human confronts the daimonic. It is in the tension between freeing release and destitute abandonment that the self-suspension in such abiding remains ready for the opportunity to carry through a possibility for "being-well" that may or may not come to pass.

If drawing a significant contrast with Creon has given us some direction for understanding the sense of *to phronein* at work in the final chorus, there is another indirect clue that can help. With the final chorus the play as such comes to an end. In that ending the enactment of the play comes to its fulfillment. But what of the experience of that enactment? What of catharsis? Is there a relation between the dynamic at work in tragic catharsis and the sense of *to phronein* in the final chorus?

In catharsis we undergo Creon's going under in the space that the play opens. The intimacy of that space opens the possibility for a kind of movement: the audience yields where Creon refuses—not to Antigone, but to the abandonment that determines their mutual destiny. The audience undergoes a release that is also an abandonment within the stillness that Creon refuses. In undergoing that refusal within the intimacy of the play, the audience abides a self-suspension that happens as a stillness-in-movement, a yielding that gives them back their situation as human beings facing daimonic otherness. If this description of catharsis touches something essential, is there then a cathartic dimension of *to phronein?*

In its root of mindful attentiveness, *to phronein* arises out of the simplicity of pausing. Within that simplicity is self-suspension; within such suspension is a holding back that allows for the expanse of abiding at the limit. Within such abiding is the stillness-in-movement by which the *deinon* of yielding is undergone and transmuted into a capacity for following along with the unfolding of the human encounter with daimonic otherness. In other words, there is the possibility in the *Auseinandersetzung* at work in *deinon* of a turn from its governance by terrifying dread to that of awe— and within awe, the opportunity for the kind of astonishment that opens the listening at work in first raising and then following the unfolding of a thoughtful question. It is within the transformational dynamics of such a "following along" with the encounter with daimonic otherness that human being finds whatever opportunity it has for "being-well."

In this transformation of the *Auseinandersetzung* at work in *deinon* we suddenly have come across one possible source for the original attunement of Greek thinking. In that source *Gelassenheit* also finds its roots. In the disposition of the co-respondence at work here we find the clue to the attunement by which we can enter into a genuine confrontation with Greek thought, and thereby, according to Heidegger, the possibility of opening the path to "another thinking." Do we know, yet, how to follow out this clue?[13]

14 Appetite and Violability: Questioning a Platonic Metaphor

JANE LOVE

So long as we have the body, and the soul is contaminated by such an evil, we shall never attain completely what we desire, that is, the truth. For the body keeps us constantly busy by reason of its need of sustenance, . . . and fills us with passions and desires and fears, and all sorts of fancies and foolishness, so that as they say, it really and truly makes it impossible for us to think at all.[1]

Now the divine intelligence, since it is nurtured on mind and pure knowledge . . . rejoices in seeing reality for a space of time and by gazing upon truth is nourished and made happy. . . . It beholds absolute justice, temperance, and knowledge, . . . that which abides in the real eternal absolute, and in the same way it beholds and feeds upon the other eternal verities.[2]

It is a commonplace in Plato's thinking that the influence exerted by the body on the soul is pernicious. This notion of the body's inferiority becomes increasingly complex as we look more closely at the relationship between the soul and the body, for although Socrates regards the body as dispensable for philosophy, in his words we find bodily concerns intertwined with the soul's concerns, not always to express a nuisance, and not necessarily meant literally.

The two passages quoted earlier—the first from the *Phaedo,* and the second from the *Phaedrus*—are striking in Socrates' use of appetite as a metaphor to describe the soul's relation to the Real. Elsewhere in the dialogues, appetite is condemned as the soul's chief distraction from its contemplation of ultimate reality; what, then, recommends appetite as a metaphor intended to characterize the soul? Surely some sort of kinship between the soul and appetite is implied by their participation in the same metaphor; unless, of course, we understand and agree to abide by the unspoken rule enjoined by the initiator of the metaphor: that its use is ad hoc, so to speak, governed by the speaker's intention, and not license for others to draw uncensored relationships from the richness the metaphor gathers together. The metaphor of appetite, as used by Socrates in the *Phaedrus,* is strategic in this sense: we are trusted to understand that any kinship between bodily appetites and the soul is not only *not* implied by the metaphor, but that the metaphor as such acts as a sort of quarantine device for the perniciousness of appetite. The metaphor of appetite is meant to protect the purity of the soul.

But suppose we violate this trust, undermine the discretion of the metaphor—what sort of body-soul relationship emerges within the metaphorical space of appetite? What might be the philosophical consequence of such a relationship? I wish to explore these questions, as well as the two distinct, but related, powers of metaphor: its power when it is wielded strategically, and its power when its strategic discretion is violated. It seems that metaphor spans innocence, from the naïve innocence of one who trusts that the reader will obey one's intentions in reading the metaphor, to a wholly other innocence residing silently within the metaphor itself, an inscrutable literalism.

My intention here is not so much to argue closely an interpretation of the Platonic text, but rather to broach this "other" innocence by deliberately reading toward what is un-Platonic in the metaphor of appetite. I begin by examining Socrates' depiction of the soul as a chariot drawn by a notoriously ill-matched pair of horses. The disparity of appetites in the two horses raises the question of what appetite, apart from the values assigned to its objects, itself signifies: a mortality marked by contingency, by violability, which leads to a curious reading of both the soul's relation to the Real and the body's relation to that relation. We find that the body, through the contingency imposed by its mortality, safeguards, rather than obstructs, the soul's relation to the Real. The metaphor of appetite thus permits an inversion of Platonic intention and also, perhaps, a glimpse into the strangeness of metaphor itself.

Two Horses, One Harness

We will begin by returning to the two passages quoted at the beginning. In the first passage, from the *Phaedo,* Socrates makes a point concerning the immortality of the soul: The true philosopher does not fear death, because the body has never been anything but detrimental to the practice of philosophy. Surely those who have spent their lives in the pursuit of wisdom can only welcome death as freedom from the persistent distractions of the body. This passage describes the body as an affliction suffered by the soul, or an infliction of substance upon the soul, substance that perniciously influences the mind through "passions and desires and fears, and all sorts of fancies and foolishness." To rid himself of this affliction, Socrates says that the philosopher must spend "all his life fitting himself to live as nearly in a state of death as he [can]"; "the true philosophers practice dying..." (*Phaedo* 67E).

Philosophers practice dying by withdrawing from commerce with the body and turning to "gaze upon truth" (*Phaedrus* 247C), by which, as we are told in the second passage, the soul is "nourished and made happy," as it "beholds and feeds upon the other eternal verities." The soul is distracted from this feast of divine intelligence "by reason of [the body's] need for sustenance." "What we desire, that is, the truth," is obstructed by the "passions and desires and fears" generated by our bodies. Taken together, these two passages suggest that the body plays a strangely insinuating role in the process by which the literal subject of the *Phaedo* passage (the body's desires, appetites, passions) becomes the metaphorical subject of the *Phaedrus* passage (the soul's desires, appetites, passions). In the process, appetite shifts from being the object of revulsion (when belonging to the body) to depicting desire for intellectual contemplation (when belonging to the soul).

This metaphor of appetite is applied extensively to the soul throughout the *Phaedrus,* especially in Socrates' second speech on love, in which he describes the soul as follows:

> We will liken the soul to the composite nature of a pair of winged horses and a charioteer. Now the horses and charioteers of the gods are all good and of good descent, but those of other races are mixed; and first the charioteer of the human soul drives a pair, and secondly one of the horses is noble and of noble breed, but the other quite the opposite in breed and character. Therefore in our case the driving is necessarily difficult and troublesome. (246B)

> The horse that stands at the right hand is upright and has clean limbs; he carries his neck high, has an aquiline nose, is white in colour, and has dark eyes; he is a friend of honour joined with temperance and modesty, and a follower of true glory; he needs no whip, but is guided only by the word of command and by reason. The other, however, is crooked, heavy, ill put together, his neck is short and thick, his nose flat, his color dark, his eyes grey and bloodshot; he is the friend of insolence and pride, is shaggy-eared and deaf, hardly obedient to whip and spurs. (253D–E)

Socrates goes on to describe the behavior of the dark horse when aroused by appetite: he "no longer heeds the pricks or the whip of the charioteer, but springs wildly forward," and when stopped by the charioteer he "breaks forth into angry reproaches, bitterly reviling his mate and the charioteer for their cowardice and lack of manhood." It is clear from this that the dark horse is enslaved by his appetites. But it is less obvious that the white horse is driven by appetite as well, as we see when Socrates says, "But the reason of the great eagerness to see where the plain of truth is, lies in the fact that the fitting pasturage for the best part of the soul is in the meadow there, and the wing on which the soul is raised up is nourished by this" (248B). The language of nourishment, feeding, and desire recalls the language of appetite used in the *Phaedo* to describe the body's impingement upon the soul's contemplation of reality. This description of the soul's communion with the divine intelligence suggests that the dark horse (signifying the body) and the white horse (signifying the soul) are harnessed together by appetite.

The metaphor of appetite suggests that although body and soul each suffer the demands of appetite in their distinct and respective fashions, the commonality of appetite to each horse persists through and underlies these differences of focus and expression. This suggests that the value Plato assigns to each horse (good to the white, bad to the dark) is not so much because one horse possesses appetite, since in fact both horses possess it, but rather in virtue of the *object* of appetite: sensual appetite is deplorable, whereas intellectual appetite is virtuous. Already, however, this reading of the metaphor is indiscreet; it breaches the etiquette demanded of readers toward metaphors. We are expected to understand, and accept, that the appetite of the dark horse is literal and therefore base, evil, and corrupt, whereas the appetite of the white horse is metaphorical and therefore untainted, transcending the sensual origins of appetite, and therefore not *really* appetite at all.

Metaphor is peculiar in that it serves to describe and to preserve distinctions—as between sensual and intellectual appetite—at the same time that it undercuts such distinctions to point toward a more essential nature. If appetite spans the sensual as well as the spiritual, then it is not solely a matter of the body but also of a relation that can be characterized independently of its objects and that, in fact, mediates the relationship between the end points of its span, between body and soul. What sort of relation, then, is expressed in appetite?

A Brief Meditation on Appetite

Although we speak of different appetites (for sex, food, drink, and other pleasures or desires), the word *appetite* generally refers to the body's need and desire for food. We eat in response to hunger, which may be physical or emotional—an emptiness within, or the fear of inward emptiness. Over the course of hours and days we fill and empty ourselves, again and again, and both the fullness and the emptiness bespeak the body's need for nourishment. The body is not self-sustaining; it is self-regulating only within the limits of its responsiveness and is most itself within the economy of exchanges—respiration, evaporation, elimination—that are required to sustain it. The body enacts itself through its needs, and what it needs includes nourishment, the assimilation of food in service of the body; what it enacts is the transmutation of substance, as in alchemical practice.

As James Hillman points out in the following passage, the metaphorical power of alchemy lies in how it replicates the relation of the soul to the body and to material reality:

> Fundamental to [alchemy] was one basic idea: the soul is lost in its literal perspective, its identity with material life. It is stuck in coagulations of physical realities. This perspective of reality needs to break down and fall apart, to be skinned alive and sensitized, or blackened by melancholic frustration. Habits and attitudes that obscure psychic insight and have lost psychic significance need to be dissolved, or made to stink, becoming monstrous and repulsive, or grindingly rubbed away.[3]

Hillman's language here recalls the passage from the *Phaedo* (66B–C) quoted earlier: the body as the soul's link to material reality is despised; the soul is seen as the body's victim. The alchemical transmutation of substances, however, asserts the power of the soul to alter and subjugate material reality. Hillman writes:

> Freeing the psyche from its material and natural view of itself and the world is an *opus contra naturam,* a work against nature.... Although working with natural materials such as urine, quicksilver, or antimony, alchemy changed these substances into fantasies. It recognized the substantial nature of fantasy and the fantasy aspect of all natural substances. This was its true *opus contra naturam:* the transmutation, within the alchemist himself, of the natural viewpoint into the imaginal viewpoint. (RVP 91)

In other words, the soul insinuates itself into the body, as well as vice versa. The insinuated soul is, in fact, the agent of transubstantiation in alchemy, and the soul's effective purchase on material reality is a matter of perspective. If, as Hillman writes, "the soul is lost in the literal perspective," then the soul frees itself by shifting back to its own (the "imaginal") perspective. Such a shift is made possible by virtue of "the substantial nature of fantasy and the fantasy aspect of all natural substances"—by virtue, that is, of perspectives in which both body and soul participate, as both the dark horse and the white horse participate in appetite—as metaphor participates in the interplay of perspectives or meanings that resides in words.

Metaphor turns upon such an interplay: an overlapping, perhaps, or a kinship that acknowledges the blood relations among things, both the legitimate and the illicit, the bastard. Meaning is carried across from one perspective to another in a movement that marks the span of something deeper. The body's hunger and the soul's hunger, taken together, reveal something of the span of hunger itself, its meaning, as it gathers literal and soulish perspectives in a meeting place, an alchemical point at which transubstantiation, the shift in perspective from body to soul, is possible.

Mortality as Violability

The metaphor of appetite and the practice of alchemy, then, converge upon transubstantiation; the alchemy of digestion, the appetite of the alchemist for gold, depend upon one thing becoming another, one meaning giving way to another meaning, a confluence of meaning, possibility, and perspective, in which something becomes something else. Food, when eaten, becomes the eater, and death is implicit in this process. If the body does not vicariously participate in death in this way, then it will do so by its own dying. In naming the body's need and desire for nourishment, appetite also names the body's mortality.

It is obvious that the body can fail to receive its proper nourishment and die. The soul, too, however, is subject to starvation and to a kind of death as well, due to its appetite for the Real. This possibility is described in Socrates' account of the soul's original experience of the Real, an account that begins as follows:

> But at that former time they saw beauty shining in brightness, when, with a blessed company—we following in the train of Zeus, and others in that of some other god—they saw the blessed sight and vision and were initiated into that which is rightly called the most blessed of mysteries, which we celebrated in a state of perfection, when we were without experience of the evils which awaited us in the time to come, being permitted as initiates to the sight of perfect and simple and calm and happy apparitions, which we saw in the pure light, being ourselves pure and not entombed in this shell which we carry about with us and call the body, in which we are imprisoned like an oyster in its shell. (*Phaedrus* 250B–C)

For Plato, this vision of the Real is originary and transcendental, and while the mortality conferred on us by our bodies interferes with this vision, mortality per se cannot, in Plato's view, be said to be constitutive of the soul's relation to the Real. In another view, however, it becomes apparent that the vision of the Real participates in the metaphor of appetite, since it is directed upon what Socrates has earlier described as the "plains of truth," where the "fittest pasturage for the best part of the soul" lies. The vision of the Real awakens the appetite of the soul. This vision has the same fragile contingency as the body and requires the same care; this contingency recalls what Socrates says when he describes the transmigration of souls: "Then a human soul may pass into the life of a beast, and a soul which was once human may pass again from a beast into a man. For the soul which has never seen the truth can never pass into human form" (*Phaedrus* 249B). To have "seen the truth" is what makes the human soul a human soul; to forget that it *has* seen the truth is what costs the human soul its humanity.

Continuity is implied in the soul's vision of the Real, even though the human soul does not attain an unbroken view—humanness, in fact, is distinguished by an interrupted vision of the Real, as only the gods are allowed an uninterrupted vision. The human soul, then, takes shape in the violation of what is, or should be, essentially continuous. This violation is constitutive of the human soul as such, and, for Plato, it is apparent both in the body's distraction of the soul's gaze from the Real and in the soul's possible diminishment from human to animal. This transmigration of the soul is itself based in a particular conception of the soul's immortality.

In the *Phaedo,* the immortality of the soul is conceived of as the soul's continued and repeated survival of the body's death. That the life of the soul extends beyond that of the body might, however, be conceived differently in terms of the soul's mortality, rather than immortality—a mortality that, to be sure, extends beyond that of the body, but, like the body's, is also the expression of a crucial dependency that is subject to violation. Like the relation of the body's mortality to its appetite for food, the soul's mortality is coextensive with the soul's appetite for—and the consequent recovery, renewal, and preservation of—the soul's vision of the Real. The soul's mortality, in this sense, then, is what warrants the soul's appetite for the Real, what attests to the violability of that relation, a violability that itself creates the need for the recovery and renewal of the vision of the Real. Violability holds the soul's gaze in thrall to the Real at the same time that it threatens this gaze, and in doing so originates the soul's appetite for the Real.

Violability, then, maintains the essential relationship of the soul to the Real. It does this by bringing the mortality of the body—through its appetites—to bear upon the mortality of the soul, in such a way that the soul's immortality is rendered not absolute and inviolate but instead commensurate with the soul's relation to the Real—a relation that is itself anything but absolute: a relation that can die.

The Body as Guardian

Death is the outer limit of appetite; it is what begins where appetite fails, what generates the need for appetite. The generation of opposites forms the basis of Socrates' argument for the soul's immortality in the *Phaedo* (70E–71E), in which he holds that being dead and being alive are opposites that necessarily generate each other, back and forth, the dead being reborn and the living returning to death, each bounded by the other, each the guardian of the other: death ensures the recovery of life. To practice dying (as philosophers should) is to push into the outer limits of the body's appetite, into the region of guardianship for the body's opposite, the soul. The body, in fact, is the guardian of the soul; this guardianship, however, exerts its protection perversely. Its role is not to defend or nurture the soul from without, but to provoke the inner desire of the soul for the Real by placing itself between the two. In this way, the body, through its distractions and obsessions, requires that the soul experience genuine appetite. The body is the violation of the soul that requires and threatens, enforces and obstructs the soul's vision, and in this way the body, through its own appetites, not only affects but *effects* the soul's appetite for and relationship to the Real. The soul's mortality is commensurate with the body's (even though the two are not coextensive), and the soul's impulse toward and its appetite for the Real are necessities safeguarded by and reflected in the body. Appetite belongs to the soul and is proper to the soul. The tie linking soul and body, then, is not simply a matter of the soul's corruption but the soul's meaning, its nature, which is inextricably bound to the Real as well as to the body. The resulting tension in the soul as, in response, it spans these two claims suggests a kind of symmetry between the body and the Real, like the symmetry shared by the two horses in respect to appetite. The metaphor of appetite, when questioned, reveals that what appears in Plato as antipathy between the body and the soul actually arises from a deeper *affinity* of body and soul with respect to violability. The antipathy between the body and the Real, perhaps, also belies a fundamental kinship.

If it does, if the metaphor will bear us this far away from its intended purpose, then in the span marked by this distance something of metaphor itself may begin to emerge, something of the peculiar dimension that it opens for thinking. Getting to this far point of affinity between the body and the Real requires an excursion, one that brings the two face to face. Such an encounter takes shape as an experience, and, as the needs of the psyche will have it, the abstract, impersonal authority of the Real becomes personified as divinity in this experience. For Heidegger, the span (which I have adopted here as a metaphor of metaphor) is granted by our recognition, through the unfamiliar, the alien, of divinity.[4] What is needed, then, is an encounter with divine authority, a stand-off with god. Lot's wife comes to mind.

An Excursion into the Span

Some distance out from the city, up into the mountains, back-lit by the fires, she turns to look back, having been told not to do this. Her disobedience asks why she should not look, and her fate is the answer: in turning back to look, and thus knowing herself to be safely outside the burning city, beyond the destruction, she becomes blameless in the distance of her gaze. Her vantage from the mountains—raised up and removed— places her at a reflective distance. Not only is she saved, but reflection grants her a god's eye view of the destruction. In turning to take up this divine perspective, she does not die so much as she loses her mortality; she becomes inanimate.

Where did her desire to turn originate? Does simple curiosity justify such consequences, such harsh punishment? But this itself is crucial: we do not know whether the fate of Lot's wife is the consequence of an act from which the directive not to turn was meant to protect her, or whether her fate is punishment for disobedience. When God says, "Do not look back," is this the threat of the Old Testament's violent, angry father, or is it the warning of a watchful, protective father?

The desire to turn and look is born precisely in this uncertainty, this ambivalence in authority that leaves open the mortal relationship with the divine. The human question arising from this uncertainty is, simply, are we loved? Lot's wife turns on this pivot, this equivocation between love and power; her body turning unveils the question; her backward glance interrupts the divine voice, questioning its authority and the limits it inscribes for her, whether they are inscribed in love or simply in power. The assurance held out by the authority, the assurance for safe passage if it is but obeyed, is not enough. As Lot's wife's turning usurps a divine perspective, a *reflective* perspective, it also enacts the human rupture with the divine that occurs when limits are at issue, open to question, rather than taken for granted. And it is no accident that bodies are forfeit in taking this risk.

The issue of human connection with and relation to the divine (or to the Real) comes to rest over and over with the body, until one finally begins to suspect some secret complicity beneath all the antagonism. The complicity appears in the limits, the absolutes, that both divinity and the body force upon us, one in virtue of the other. In manifesting the limits of mortality, the body poses the same questions raised in the encounter with divinity: Are these limits constitutive for us, is knowing them knowing ourselves? If so, then is this knowledge equally countenanced by the divine, is it animated by a divine awareness at least commensurate with our own, and itself equally constituted by the limits of mortality? The psyche apprehends limits in terms of authority, a personified power, and hence a power capable of recognition or indifference; it is this question—Recognition or indifference? Love or power?—that underlies all the others. Incarnation is final with us, and this fact brings divinity and authority to reside in the flesh; the body authorizes all other limits. The turning away from the body into reflection (the philosophical practice of dying) simply pursues embodiment elsewhere, as anyone knows who has ever fallen in love with the specific gracefulness of a body of thought. The compulsion within such a love is not so much for the relative truth, or accuracy, or usefulness of the thinking but for this body that thinking inhabits, that makes conceptual expression possible in conceptual space and time, that gives thinking coherence, beauty, integrity, and the capacity for extending and generating these qualities through the thinking of others.

Metaphor and Innocence

So this question arising from the confrontation with limits—Are we loved?—does not turn away, but accepts limits as given, attending instead to the manner of presentation: Do they occur in awareness that is reciprocal with our own? Does care for us reside alongside knowledge of us? This question, Are we loved? opens two channels for our response, fear and recognition: the fear that we are not loved, and the recognition that we are. The soul spans these two channels, which respectively flow toward body and mind, sensual knowledge and rational knowledge; the soul finds itself in this between.

In a different context, Heidegger speaks of the between as that which, reaching from the earth to the sky, is measured out for the dwelling of man (PLT 220). Perhaps the function of metaphor can be thought of in the same way, as a spanning of the "between" that rests within the poles of, or the movement from, literal to metaphorical. For Heidegger, the possibility of measuring lies with the disclosure of the unknown, insofar as it remains unknown and against which man's familiarity shines forth. Something similar happens within a metaphor, although reversed: as meaning is carried across the span, the meaning itself, like man in his measuring, shines forth. But what shines forth is what is known; the familiarity of meaning is what allows the metaphor, and the discretion of metaphor protects this familiarity. And yet behind this shining forth stands, obscured, the between itself, which is unknown as long as the metaphor goes unquestioned.

Once questioned, however, metaphor reveals an innocent literalism at its core. Difference is always assumed in the metaphorical leap, difference that the leap proposes to bridge. But what supports the bridge, what possibility goes unthought? There is this silent space within the metaphor, bearing everything, and this silent forbearance is both literal and innocent, as are we in the face of it, until we begin, indiscreetly, to question the metaphor, to unfold the literal. The radical affinity of the body and soul is what permits the literal to seek expression in the metaphor of appetite. This affinity is at once innocent and inscrutable—innocent in that it pre-empts the strategy of the metaphor, and inscrutable in its consequences for thinking. How can we greet what is innocent? What is required of us in being wholly present to what keeps silent counsel in thinking, dreams itself in our thoughts? Submission and transgression, sensual intelligence, synesthesia extending beyond the senses to gather in thinking itself—these mark a threshold embedded deep within the metaphor of appetite. The affinity of body and soul, body and Real, opens up a transcendent sensuality, a sensual metaphysics, that will not be glimpsed through any clear, reflective vision, or be spoken in clear, reflective language. Instead, innocence seems to require of us that we suffer, that we undergo our embodiment without the protection of transcendence or reflection. Perhaps Plato's metaphor, ironically, finds its deepest resonance in the idea of philosophical suffering, rather than in that of transcendence.

Part 5

Shattering Identities

15

Monstrous Reflection:
Sade and Masoch—
Rewriting the History of Reason

DOROTHEA OLKOWSKI

In the essay "Plato and the Simulacrum," Gilles Deleuze inquires into the meaning of Nietzsche's announced task of overthrowing Platonism. This phrase, says Deleuze, seems to mean "abolishing the world of essences *and* the world of appearances."[1] But such a task, he continues, would not have been unique to Nietzsche, since this is basically the program of Hegel and even Kant. Therefore it becomes necessary to ask again what we mean by overthrowing Plato. It appears that what Deleuze has in mind is something less abstract, less strictly philosophical and perhaps more psycho-logical, but not in a way that leads to psychologism, rather, in a way that comes to question the most fundamental logical structures of Plato's philosophy as well as its foundational role in the establishment of morality.

Like Nietzsche, Deleuze asks about the motives of Platonism and attempts to bring these motives to light: What about the Platonic "will" to select and sort out in a certain manner? What about the Platonic distinctions between the thing and its images, the original and the copy, the model and the simulacrum? (PS 45). We would be mistaken, he claims, if we were to be satisfied with thinking that this is a superficial process for delimiting specifications in the search for definitions, because the Platonic method of division (into types of souls, classes of men, orders of work) is far more profound in a number of ways. Deleuze writes that, for example,

> in the *Phaedrus,* the myth of circulation of souls seems to interrupt the effort of division; so, in the *Statesman* does the myth of archaic times.... the myth really interrupts nothing. On the contrary, it is an integrating element of division itself. It is the property of division to transcend the duality of myth and of dialectic and to join, internally, the power of dialectic with that of myth. The myth, with its constantly

circular structure, is really the narrative of foundation. It allows the construction of a model according to which different claimants can be judged. In effect, that which must be founded is always a claim. (PS 46)

Throughout the dialogues of Plato, then, the myth serves as the foundation, the standard, the model. In the *Phaedrus* the false claimants are those sensual souls who see a part but not the whole of truth and soon forget even this.[2] The true claimants are those souls who are most like the gods and so are best able to keep their chariots headed in the direction of the heavens and thus have seen and remember the realm of Ideas (PH 248). Between the true claimants and the false lies a hierarchy of degrees of claimants, and the role of the Platonic text, according to Deleuze, is to "hunt down the false claimant" (PS 46). This, he says, is the motive of the Platonic text, to divide the claimants according to their degree of reality and in so doing to distinguish the true claimants, the true copies, from the simulacra who, in the Platonic text, "embody the evil power of the false claimant" (PS 47), and whom, just like the iron men in the *Republic,* Plato wishes to keep in their place, for if they should come to rule, the state would be ruined.[3]

Given this job of hunting down the false claimant, it becomes necessary, according to Deleuze, not only to make the distinction between Idea and copy, but to make a second, perhaps more profound distinction between copies or likenesses that are well-grounded claimants united with the Ideas by resemblance, and *simulacra,* false claimants "built on a dissimilitude, implying a perversion, an essential turning away."[4] *Evil power, false claimant, perversion, essential turning away*—each of these terms indicates that the process of division is at the basis of what are for Plato moral determinations. The copies *(ikons)* are good images insofar as their resemblance is not simply an external semblance but is possible only as *mediated* by the Ideas. This means, writes Deleuze, that their claim is internal and spiritual; their resemblance is derived from the Ideas (PS 48). Simulacra, by contrast, are for Plato a perversion, an evil power not because they are a copy of a copy, a degraded *ikon,* but precisely because they *fail* to resemble the Idea at all. They are merely imitative; they lack resemblance while retaining an image (PS 48).

In the *Phaedrus,* Socrates distinguishes nine degrees between the *ikon* and the simulacrum, starting with the lover of wisdom or beauty and ending with the tyrant (PH 248). In the *Republic,* this hierarchy is explicitly delineated in political and moral terms. The good and just man corresponds to the aristocratic form of government. Beneath him we find the timocratic, the oligarchic, the democratic, and the dictatorial man (REP 545a). This last, the tyrant, yielding to lawlessness in the name of liberty, is driven to a kind of frenzied madness led especially by lust (REP 572d–e). He will steal from his parents and deceive them, and he "will not refrain from any terrible murder, from any kind of food or deed" (REP 575).

Yet there seems to be a model for even the tyrant; that is, he seems to model himself after the various kinds of imitators who have neither knowledge nor right opinion and are merely image-makers (REP 602a). Imitative artists, for example, are said to rely on the confusion of the senses. The same things appear concave or convex because our eyes are confused by colors, or the same magnitude does not appear to our sight to be of the same size when we look at it from nearby or from a distance (REP 602c). Imitative poets appeal to the excitable and varied part of the soul, setting up a "bad government in the soul of every private individual by gratifying the mindless part which cannot distinguish the small from the large but thinks that the same things are at one time small, at another large" (REP 605b). Sophists make their audiences think that the same objects are both like and unlike, both one and many, both at rest and in motion (PH 261). Imitators, in every case, dispense with the *ikon* and so with measuring, counting, weighing, calculating, with limitation in all its forms (REP 602d).

Such imitation, says Deleuze, is not simply a weak resemblance to the Idea but is the process of going mad; it is not being able to set limits. Plato rejects imitations because they can never become *ikons;* they lead to limitlessness, "a constant development, a gradual process of subversion of the depths, an adept avoidance of the equivalent, the limit, the Same, or the Like: always simultaneously more and less, but never equal" (PS 49). This same structure also operates in the area of law. Deleuze comments that in the *Statesman,* we find the figure of "the Good as father of the law, the law itself, the constitutions. Good constitutions are copies, but they become simulacra from the moment they violate or usurp the law, in escape from the Good" (PS 48). Again, for Plato, the Idea serves as the standard (as the Good in this instance), whereas the simulacrum represents evil power.

What Deleuze's reading of the Platonic texts makes clear is that in these texts Plato continually presents the simulacrum as the perversion of reason, the false claimant, and, therefore, as the evil power. Yet, in a text that serves as a significant reformulation and clarification of the literature of the Marquis de Sade and of Leopold von Sacher-Masoch, Deleuze questions this characterization of simulacra. According to his reading of these eighteenth-century texts, the perversion of reason, the evil power, lies not in the simulacra, the false claimant, as Plato would seem to be saying, but in the very nature of demonstrative and dialectical reason itself, in the symptomatologies called *sadism* and *masochism.*

As if to emphasize this discovery, Deleuze makes no claim for exalting the texts of Sade and Masoch above the violent texts they seem to resemble on the basis of anything like literary merit. There is no question that the language of Sade and Masoch operates in accordance with the literature of pornography.

> What is known as pornographic literature is a literature reduced to a few imperatives (do this, do that) followed by obscene descriptions. Violence and eroticism do meet, but in a rudimentary fashion. Imperatives abound in the work of Sade and Masoch; they are issued by the cruel libertine or by despotic women. Descriptions also abound (although the function of the descriptions as well as the nature of their obscenity are strikingly different in the two authors). ...Everything must be stated, promised and carefully described before being accomplished.[5]

However, Deleuze wishes to augment this description with the observation that these texts do function on a basis that prescribes more than the elementary functions of ordering and describing; they can be regarded as a kind of "pornology," the science of a symptomatology, that includes not only pornographic violence and eroticism but also an anthropology that reveals something significant about man, culture, and nature, about pornography itself, because it embraces new forms of expression (MAS 16, 17).

When Deleuze asks what seem to be the urgent questions regarding these texts—that is, "How are we to account for the violent language linked with eroticism?" and, What is the point of the excessive and abundant language of Sade and Masoch in this context?—Deleuze answers in a rather Platonic manner, "Look to the organization of language in these texts" (MAS 16). Then Deleuze asks about these texts the same questions he asked about the Platonic texts: What about the (Platonic) "will" to select and sort out in a certain manner? What about the (Platonic) distinctions between the thing and its images, the original and the copy, the model and the simulacrum?

The answer to these questions requires some insight into the organization of language in these texts. Deleuze points to the necessity of recognizing that language does not function in the same manner in Sade and Masoch. In Sade he finds "an astonishing development of the demonstrative use of language" (thus of demonstrative rationality), and, discursively, an "affinity with Spinoza" with regard to Sade's "naturalistic and mechanistic approach imbued with the mathematical spirit"[6] (MAS 18, 19). With this, Deleuze invites us to compare Sade's own commands for the ordering and arrangement of bodies to Spinoza's definitions of bodies in relations of motion and rest, in modes of speed or slowness or in the capacity of affecting or being affected (SPP 123–24). Such a conception also accounts for the repetitions, the multiple illustrations, the adding of victim upon victim, the purely impersonal element of perversion as an Idea of reason (MAS 19). What the Sadian libertine wishes to demonstrate is that reason itself, the very process of demonstration, is a form of violence, a form of violence carried out by the calm and logical demonstrator (MAS 18).

> The descriptions, the attitudes of the bodies, are merely living diagrams illustrating the abominable descriptions; similarly the imperatives uttered by the libertines are like the statements of problems referring back to the more fundamental chain of sadistic theorems: "I have demonstrated it theoretically," says Noirceuil, "let us now put it to the test of practice." (MAS 19)

Similarly, in Masoch's text, according to Deleuze, imperative and description serve a "transcendental" function, though one which Deleuze identifies with the need of a victim to educate and persuade a torturer. "The educational undertaking of Masoch's heroes, their submission to a woman, the torments they undergo, are so many steps in their climb to the Ideal.... The naked body of a woman can only be contemplated in a mystical frame of mind, as in the case of *Venus*"(MAS 20). In the texts of Masoch, this ascent from the human to the Idea takes place only under the whip. It is, says Deleuze, the melding of Mephistopheles to Plato (MAS 22). In short, Masoch's pornological torture exemplifies a dialectical rationality (MAS 21).

But how can this be? On what basis can Deleuze claim that a transcendental function exists in Sade and Masoch? How can he credibly account for violence in terms of demonstrative and dialectical reason, that is, in the very structure and organization of philosophical thinking? Let us return to what earlier was mentioned briefly about the Idea and the law. There is in Plato the notion of the Good as father of the law, the law itself, the constitutions. Good constitutions are copies of the Idea. But constitutions and laws are only the delegated powers representing the Good. "If men knew what the Good was or knew how to conform to it, they would not need laws" (MAS 71). By the eighteenth century this "classical" conception of law was more or less overthrown.

> In *The Critique of Practical Reason* Kant gave a rigorous formulation of a radically new conception, in which the law is no longer dependent on the Good, but on the contrary, the Good itself is made to depend on the law. This means that the law no longer has its foundation in some higher principle from which it would derive its authority, but that it is self-grounded and valid solely by virtue of its own form. (MAS 72)

This allows us to speak of the "Law," the pure form of lawfulness independent of content. According to the Platonic scheme, "laws would seem to be written copies of scientific truth in the various departments they cover, copies based as far as possible on the instructions received from those who really possess the scientific truth on these matters."[7] Since only the true statesman who has real knowledge is qualified to change these laws, the rest of the citizens must simply follow the laws without altering them. But with the Kantian reformulation, law is no longer grounded on the superior principle of real knowledge or, as Deleuze says, on the Good. What occurs instead is the dominance of the law alone. The good is now derived from the "Law" and one obeys the Law without knowing what it is based on (MAS 72).[8]

This revised notion of the Law is at the basis of both Sade and Masoch's subversion. For if their literature is a perversion of reason within reason, it is also a subversion of Law as delimited by Kant. Both wish to subvert the law by transcending it (back in the direction of Plato) to a higher power, an Ideal. Thus Deleuze notes that, for Sade, the tyrant is made possible by the very existence of the Kantian Law, and tyranny is the language of Law. Sade's libertines speak the "counterlanguage" of tyranny, which is the language of absolute impersonal Evil. Countering Kant, Deleuze claims that rational and intelligible transcending and subversion of the Law in the direction of Evil, the supreme principle of wickedness, is precisely a function of that same intelligibility (MAS 76). This returns us to the correlation of violence and eroticism, the obscenity of Sade's descriptions. Transcendence of law in the direction of absolute Evil is the demonstrative function of Sade's language. Transcendence of law comes about through a process of negation—negation as a partial process in which destruction is merely the reverse of creation and change, disorder simply a variation of order, death one step in the organization of life (MAS 24). But this kind of negation is profoundly dissatisfying to the libertine who strives, through the repetition and amplification of his crimes, to attain perfect negation, a negation that no longer bears any relation to positivity. So Noirceuil confides to Juliette prior to informing her of the impending visit of a young woman whose husband he has imprisoned "in order to get possession of the wife": "Crime, such is my wish, must stamp every instant of my career...."[9]

But as the Kantian critique has shown, experience is constituted out of a negation that is only a partial negation and remains part of positivity; pure human intelligibility can never be more than the "object of an Idea," "a delusion of reason itself," "an exorbitance specific to reason itself" (MAS 25). Hence the rage and despair of the sadistic hero when he realizes how paltry his own crimes are in relation to the Idea which he can reach only through the omnipotence of reasoning. He dreams of a universal, impersonal crime, or as (the libertine) Clairwil puts it, a crime "which is perpetually effective, even when I myself cease to be effective, so that there will not be a single moment of my life, even when I am asleep, when I shall not be the cause of some disturbance" (MAS 25–26).

The problem for the libertine is that he can demonstrate this theorem only with the partial, inductive processes of experience. He strives to overcome this with the aid of coldblooded demonstrative reason. Thus, notes Deleuze, the pornologist Sade never demonstrates enthusiasm for his crimes and the libertine condemns even the enthusiasm for evil; it reflects the partial nature of negation and implies a residue of the Good (MAS 26). The only pleasure allowed is disinterested pleasure in the operations of demonstrative reason; it is the descriptions themselves, the repetitions of violent acts produced in a calm, logical manner (without self-interest) that serve to demonstrate the reality of the Idea of Evil.

The subversion of Law carried out by Masoch orients itself in an entirely different manner. If Sade attempts to transcend the power of the Law in the direction of absolute Evil, Deleuze believes that Masoch's texts achieve their effects contrarily, through a scrupulous application of the law "to demonstrate its absurdity and provoke the very disorder that it is intended to prevent or to conjure" (MAS 77). Like the Sadist, the Masochist derives no real pleasure from the superficial aspects of his actions, in this case from the punishment he causes to have inflicted upon himself. Such punishment is merely regarded as the strictest adherence to the Law, after which the masochist is free to engage in and find pleasure in the very activities the Law forbids, because he has already paid for his pleasure with suffering. Suffering under the Law is the premiss from which the conclusion of pleasure will then be drawn, making the masochist the logician of consequences that subvert Law (MAS 78).

This, says Deleuze, is what accounts for the relative lack of obscene descriptions in Masoch's texts: there is always the appearance of adherence to the Law. Furthermore, the dialectical ascent to the Ideal is complicated by the organization of masochism which demands "a victim in search of a torturer... who needs to educate, persuade and conclude an alliance with the torturer in order to realize the strangest of schemes" (MAS 19), while advancing the techniques of dialectical reversal, disguise, and reduplication.

> Plato showed that Socrates appeared to be the lover but that fundamentally he was the loved one. Likewise the masochistic hero appears to be educated and fashioned by the authoritarian woman whereas basically it is he who forms her, dresses her for the part and prompts the harsh words she addresses to him. It is the victim who speaks through the mouth of his torturer, without sparing himself. (MAS 21).

Such transpositions and displacements produce several levels of experience, reversals and reduplications of roles and discourse that are fundamental to the dialectic (MAS 21).

Moreover, if, as Deleuze claims, Sade's task is to reveal the violence of reason in the form of a pure impersonal negation, demonstrating this through the multiplication and condensation of the ordinary evils of experience, Masoch's dialectic proceeds toward its Idea by the more "delicate mechanism of disavowal."

> Disavowal should perhaps be understood as the point of departure of an operation that consists neither in negating nor even destroying, but rather in radically contesting the validity of that which is; it suspends belief in and neutralizes the given in such a way that a new horizon opens up beyond the given and in place of it. (MAS 28)

Thus Masoch does not seek either to negate or destroy the world nor to idealize it (as Sade does in the name of Evil) but to disavow it, thereby suspending it, escaping into a world of dreams, a phantasy, a pure ideal reality that he creates (MAS 30). It is a world in which Law has been subverted while seemingly being satisfied.

Returning then to Plato and the simulacra, it becomes clear now that the Platonic judgments against false claimants and simulacra do not come into play here. What we have with Sade and Masoch, sadism and masochism, is the violence of reason itself, the perversion of reason from *within* by virtue of the logical and discursive structure of reason itself. Pornography arises not from without but as a function of what has historically been understood as the only methodology suitable to philosophical thought. What then of the distinction between *ikon* and simulacra, if these perversions are not simulacra but visions of the Idea? In *Logique du sens,* Deleuze writes again of the distinction throughout the Platonic texts between *ikon* and simulacra, in terms that can be located in *Cratylus, Philebus,* and *Parmenides,* among others:

> Plato invites us to distinguish two dimensions: 1) that of limited and measured things, fixed qualities that might be permanent or temporary, but always presupposing stops as well as rests, the establishment of presents, the assignation of subjects: such a subject at such a size, such a smallness at such a moment; 2) then, a pure becoming without measure, a veritable becoming-mad that never stops, in two senses at once, always escaping the present, making past and future coincide, the most and the least, the too much and the not-enough in the simultaneity of a tractable matter.[10]

We recognize immediately the profound duality of what receives the action of the Idea and what does not, what instead contests the very possibility of both a model and a copy (LS 10). As Deleuze's text on Sade and Masoch has indicated, model and copy are not, as Plato thought, functions of the Good and its perversions, less and less discernible copies. Rather, the distinction in these texts seems to bear a particular relation to language. There are the measured things under Ideas and, then, the mad element that subsists, a flux of words, a discourse maddened, disconnected, that never ceases to glide and slide on this flux (LS 10). This is, says Deleuze, a dimension of language that evades the present and so evades *identity,* maintaining instead the infinite identity of two senses at once. We can see this operating in a text that subsists beneath the Kantian Law:

> Said the Queen, "Were you ever punished?" "Only for faults," said Alice. "And you were all the better for it, I know!" the Queen said triumphantly. "Yes, but then I had done the things I was punished for," said Alice, "that makes all the difference." "But if you hadn't done them," the Queen said, "that would have been better still; better, and better, and better!"[11]

Or in yet another text that goes right to the heart of the question of identity, its gliding and sliding character:

> "Who are you?" said the Caterpillar.... Alice replied, rather shyly, "I—I hardly know, Sir, just at present—at least I know who I was when I got up this morning, but I think I must have been changed several times since then." "What do you mean by that?" said the Caterpillar sternly. "Explain yourself." "I can't explain *myself,* I'm afraid, Sir," said Alice, "because I'm not myself, you see." "I don't see," said the Caterpillar. (AAW 75–76; emphasis added)

In Lewis Carroll the full paradox of the simulacrum finds expression, not as Evil but as the manifestation of a pure event. Here we encounter the overthrow of Platonism, which desires to repress the simulacrum and confine it within the cave, for "the simulacrum is not simply a false copy, but... it calls into question the very notions of copy... and of the model," and with that the entire structure of identity (PS 47, 50). In Carroll's tales the simulacrum "breaks its chains and rises to the surface," asserting itself over the *ikon* (PS 51, 52). Instead of being a model that serves as the Idea for its copies, which are in turn more or less perfect imitations of that model with more or less perfect *identity* to the model, the simulacrum plays havoc with space, time, and identity, the very principle of noncontradiction. This is not, as Plato claims, Evil nor is it the perversion of the Good; rather, it is much closer to what from the perspective of the principle of identity and noncontradiction is continually condemned as madness, vertigo, limitlessness, the impossibility of mastery insofar as there is nothing, no limit bringing persons or events to resemble themselves, to be the Same as or like themselves. "Difference as a primary power," says Deleuze (PS 53).

In *Alice's Adventures in Wonderland* and *Through the Looking Glass* we encounter the full force of sophistry. Like Plato's tyrant, the text of Alice follows that of the sophists who, for Plato, have neither knowledge nor right opinion and are merely image-makers, making the same objects appear alike yet unlike, one yet many, at rest yet in motion. Says Deleuze, "When I say 'Alice grows,' I mean she becomes larger than she was, but by the same token, she becomes smaller than she will be. Of course she is not larger and smaller at the same time, but it is at the same time that she *becomes* it" (LS 9). The point of all this becoming is continuously to evade the present, to collapse the distinction between before and after, past and future, so as to make place for the two senses at once, affirmation of two meanings at once (LS 9). To assign a specific size at a specific moment is to stop becoming for the sake of measuring things and placing them under Ideas, for the sake of our ability and need to represent things. Yet even when such representation occurs (and it is what always occurs within philosophical thinking insofar as it demands the intelligibility and certainty of a representational system), the "mad" element continues; it subsists below the order imposed by Ideas and received by things (LS 10). The simulacra remains pure, unlimited becoming insofar as it evades the action of the Idea (LS 10).

Because it subsists and is not merely eliminated or annihilated by the representations that seek to assign it a place within a measured system, the most important function of the simulacra is to contest the authority and primacy of both the model and the copy, to contest the very function of representation, and this, just like the Platonic fixing of limits, takes place in the sphere of language (LS 10). Language fixes the limits of becoming by measuring, establishing past, present, future, rest, likeness, and identity. But language is also capable of *exceeding* those limits, inaugurating the series of reversals that constitute Alice's adventures, so that one is punished before being guilty, serves the cake before cutting it, and cries before being hurt. In these and all such reversals, the possibility of permanently establishing one's identity is lost (LS 10). So writes Deleuze, "When the substantives and adjectives founder, when the names of stopping and rest are overtaken by the verbs of pure becoming and slide in the language of events, all identity is lost for me, the world and God" (LS 11).

What has been accomplished here? What about the overthrow of Platonism? What about the distinction between phantasm and *ikon?*

Regarding the first question, let us be very cautious, for the struggle between copy and simulacrum is, as Deleuze points out, a concern of modernism, not of ancient Greece. And this means that the danger is always present that philosophers will not see that it is in Plato that the distinction was first made and understood.

> It is between the destruction which conserves and perpetuates the established order of representations, models, and copies, and the destruction of models, and copies which sets up a creative chaos, there is a great difference; that chaos, which sets in motion the simulacra and raises a phantasm, is the most innocent of all destructions, that of Platonism. (PS 56)

If Platonism is itself this first and innocent destruction, perhaps modernism will prove to be the other, though "innocence" is hardly to be expected there.

With regard to the second question, Deleuze is seeking to remove the sliding and gliding event of the simulacrum from condemnation. Not simply an evil factor to be annihilated or to be kept chained in the depths, accused, feared, committed to the margins of philosophy, simulacra have in Deleuze's reading, as in Plato's, broken the chains, risen to the surface, so as to be brought into play and into language, thought, and knowledge, yet without ever being assimilated into Ideas. How this happens is to a very large degree the main focus of all of Deleuze's writing, but especially it is the project of *Logique du sens*. And it may well be that until philosophers commit themselves to a questioning investigation of the logic of *meaning (sens)* and fully commit thought to the overthrow of Plato's logic (something Deleuze believes he has accomplished in his own logical investigations), language itself will remain chained, unable to rise to the surface of thought.

16 Abjection and Oppression: Dynamics of Unconscious Racism, Sexism, and Homophobia

IRIS MARION YOUNG

My body was given back to me sprawled out, distorted, recolored, clad in mourning in that white winter day. The Negro is ugly, the Negro is animal, the Negro is bad, the Negro is mean, the Negro is ugly; look, a nigger, it's cold, the nigger is shivering, because he is cold, the little boy is trembling because he is afraid of the nigger, the nigger is shivering with cold, that cold goes through your bones, the handsome little boy is trembling because he thinks that the nigger is quivering with rage, the little white boy throws himself into his mother's arms; Momma, the nigger's going to eat me up.

All round me the white man, above the sky tears at its navel, the earth rasps under my feet, and there is a white song, a white song. All this whiteness that burns me. . . .

I sit down at the fire and I become aware of my uniform. I had not seen it. It is indeed ugly. I stop there, for who can tell me what beauty is?[1]

Suffering racial oppression involves, among other things, existing as a group perceived as having ugly bodies, and being feared, avoided, or hated on that account. People oppressed by racism, moreover, are by no means the only ones characterized by ugly or fearful bodies. Although a certain cultural space is reserved for revering feminine beauty, for example, in part that very cameo ideal renders most women's bodies drab, ugly, fleshy, loathsome by comparison. Old people, gay men and lesbians, disabled people, and fat people are other groups perceived to have ugly, fearful, or loathsome bodies.

In this chapter I explore some of the meaning and dynamics of racism, sexism, homophobia, ageism, and "able-ism" (prejudice toward the disabled) as they structure everyday interaction and subjectivity at non-discursive levels of practical consciousness and unconsciousness. Despite our society's explicit normative and legal commitment to equality and respect for all persons on their individual merits, group identifications nevertheless continue to structure relations of privilege and oppression through feelings, bodily reactions, images and stereotypes, linguistic and behavioral habits. People behave differently toward one another according to their group identification. In particular, whites behave toward people of color, men toward women, straights toward gays, the young and middle-aged toward the old, the able-bodied toward the disabled often with symptoms of avoidance, objectification, disgust, dislike, or discomfort. Through Julia Kristeva's category of the abject, I explore how the habitual and unconscious fears and aversions that continue the perception of some groups as having despised and ugly bodies at least partly arise from anxieties over loss of identity. Since these structures of oppression lie beneath discursive consciousness, they cannot be addressed by law or policy. I conclude by discussing the meaning of "consciousness raising" as a social strategy for mitigating these sources of oppression.

Conscious Acceptance, Unconscious Aversion

Those of us who argue that racism, sexism, homophobia, ageism, and able-ism are basic oppressions in contemporary social relations cannot dismiss an illusory the common conviction that ideologies of natural inferiority and legitimate group domination no longer exercise significant influence in our society. Nor can we plausibly regard the aversions and stereotypes that, we claim, perpetuate oppression today as simple, though perhaps weakened, extensions of the grosser xenophobia of the past. To be clear and persuasive in our claims about contemporary group oppression and its reproduction, we should affirm that explicit and discursively focused racism and sexism largely have been discredited. We must theorize a different social manifestation of these forms of group oppression corresponding to specific contemporary circumstances, which have both continuities and discontinuities with past structures.

To formulate such an account I adopt the three-leveled theory of subjectivity that Anthony Giddens proposes for theorizing about social relations and their reproduction.[2] Action and interaction, says Giddens, involve discursive consciousness, practical consciousness, and the basic security system. Discursive consciousness refers to that aspect of action and situation that is either verbalized, founded on explicit verbal formulas, or can be easily verbalized. Practical consciousness, on the other hand, refers to those aspects of action and situation that involve often complex reflexive monitoring of the relation of the subject's body to those of other subjects and to the surrounding environment, but that are on the fringe of consciousness, rather than in focused discursive attention.[3] Practical consciousness names the habitual, routinized action that enables persons to accomplish focused, immediately purposive action. For example, the action of driving to the grocery store and buying goods on my shopping list involves a highly complex set of actions at the level of practical consciousness, like driving the car itself and maneuvering the cart in the grocery store, where I have acquired a habitual sense of the space in relation to the items I seek.

Basic security system for Giddens designates a base level of identity security and sense of autonomy required for any coherent action in a social context; one might call it the subject's ontological integrity. Psychotics are people for whom a basic security system has broken down or never formed, either in all situations or some. Giddens's theory of structuration assumes that social structures exist only in their enactment through reflexively monitored action, the aggregate effects of those actions, and the unintended consequences of action. Action, in its turn, involves the socially situated *body* in a dynamic of trust-anxiety in relation to its environment and especially in relation to other actors.

> The prevalence of tact, trust or ontological security is achieved and sustained by a bewildering range of skills which agents deploy in the production and reproduction of interaction. Such skills are founded first and foremost in the normatively regulated control of what might seem...to be the tiniest, most significant details of bodily movement and expression.[4]

What psychoanalysis refers to as *unconscious experience* and *motivation* relates to this basic security system. On the one hand, the personality development of each individual represses some experiences in the construction of a basic sense of competence and autonomy. An independent unconscious "language" results from the splitting off of some experiential material from self-identity; it emerges in bodily behaviors and reactions, including gestures, tone of voice, and even, as Freud discussed, certain forms of speech or symbolization themselves. In everyday action and interaction, the subject reacts, introjects, and reorients in order to maintain or reinstate that basic security system.

I propose to use this three-level model of subjectivity to understand a shift in the experience of group difference. Nineteenth- and early twentieth-century social structures of racism, sexism, homophobia, ageism, and able-ism, on the one hand, and their contemporary structures, on the other, differ in that the former appear at the level of discursive consciousness, whereas in contemporary society for the most part they do not. In contemporary society racism and sexism exist primarily at the level of routine habits and assumptions of practical consciousness, and in the unconsciously motivated reactions and symbolic associations that are part of the process of maintaining a basic sense of integrity and autonomy.[5] Whereas in the nineteenth-century social structure of explicitly sanctioned inequality and domination there is a homology among these three levels, contemporary society produces a dissonance between discursive consciousness, on the one hand, and practical consciousness and basic security system, on the other. This dissonance aggravates some of the routinized and unconscious manifestations of racial, sexual, homophobic, ageist, and able-ist fears and aversions.

Commitment to formal equality for all persons tends to support a public etiquette that negatively sanctions speech and behavior that call attention, in public settings, to a person's sex, race, sexual orientation, class status, religion, and the like. In a fine restaurant, waiters are supposed to be deferential to all patrons—whether Black or white, trucker or surgeon—as though they were aristocrats; on the supermarket line, on the other hand, nobody gets special privileges. Public etiquette demands that we relate to people as individuals only, according everyone the same respect and courtesies. Calling attention to a person's being Black, or Jewish, or Arab, or old, or handicapped, or rich, or poor, in public settings is in distinctly poor taste, as is behaving toward some people with obvious superiority or condescension, while deferring to others. Contemporary social etiquette remains more ambiguous about calling attention to a woman's femininity, but the women's movement has helped create social trends that make it poor taste to behave in deferring or patronizing ways to women as well. The ideal promoted by current social etiquette is that these group differences should not matter in our everyday encounters with one another, that especially in formal and impersonal dealings, but more generally in all non-familiar settings and situations, we should ignore facts of sex, race, ethnicity, class, physical ability, and age. These personal facts are supposed to make no difference to how we relate to and treat one another.

Where discursive beliefs, norms, and rules hold that group identification should not affect the way people relate to one another, the expression of the significance of group differences and the reproduction of group privilege and oppression take place largely at the level of practical consciousness and expressions of unconscious meanings and reactions. As long as group differences matter for self and other identification—as they certainly do in our society—it is not possible to ignore those differences in everyday encounters. In my interactions a person's sex, race, and age directly affect behaviors such as eye contact, touching, body openness, physical distance, and the like. These personal factors may be more or less salient in the situation, but they affect behavior at least at a background level. When a person's class status, occupation, sexual orientation, and other forms of group status are known or suspected, moreover, these also affect behavior.

Such reactions to members of other groups and the feelings they provoke are repressed in a double sense, for two reasons. First, because encounters among members of differently identifying groups often involve issues of basic security and identity for the participants, the feelings are repressed because of the anxieties they produce. Over and above this, the liberal imperative not to allow differences to make a difference imposes a sanction of silence about these observable behaviors that, according to that imperative, are not supposed to happen.

This tension between discursive ignorance of differences and practical and unconscious affective and bodily differentiations certainly is better than a situation that socially condones excluding, demeaning, or condescending behavior toward some persons because of their group identifications or their physical characteristics (behaviors unfortunately not absent from our society). It is better for those who are marked out and oppressed to know that we have a formal right to go anywhere and expect to be treated with basic respect that to be confined to a status and place that is overtly enforced in speech, manners, and other social rules. It reduces some of the most emotionally uncomfortable effects of oppression to have some confidence that one's plain dress, or skin color, or sex will not provoke undisguised stares, whispers, and direct remarks in daily encounters.

A unique discomfort results, however, from oppressive behaviors that are jettisoned to the margins of some people's consciousness and forbidden from speech. A Black man walks into a large room at a business convention and finds that the noise level reduces—not to a hush, but definitely reduces. A woman at the real estate office with her husband finds the dealer persistently failing to address her, to look at her, even when she speaks to him directly. A woman executive is annoyed that her male boss usually touches her when they talk, putting his hand on her elbow, his arm around her shoulder, in gestures of power and fatherliness. An eighty-year-old man whose hearing is as good as a twenty-year-old's finds that many people shout at him when they speak, in babylike short sentences that they might also use to speak to a preschooler.[6]

Members of oppressed groups constantly experience such behaviors of avoidance, aversion, expressions of nervousness, condescension, and stereotyping. For them such behaviors—indeed, the whole encounter—is often a focus of discursive consciousness. Such behaviors throw them back onto their group identity, making them feel noticed, marked, or conversely invisible, not taken seriously, or worse, demeaned. The dominant social etiquette, however, finds indecorous and tactless the calling attention to difference discursively in public. The discomfort and anger of the oppressed at these behaviors of others toward them must therefore be borne in silence if they are to remain included in those public contexts. When the more bold of us call attention to such treatment and assert that these behaviors are signs of systematic oppression, we are accused of being picky, of overreacting, of making something out of nothing, or of completely misperceiving the situation. The courage to bring to discursive consciousness behaviors and reactions occurring at the level of practical consciousness is met with denials and with powerful gestures of silencing.

Thus far I have discussed unconscious group-based aversions expressed in everyday face-to-face encounters. The effects of unconscious racism, sexism, homophobia, ageism, and able-ism, however, are by no means restricted to such encounters, but permeate much of the cultural meaning expressed in attitudes, media images, and assumptions. Since overt hatred of groups that are different is generally unacceptable, such xenophobic aversions often receive expression through widespread association of certain policies, actions, events, types of people, life styles, and so on, with particular groups.[7] Public housing projects, for example, are associated with Black and Latino people in the minds of many, and gut opposition to the construction of such projects will often be motivated by unconscious aversions to those people.[8] AIDS has clearly come to be associated with gay people, and homophobia clearly influences both much AIDS policy and how people with AIDS are treated. Group-based fears and aversions residing at the level of practical consciousness and basic security system, whether in the form of interactive behaviors of cultural images and associations, operate with far-reaching consequences on actions and policies affecting people of color, women, gay men and lesbians, old people, and disabled people, usually to their disadvantage.

Xenophobia and Abjection

With the concept of the abject that she develops in *Powers of Horror,* Julia Kristeva offers, I suggest, a means of understanding these behaviors and interactions that express group-based fear or loathing.[9] The concept of the abject theorizes one way that the subject is split between a discursive symbolic mode, on the one hand, and presymbolic relation to the mother's body, on the other.[10] Abjection does not produce a subject in relation to objects, the ego, but rather the moment of separation, the border between the 'I' and the other, before an 'I' is formed, that makes possible the relation of ego and its objects. Before desire—the movement out from a self to the objects on which it is directed—there is bare want, lack, loss and breach that is unrepresentable, that exists only as affect.

Abjection is the feeling of loathing and disgust the subject has in encountering certain matter, images, and fantasies; what is horrible and to which one can respond only with aversion, with nausea and distraction. The abject is at the same time fascinating; it draws the subject in order to repel it. The abject is meaningless, repulsive in an irrational, unrepresentable way. Kristeva claims that abjection arises from that primal repression in which the infant struggles to separate from the mother's body which nourishes and comforts, the reluctant struggle to establish a separate corporeal schema, in tension and continuity with the mother's body which it seeks to incorporate.

For the subject to enter language, to become a self, it must separate from its joyful continuity with the mother's body, to acquire a sense of border between itself and the Other. In the primal fluidity of maternal *jouissance* the infant introjects the Other. Thus the border of separation can be established only by expelling or rejecting the mother, who until then is not distinguished from the infant, so that the expulsion that creates the border between inside and outside is an expulsion of itself, its continuity. The infant struggles with its own drives in relation to the Other, to attain a sense of body control, but the struggle is reluctant, and the separation experienced as a loss, a wound, a want. The moment of separation can be only "a violent, clumsy breaking away, with the constant risk of falling back under the sway of a power as secure as it is shifting" (PH 13).

The expelled self turns into a loathsome menace because it threatens to reenter, to obliterate the border established between itself in fullness and the rejected self. The separation is tenuous; the subject feels it as a loss and yearns for, while rejecting, a reenclosure by the Other. The defense of the separated self, to keep the border firm, is aversion from the Other, repulsion, for fear of disintegration.

Abjection is expressed in a person's reaction of disgust, for example, to body excretions—matter expelled from the body's insides: blood, pus, sweat, excrement, urine, vomit, menstrual fluid, and the smells associated with each of these. The process of life itself consists in the expulsion of what is inside in order to sustain and protect my life. I react to the expelled with disgust because the border of myself must be kept in place. The abject must not touch me for fear that it will ooze through, obliterating the border between inside and outside, which is necessary for my life, but which arises in the process of expulsion. If by accident or force I come to touch the abject matter, I react again with the reflexes of expelling what is inside me: nausea.

Abjection, then, Kristeva says, is prior to the emergence of a subject in opposition to an object, making possible that distinction. The movement of abjection makes signification possible by creating a being capable of dividing, repeating, separating. The abject, as distinct from the object, does not stand opposed to the subject, at a distance, definable. The abject is other than the subject, but only as just the other side of the border. So the abject is not opposed to and facing the subject, but next to it, too close for comfort. "The 'unconscious' contents remain here *excluded* but in a strange fashion; not radically enough to allow for a secure differentiation between subject and object, and yet clearly enough for a defensive *position* to be established—one that implies a refusal but also a sublimating elaboration" (PH 7).

The abject provokes fear and loathing because it exposes the border between self and other as constituted and fragile, and because it threatens to dissolve the subject by dissolving the border. *Phobia* is the name of this fear, an irrational dread that latches on to a material with obsessed fascination, simultaneously attracted and horrified. Unlike fear of an object, to which one reacts with attempts at control, defense, and counteraction, phobic fear of the abject is a paralyzing and vertiginous dread of the unnamable.

Abjection, Kristeva says, is an experience of ambiguity. "Because, while releasing a hold, it does not radically cut off the subject from what threatens it—on the contrary, abjection acknowledges it to be in perpetual danger" (PH 9). The abject arises potentially in "whatever disturbs identity, system, order. What does not respect borders, positions, rules" (PH 4). Any border ambiguity may become for the subject a threat to its own borders, a revelation that the separation between self and Other is the product of a violent break, an irretrievable loss, a lack without name or reference. The subject reacts to this abject with loathing as the means of restoring the border separating self and Other.

This account of the meaning of the abject enhances, I suggest, an understanding of a body aesthetic that labels some groups as ugly or fearsome and produces aversive reactions to members of those groups. Racism, sexism, homophobia, ageism, and able-ism are partly structured by abjection, an involuntary, unconscious judgment of ugliness and loathing. The account does not explain why some groups become associated with degeneracy, fearful sexuality, or death, but once they do, these associations lock into the subject's identity anxieties. The subject reacts with fear, nervousness, and aversion to members of these groups because they represent a threat to identity itself, a threat to what Giddens calls the *basic security system.* People from groups marked as different fulfill the function of what lies just on the other side of the borders of the self, too close for comfort and threatening to cross or dissolve the border.

Xenophobia as abjection is present throughout the history of modern consciousness, structured by a medicalized Reason that categorizes some bodies as degenerate. I suggest that the role of abjection increases, however, with the shift from a discursive consciousness of group superiority to such group superiority lived primarily at the levels of practical consciousness and the unconscious.

When racism, sexism, heterosexism, ageism, and able-ism exist at the level of discursive consciousness, the despised groups are literally objectified. Scientific, medical, and moral discourse constructed these groups as objects, having their own specific nature and attributes, different from and over against the naming subject, who controls, manipulates, and dominates the object. When these group-based claims of superiority and inferiority recede from discursive consciousness, however, the dominant subject no longer projects these groups as clearly identifiable objects different from and opposed to itself. Women, Blacks, homosexuals, the mad, and the feebleminded are no longer distinctly identifiable creatures with degenerate and inferior natures. They are no longer unambiguously Other. In xenophobic subjectivity they recede to a murky affect without representation.

The tension between wanting to distinguish oneself from the others and yet having to admit that they are basically the same, creates the sort of border crisis ripe for the appearance of the abject. Now the Other is not so different from me as to be an object—indeed, discursive consciousness asserts that the Blacks, women, homosexuals, disabled people are like me. But at the level of practical consciousness they are affectively marked as different. In this situation, those in the despised group threaten to cross over the border of the subject's identity because discursive consciousness will not name them as completely different.[11] The face-to-face presence of these others, who do not act as though they have a "place," a status to which they are confined, thus threatens my basic security system, my basic sense of identity, and I must turn away with disgust and revulsion.

Homophobia is the paradigm of such border anxiety. The construction of the idea of race, its connection with physical attributes and lineage, still makes it possible for a white person to know that she is not Black or Asian. But as homosexuality has become increasingly de-objectified, no specific characteristics—physical, genetic, mental, or "moral character"—mark off homosexuals from heterosexuals. It thus becomes increasingly impossible to assert any difference between homosexual and heterosexual except their choice of sexual partners. Homophobia is one of the deepest-held fears of difference precisely because the border between gay and straight is constructed as the most permeable; anyone at all can become gay, especially me, so the only way to defend my identity is to turn away with irrational disgust. Thus we can understand why people who have fairly successfully eliminated the symptoms of racism and sexism nevertheless often exhibit deep homophobia.

Ageism and able-ism also exhibit the border anxiety of the abject; for in confronting old people or disabled people I confront my own death.

Kristeva believes that the abject is connected with death, the disintegration of the subject. The aversion and nervousness that old people and disabled people evoke, a sense of their being ugly, arises from the cultural connection of these groups with death. Thomas Cole shows that prior to the nineteenth century old age was not linked to death; indeed, just the opposite was the case. In a time when death might come to persons at any age and often took children and young adults, old age represented a triumph over death, a sign of virtue. During this time of patriarchal family domination, old people were highly regarded and venerated. Now, when it has become increasingly likely that people will live to be old, old age has become associated with degeneracy and death.[12] At a time when most people can expect to be old, old people produce a border anxiety like that structuring homophobia. I cannot deny that the old person will be myself, but that means my death, so I avert my gaze from the old person, or treat that person as a child, and I want to leave his or her presence as soon as possible. My relation to disabled people has a similar structure. The only difference between myself and the wheelchair-bound person is my good luck. Encounter with the disabled person again produces the ambiguity of recognizing that the person whom I project as so different, so other, is nevertheless like me.

At several points in this discussion I have used the first person in describing the experience of abjection a person has in encountering Blacks, Latinos, Asians, Jews, gays, lesbians, old people, disabled people, sometimes women. The question must arise, though, what about the subjectivity of members of these groups themselves? The form of cultural imperialism in the modern West provides and insists on only one subject position, that of the unified, disembodied reason identified with white bourgeois men. Thus the subjectivity of members of culturally imperialized groups tends to stand in the same position as the privileged groups. From that supposedly neutral subject position all these despised and deviant groups are experienced as the abjected Other. This means that Blacks themselves may have aversive reactions to other Blacks, but more especially to other racially marked groups; gay men and lesbians themselves exhibit homophobia; old people denigrate the aged; and women are sometimes sexist. That is, insofar as members of these groups assume the position of subjects within the dominant culture, they experience members of their own group abjectly.

Even if they do not strictly assume that position of subjectivity, members of these groups carry the cultural knowledge that dominant groups fear and loathe them, and to that extent carry the position of the dominant subjectivity toward themselves and other members of the group with which they identify. Simultaneously, however, people oppressed through cultural imperialism live a subjectivity different from the dominant subject position. They also have a sense of themselves and one another as ordinary, companionable and humorous. The very drive to unity of the subject that produces the culturally dominant meaning of some groups as abject produces for those groups a plural or split subjectivity. This strain drives some of them crazy; but it drives others to cultural revolution.

Consciousness Raising as a Strategy for Justice

I have argued that a dissonance exists in many people between conscious and unconscious ways of relating to group difference. Discursive consciousness is committed to equal respect and equal treatment for all persons. Racist, sexist, heterosexist, ageist, and able-ist behaviors and reactions continue to be acted out, however, at the levels of practical consciousness and basic security system, reproducing group privilege and oppression. Group oppressions are enacted in this society not primarily in official laws and policies but in informal, often unnoticed and unreflective speech, bodily reaction to others, conventional practices of everyday interaction and evaluation, aesthetic judgment, and the jokes, images, and stereotypes pervading visual, oral, and print media.

If cultural habits of bodily comportment, interactive reactions to others, aesthetic judgments about people's bodies contribute to oppression, then they should be condemned and changed. This obviously cannot imply that they should or can be the subject of legislation or formal rules. One cannot pass a law regulating the appropriate distance people ought to stand from one another, or whether and how they should touch. While aesthetic judgment always carries implicit rules, and the project of revaluing some people's bodies involves changing those rules, aesthetic judgment cannot be formally regulated. The injunction, "Be just," in such matters amounts to no more and no less than a call to bring these phenomena of practical consciousness and unconsciousness under discussion, that is, to *politicize* them. The process of politicizing the habits, feelings, aesthetic judgments of a dominant cultural framework in order to undermine their oppressive consequences has been labeled by these movements *consciousness raising*.

The phrase *consciousness raising* was first used by the women's movement in the late 1960s to describe a process in which women share their experiences of frustration, unhappiness, anxiety, and find common patterns of oppression structuring these very personal stories. They found that "the personal is political," that what was initially experienced as a private, personal problem, in fact has political dimensions and exhibits an aspect of power relations between men and women. Aspects of social life that appear to be given and natural, come into question and appear as social constructions and therefore changeable. The process by which an oppressed group comes to delineate and articulate the social conditions of its oppression and to politicize culture by confronting the cultural imperialism that has denigrated or silenced their specific group experience, is a necessary and crucial step in confronting and reducing oppression.

By the late 1970s many feminists used consciousness-raising methods to address other oppressions. The soul searching generated by angry accusations that the women's movement was racist, engendered forms of discussion addressing concretely women's experiences of group differences and seeking to change relations of group privilege and oppression among women. Women's groups structured small intensive discussions designed to bring to the discursive consciousness of the participants the feelings, reactions, stereotypes, and assumptions they had about women of other groups, as well as how their behavior toward these women might participate in and reproduce relations of privilege and oppression between them.

By proposing consciousness raising as a strategy for achieving social justice—only one among many necessary strategies, of course—I intend to generalize such a process of bringing unconscious behaviors and images to discursive awareness. Commitment to justice as the reduction or elimination of oppression requires that social agents ask whether or how cultural images, stories, expectations of speech and comportment, interactive habits, and the like foster the oppression or domination of some people and how they might be changed. To politicize culture is to assume that culture, while indeed a matter of tradition and habit, is nevertheless a social product and thus not in any way necessitated.

Thus culture is a matter of social choice in the sense that we can choose to change the elements of culture and to create new ones. Sometimes such change can be facilitated by passing laws or establishing policies. Nicaragua has a law against the use of women's bodies for advertising commodities. A glossy magazine can establish a policy of having more articles, photographs, and ads that depict Blacks in ordinary life activities. Cultural change rarely occurs, however, as a result of a simple decision by a collective to adopt new images or habits after discussing and coming to agreement about what is wrong with the existing ones. Cultural change usually does not occur by edict but through discussion, experiment, and play. The requirements of justice, then, concern less the making of such changes than the provision of institutional means for fostering consciousness-raising discussion and making forums and media available for the exhibition of experiments and expressions. The politicization of culture is an ongoing process launched by starting discussion and keeping it going, and by not listening to silencing or dismissive reactions. Institutionalized consciousness-raising policies can take many forms, and I will give just two examples.

In recent years some enlightened corporations who also wish to stave off conflict and possibly lawsuits have instituted consciousness-raising workshops with male managers and other male employees on issues of sexual harrassment. The very concept of sexual harrassment resulted from feminist consciousness raising among women no longer willing to accept as inevitable some individual behaviors they found annoying, humiliating, or coercing. Bringing men to the point of being able to identify behaviors that women collectively tend to find annoying, humiliating, or coercing, however, and explaining why women find them so, has been no easy task.

Differential privilege of members of different racial groups is perpetuated in part by the process of schooling. If my account of unconscious aversion as a typical dynamic of racism is at all accurate, many if not most teachers unconsciously behave in different ways toward Blacks or Latinos than whites. A school system committed to racial justice can distribute literature describing processes of unconscious differential treatment and conduct consciousness-raising workshops where teachers reflect on and discuss their own behavior and attitudes toward students of different races.

Such consciousness raising can be considered a kind of social therapy, confronting the anxieties and fears of difference expressed by the abject. One aspect of the task is to dislodge the association between issues of identity and fears of identity loss, on the one hand, and particular groups projected as different, on the other. Issues of separation, identity, fears of identity loss, and death will be with us as long as humans have consciousness; but these issues need not be played on the register of group differences. Since to some degree contemporary denials or devaluations of group difference express such a mastering subjectivity, for consciousness raising to be ultimately effective requires not only severing the link between identity and fear of difference, but in loosening the desire for unity in the experience of subjectivity and identity itself. The straight, rational, organized, articulate, consistent paradigm of the "mature" person must give way to a personality less preoccupied with "self-control" and more open to entrance from others. Cultural revolution, that is, entails revolutionizing the subject's self-recognition, to allow for a plural and shifting process, rather than insisting on being a single coherent identity.

17 Lacanian Castration: Body-Image and Signification in Psychoanalysis

RICHARD P. BOOTHBY

Jacques Lacan made his reputation as the man who brought structuralist linguistics to psychoanalysis. According to Lacan's celebrated formula—the phrase that has been the rallying cry for a revolution in French psychoanalysis—"the unconscious is structured like a language." In Lacan's view, the concepts of structural linguistics, forged during Freud's lifetime but unavailable to him through "an accident of history," offer an ideal framework for theoretically rendering the psychoanalytic experience. Lacking them, Freud relied on analogies to nineteenth-century physics and biology to form many of his basic concepts. Freud's true discovery, Lacan claims, concerns the function of the linguistic signifier in the unconscious.

> If what Freud discovered and rediscovered with a perpetually increasing sense of shock has a meaning, it is that the displacement of the signifier determines the subjects in their acts, in their destiny, in their refusals, in their blindnesses, in their end and in their fate, their innate gifts and social acquisitions notwithstanding, without regard for character or sex, and that, willingly or not, everything that might be considered the stuff of psychology, kit and caboodle, will follow the path of the signifier.[1]

Given the radicality of Lacan's emphasis on speech and language in psychoanalysis, it may seem strange that Lacan also reserves such a privileged place for Freud's theory of castration. In fact, perhaps the most provocative thing about Lacan's "return to Freud" consists less in his linguistic reinterpretation than in the way Lacan recenters psychoanalysis on the phallus and castration, concepts that probably have been attacked more repeatedly and more strenuously than any others in Freud's legacy.

Lacan's position is unequivocal: "it is castration that governs desire, whether in the normal or the abnormal."[2] Statements like these have provoked some feminists to charge that Lacan is essentially a retrograde thinker, fancying up unhappily traditional ideas with modish post-structuralist dressing. Lacan has also drawn criticism from deconstructionists, who claim that his phallocentrism betrays him as a closet metaphysician. In spite of such criticisms, Lacan continues to insist on the importance of castration. Indeed, castration might well be offered as the master problem of Lacanian psychoanalysis. How are we to understand this emphasis on literal anatomy?

Lacan's return to the phallus may be a little puzzling in itself, but our perplexity is deepened when we realize that the two typically Lacanian themes just mentioned, those of language and the phallus, are intimately bound up. Lacan locates in the acceptance of castration the key moment in which the child's relation to language is crystallized. He claims that "the phallus is the privileged signifier of that mark in which the role of the logos is joined with the advent of desire."[3] The question remains, however, what sense we are to make of the relation of castration and signification. For all its central importance for Lacan, the concept of castration remains a difficult and elusive one. In this chapter, I want briefly to address the topic of castration in Lacan's work in an attempt to present the main lines of his thinking in an integrated conception. This task involves determining the meaning of castration within the three fundamental registers that inform all of Lacan's work: the Real, the Imaginary, and the Symbolic. We may hope that a discussion of Lacan's view of castration not only will contribute to clarifying a difficult but crucial concept but also will afford some insight into the relation of the three basic Lacanian registers to one another.

Rereading Freud's Theory

On the topic of castration, as elsewhere, Lacan may be said to return to Freud, but only by substantively reinterpreting him. The standard view of castration and its central role in the Oedipus complex is familiar enough, especially in the case of the little boy. Engrossed in an amorous relation with his mother, the little seducer is forced to abandon his attachment under threat of castration by the father, with whom the boy, in mourning for his bitter loss, will subsequently identify. Lacan reconceives this Freudian scheme in several fundamental ways. First, Lacan reorders the interpersonal dynamics of the Oedipus complex according to a differing conception of the nature of human desire. Lacan invokes Hegel to emphasize that it is not the other qua object that is desired, but rather the other as him- or herself desiring. Human desire is essentially desire of the other's desire. For Lacan, then, the key issue in the Oedipus complex is not the availability of the mother to the desire of the child but rather the position of the child in relation to the desire of the mother. The narcissism of the pre-Oedipal period is centered on the child's desire to be the privileged object of the mother's desire; that is, to offer himself as what is lacking to the mother. The specter of the phallus thus arises in the child's imagination not because a part of his body is threatened by the father but because the phallus is taken to signify the mother's desire. Prior to the Oedipal stage, the child longs to *be* the phallus of the mother.[4]

Lacan rereads the drama of desire in the Oedipus complex; so, too, he radicalizes the theme of loss. Castration involves coming to terms with what one is not, with what one does not have, with what one cannot be. The relation of castration to loss, limit, and ultimately to the recognition of finitude can be glimpsed in the interpersonal triangle just discussed. The child loses its privileged position as the be-all and end-all of the mother's attentions when the realization dawns that her desire gravitates toward a third object: the father. But the link between castration and loss ultimately derives from the nature of desire itself. Lacan sharpens and deepens Freud's insight that the love object is essentially a lost object, indeed, a lost object that was never possessed. Human desire turns around a fundamental lack, a *manque à être* or "want of being." Castration thus means recognizing that something crucial is always already lost, and irretrievably so. Castration is therefore related in an essential way to the encounter with desire. In castration, the human subject confronts the intrinsic unfulfillability of its desire. Once again, castration is only incidentally related to a paternal threat of violence. Castration anxiety arises in the unfolding of an essential maturational task. It is not merely a possibility to be feared or anticipated, but a task to be symbolically accomplished. Castration, claims Lacan, is a "radical function for which a more primitive stage in the development of psychoanalysis found more accidental (educative) causes."[5]

Already we can point to some important implications of Lacan's reinterpretation. Acceptance of castration means abandoning the narcissistic dream of absolute self-adequacy and submitting to an original being-at-a-loss. Lacan therefore clearly rejects the conclusion often drawn from the Freudian account that whereas the little girl is lacking or missing something by an accident of anatomy, the little boy has from the start the advantage of possessing an essential wholeness and only later comes to fear that he, too, might suffer the little girl's loss. According to Lacan, castration anxiety is not a fear over the loss of an original wholeness but a reemergence of the sense of chaos and virtual dismemberment into which every human infant is born. Far from being an unqualified advantage, therefore, possession of the penis tends to tip masculine psychology into the orbit of fetishism. The boy's own penis, which readily offers itself as a reassuring presence, the guarantor of a false promise of wholeness, becomes the prototype of the fetish object.[6]

Lacan thus reconstructs Freud's Oedipal scenario of loving and losing, but we have yet to give account of the key point of Lacan's innovation: Lacan links the Oedipus complex to language acquisition. From a Lacanian point of view, the essential function of the Oedipus complex and the castration anxiety that energizes it—the accomplishment of what Lacan calls the *paternal metaphor*—is to effect the child's submission to the law of language upon which the architecture of culture is based. In this scheme, castration forms the pivot point between the pre-Oedipal sway of the narcissistic ego, formed in the register of mimicry and resemblances that Lacan dubs the *Imaginary,* and the emergence of a speaking subject whose desire is passed along the signifying chain of a symbolic order. Castration thus becomes the central knot by which Lacan's three cardinal categories—the Imaginary, the Symbolic, and the Real—are dynamically bound together.

Imaginary, Symbolic, Real

Lacan's conception of the Imaginary, as Catherine Clement has remarked, "was a true discovery."[7] Although Lacan's focus tends to shift over his career to the Symbolic and the Real, the Imaginary remains throughout an indispensable point of reference. "The teaching of Lacan," says Philippe Julien, "is, from start to finish, a debate with the Imaginary."[8] Building on the work of Henri Wallon and inspired by findings in animal ethology and Gestalt psychology, Lacan proposes that the primitive ego is organized around an identification with the body image of another human being. In his theory of the "mirror phase," Lacan locates the moment in which the human infant first experiences a sense of its own bodily unity and wins an initial measure of coordination over the chaos of its movements through recognition and imitation of the Other. The effect of this "imaginary" gestalt, Lacan claims, "is akin to the most general structure of human knowledge: that which constitutes the ego and its objects with attributes of permanence, identity, and substantiality, in short, with entities or 'things.'"[9]

Lacan's notion of the Symbolic, indebted to the linguistics of Saussure and Jakobson and to the structural anthropology of Levi-Strauss, was conceived from the outset in dynamic opposition to the formations of the Imaginary. Therefore Lacan claims that "if this speech received by the subject didn't exist, this speech which bears on the symbolic level, there would be no conflict with the Imaginary."[10] The Symbolic is the register of language and linguistically mediated cognitions. In the symbolic order, Lacan envisions a complex system of signifying elements whose meaning is determined by their relation to the other elements of the system—a grand structure, then, in which meaning is free to circulate among associated elements or signifiers without necessarily referring to a particular object or signified. In opposition to the gestalt principles and relations of perceptual resemblance that govern the semiotics of the Imaginary, the order of the Symbolic functions in accordance with rules internal to the system itself. The Symbolic is structured not by unity but by difference, multiplicity, and opposition.

Lacan understands castration to be the structured process by which imaginary identifications give way to the law of the symbolic function. What makes this transition necessary is the alienating effect of the Imaginary. The Imaginary structures the foundations of psychic life, but, paradoxically, the achievement of psychical identity in the Imaginary involves a fundamental self-estrangement. The pernicious effect of alienation in the Imaginary is due in the first place to the fact that the human being's nascent sense of self is modeled on an other outside him. But imaginary alienation is not only a conflict of inner versus outer but also of unity versus multiplicity and stasis versus change. The very fixity over time by which the gestalt form stabilizes the first contours of psychic life introduces a denaturalizing effect that pits a rigid psychological structure against the shifting rhythms of bodily needs. The imago on which the ego is based constitutes a point of stoppage and stagnation in the ebb and flow of biological processes. As Lacan asks of the imaginary ego, "How can one not conceive that each great instinctual metamorphosis in the life of the individual will once again challenge its delimitation?"[11]

Lacan's insistence that the organization of the imaginary ego is resistant to the unfolding of incipient desire is at the heart of his distinctive appropriation of psychoanalysis. Mainstream psychoanalytic theory, especially in the United States, has centered the personality on the executive ego and its powers of adaptation to reality. Lacan, by contrast, maintains that the ego is an internal object, separate from the true subject. He emphasizes the defensive and generally repressive functions of the ego, insisting that "the ego, whose strength our theorists now define in terms of its capacity to bear frustration, is frustration in its essence."[12] Lacan denounces the reality of the ego as a tissue of misperception, or *méconnaissance,* and reassociates the true subject with the id and with unconscious desire. For this reason Lacan protests against the customary reading of Freud's famous formula *Wo Es war, soll Ich werden:* "where the id was, there the ego shall come to be." For Lacan, it is precisely because the ego is constituted only by excluding what Freud called *das Es* that the process of self-recovery announced by Freud's epigram becomes necessary and, further, it is the ego that remains the primary obstacle to the accomplishment of this process. According to Lacan's rereading: *Wo Es war,* where that refused by the ego was, *soll Ich werden,* there shall I, the subject, emerge.[13] "The subject is there to rediscover *where it was...* [namely] the real."[14]

Lacan reserves the word *Real* not only to evoke the horizon of Being beyond the psyche but also to point to the uncanny forces of desire unassimilated by the ego, what Serge Leclaire has called an *ecstatic void* beyond the Imaginary.[15] The Real is precisely what is lacking in the Imaginary and what is occluded by it. The Real is the always-still-outstanding, the excluded, the wholly uncognized. The Real, as Lacan puts it, is the impossible. And yet the Real involves a part of my own being. The fact that it remains unrepresented in the Imaginary establishes the most fundamental dynamic of psychic life. When Lacan claims that "psychoanalysis concerns the real of the body and the imaginary of its mental schema," it is precisely to emphasize the gulf that separates them.[16]

Although novel in its references and implications, Lacan's concept of the imaginary ego and its vicissitudes is not without significant correspondences in Freud's thought. It made new sense, for example, of Freud's claim that "the ego is first and foremost a bodily ego, it is not merely a surface entity, but is itself the projection of a surface."[17] Lacan's conception also recapitulates Freud's separation of the ego from the id and his emphasis on the opposition between them. For Lacan, the ego is a homogeneous but rigid and limiting form that is inimical to the heterogeneity of desire. But Lacan's view further serves to explain and integrate several key problems in Freud's theory. Most significantly, perhaps, Lacan is able to link the topography of id, ego, and superego to Freud's mature formulation of the dual instincts of life and death.[18] The tension between the narcissistic ego and the stirring of desire alienated by it gives rise to a kind of obscure revenge against the strictures of the ego and predisposes the human being toward transgression of its own imaginary identity. Lacan claims that "The libidinal tension that shackles the subject to the constant pursuit of an illusory unity which is always luring him away from himself, is surely related to that agony of dereliction which is Man's particular and tragic destiny. Here we see how Freud was led to his deviant concept of a death instinct."[19] From a Lacanian point of view, it is not the biological organism but the ego and the perceptual imagos on which it is modeled that fall subject to the obscure strivings of the self-destructive drive that Freud called a *death instinct*. The price of access to desire becomes a certain disintegration or deconstruction of the ego's gestalt unity.

The Meaning of the Cut

Returning to our theme, it is now possible to see how Lacan's conception of the imaginary unity of the ego and its violation by the heterogeneity of desire enables him to frame a new interpretation of castration. First, we are given to understand why the Oedipal child, stirred by strange, new impulses, is predisposed toward fantasies of bodily dismemberment. The key point is that castration is, after all, a specific form of bodily dismemberment. As such, it can embody in fantasy a fracturing of the ego's imaginary identity. Indeed, it is striking to observe how children three- to six-years-old relish tearing off dolls' heads and limbs, how they gleefully threaten to pluck out the eyes and bite off the fingers of caretakers and peers, or how they squirm with giddy but delighted fascination at fairy-tale scenes of violence. From a Lacanian viewpoint, these fantasmatic dismemberments serve a psychological purpose, constituting a kind of experimentation toward a transformed identity, a new emergence of desire made possible by new forms of symbolic functioning.[20]

Second, we can answer the question, Why the penis? Why does this particular organ assume such importance? The prime consideration is the familiar one: the presence of the penis in the father and its absence in the mother suggests its role as the focus of the mother's desire. But there is more to be said insofar as the penis readily lends itself to representing certain aspects of the transition from a predominantly imaginary to a predominantly symbolic mode of functioning that for Lacan is constitutive of the Oedipal drama. The penis is especially well-suited both to represent the breakdown of an imaginary gestalt and to anticipate the structure of the linguistic signifier. On the one hand, the anatomical vulnerability of the penis readily symbolizes the possibility of violation of the body's imaginary wholeness. Aside from the mother's breast, the penis is the only bodily appendage unsupported by bone and the only appendage incapable of voluntary movement. It is sensitive and easily hurt. By virtue of its very physiology, therefore, the penis designates a special point of cleavage in the imaginary unity of the body. Like the other partial objects enumerated by Lacan, "the mamilla, faeces,...the urinary flow," the phallus as an imaginary object bears the "mark of the cut."[21] What these "objects" have in common is their potential separability from the body proper. To the extent that they either literally separate from the body (feces, urine) or project beyond the general body surface in a way that suggests a possibility of separation, they readily represent fears of loss or bodily fragmentation. On the other hand, the penis displays the features of difference, and of presence, and absence that distinguish the structure of the linguistic signifier. As Freud himself was wont to emphasize, the child's knowledge of anatomy soon comes to include a recognition of the presence of the penis in the male and its absence in the female. The penis functions anatomically like a differential feature in linguistics; its presence or absence signifies male or female. It constitutes on the level of anatomy what Roman Jakobson called *the marked and the unmarked*.[22] Even in the male alone, the penis embodies a principle of difference in its alternance of flaccidity and erection.[23]

Lastly, we can now clarify the more general psychological dynamic that the specific imagery of castration helps to accomplish. We have said that fantasies of bodily violation, castration among them, help to effect a shift from a predominantly imaginary mode of functioning to a predominantly symbolic one. This shift can be variously described:

1. At the Oedipal stage, the subject that previously found its identity in the gestalt unity of the ego comes to be represented by what linguists call *shifters,* the personal pronouns whose meaning alters depending on whether they are sounded by my mouth or that of another.

2. The dyadic bond with the perceived other that structures the Imaginary gives way to triadic relations in which social exchange is mediated by the laws of language.

3. The imaginary register of perceptual presence governed by resemblance yields to a system of differences that operates through a vacillating play of presence and absence.

4. The simultaneities of the Imaginary, which ground anticipations limited to repetition of the same, now contrast with the serial unfolding of the signifying chain that finds its circuit in the diacritical web of the symbol system.

Reduced to its most absolutely basic terms, the Oedipal transition constitutes a shift from unity to complexity, from identity to difference. In progressing through the Oedipus complex, the subject ceases to be held in thrall to imaginary formations and passes into the defile of the signifying system. The psychic process moves beyond the bounds of imaginary unities and is taken up into the universe of signifiers. It is a shift that readily finds a perceptual analog in a contrast between the integrity of the body gestalt and its dismemberment into fragments. To the extent, therefore, that Lacan reads the Oedipal crisis in terms of a transition between imaginary and symbolic functions, he understands the entry of the subject into language to be concomitant with, even conditioned upon, a certain transformation in the way the integrity of the body is experienced.[24]

This idea is corroborated in a remarkable way by what may be the most famous example of language acquisition—that of Helen Keller. You will remember her recounting of that magic moment at the well-house with her teacher Anne Sullivan.[25] All at once, in a rush of insight as free and spontaneous as the flow of water over her hand, Helen Keller suddenly understood the connection between the letters traced on her left palm and the "wonderful cool something" that flowed over her right. But what was it that made possible the breakthrough at the well-house? We may be tempted to think of it as a sort of magical spark of association that leapt between Helen's two hands, the one drawn upon and the other wetted. Yet rereading Helen's recollection of the event we find that the drama at the pump-house is a story within a story. The larger story concerns a doll given to Helen by her teacher. Frustrated by Anne Sullivan's repeated efforts to spell the word *doll,* Helen smashes the doll on the floor. The interesting thing to note is her "keen sense of delight" at feeling the fragments of the broken doll. She twice remarks on it. Is it possible that the experience of the smashed doll accomplished for Helen Keller the function of imaginary violation that Lacan associated with the accession to symbols? Might the doll's fragments, as an image of the body's wholeness broken into pieces, have fulfilled the function of castration in its Lacanian meaning? These suggestive questions seem underscored by further details of Helen Keller's account. We might note, for instance, how when Helen returns to the house, empowered by her "strange new sight" of a world with names, she remembers the broken doll and, for the first time, feels repentance and sorrow. It is plausible to take this detail as an evidence of a dawning superego, the first tremor of a new sense that the named world is subject to law. Viewed from this perspective, Helen Keller's experience at the well-house presents in extreme compression some of the key elements of the Oedipal drama as Lacan conceives it.

Implications of Lacan's View

It is important to point out that my account of Lacan's theory of castration leans more heavily on his concept of the Imaginary than much of what one finds in the literature on Lacan, which often tends to give pride of place to the Symbolic. At the risk of being overschematic, this strategy allows castration to emerge more explicitly as a structured dynamic, a kind of hinge or pivot point between imaginary and symbolic functions as Lacan defines them. It also has the advantage of highlighting certain theoretical implications of Lacan's position. It is to these implications that I want now briefly to turn.

At the core of Lacan's theory of castration is the idea that the imaginary schema of the body's wholeness plays a crucial role in the unfolding of symbolic competence. The imaginary body-gestalt provides an initial organization of unitary form upon which the differentiating function of linguistic signification can go to work. The body imago functions as an originary frame or matrix over against which difference within identity can first be registered.

The Imaginary thus constitutes the proto-context for symbolic activity. It forms the original myth of human identity, but, as such, it becomes something more than a myth, a near-necessary myth. The Imaginary has a peculiar epistemological status. On the one hand, it is an autochthonous function that arises from perceptual mechanisms that are more primitive than activities of conscious judgment and reflection. Yet, at the same time, the Imaginary is essentially fictive, since it grounds a perception of sex difference that has little to do with biology. Biologically speaking, there is nothing missing in the female. We can note in passing the implications of this idea for the question of gender difference. The problem faced by any theorist is to explain how gender difference, if it is not merely a biological fact, occurs with such regularity across different cultures and epochs. Like Freud, Lacan is convinced that there is nothing biologically fixed or determined about gender identity, as the very existence of homosexuality suggests. Yet neither is sex difference purely and simply a result of learning or role socialization. From a Lacanian point of view, the psychology of patriarchal gender difference is not fixed or necessary (one might imagine other possible configurations of sexual identity), but it is, we might say, *favored* by the imaginary construal of anatomy. The structuring of desire in the unconscious is to be explained in terms of the positioning of the subject with respect to the presence or absence of the phallus as an *imaginary* object.

In the most general sense, Lacan insists on retaining the anatomical literality of "castration" to emphasize the crucial role played by the image of the body in the life of the mind. The wholeness of the body image is an important "moment," as Hegel might say, in the birth of the symbolic function. But what about the later life of signification, beyond the transformation of the Oedipus complex? Would Lacan share the view of Socrates in the *Phaedrus*, that "any *logos* ought to be constructed like a living being, with its own body, as it were; it must not lack either head or feet, it must have a middle and extremities so composed as to suit each other and the whole work"?[26] At first sight, we feel sure the answer must be "no"—it is precisely the function of castration to inaugurate another and different mode of symbolic process than that of the Imaginary and its play of body-gestalts. The emergence of the symbolic function in castration begins with the imago of the body only to violate it. This no doubt is accurate. Yet there is a great deal to be said to the contrary. In what follows, I want briefly to suggest how, even after the Oedipal transition, the Imaginary and its reverberations continue to orient the Symbolic process as Lacan conceives it.

First of all, one might say that castration is never complete.[27] The work of castration, like analysis itself, is essentially "interminable." Insofar as castration remains incomplete, the forms and demands of the Imaginary continue to exert influence over the Symbolic, bending the signifying chain into orbit around imaginary loci. There is, for example, the everyday ego-discourse that Lacan calls *empty speech*. In empty speech, the ego turns the resources of speech and language to its own purposes, augmenting the familiar defensive structures of the ego with stale, repetitive formulas of everyday sociability.[28]

Second, the incompleteness of castration, so far as it can be conceived of in various degrees, can be taken as the determinant of variable degrees of disfunction, running the gamut from neurosis to psychosis. In the case of the psychotic, castration is foreclosed more or less totally, implying that the "treasury of the signifier" is pressed *en bloc* into the service of Imaginary structures. In the psychotic discourse of Judge Schreber, for example, we find the whole machinery of speech and language imbricated within and supporting the paranoid structure of the double.[29] In neurosis, we may envisage partial or regional failures of castration, such that signification is refracted around certain key life concerns. The localization of signification in the neurotic body would be especially clear in the case of hysteria, in which the body, through its paralysis or spasming, becomes the site in which signifying relations are inscribed. The role of the imaginary body would also be especially prominent in phobia, where, if Lacan is right, the phobic object constitutes a signifier of desire, but often functions by addressing itself threateningly to the body of the phobic individual.

In empty speech and the dysfunctional processes of psychosis and neurosis, therefore, the Imaginary and its implication of the body schema may be said to retain a certain priority that restricts by foreclosure or fixation the emergence of desire in signification. But to these figures we may add a third possible form of imaginary ordering of discourse. For even if we suppose an ideal limit-case in which castration is fully realized and the desiring subject is freed from the captures of the Imaginary and submitted to the circuit of the signifying chain for the pursuit of its desire, the Imaginary and its investment in the body image seem to return yet again. This is so because, according to Lacan, the desire of the subject, even when it has been passed along the signifying chain of a symbolic order, tends to realize itself in fantasy. In speaking of the fantasm and its function, we find Lacan at his most cryptic, appealing to the notions of *das Ding* and of the *objet petit a*. But the fantasm ever remains a manifestation in a perceptual register and thus retains a quasi-imaginary character. As Lacan says of it in his first seminar, the Imaginary and its reflection of the body image remains "an essential dimension of the human, which entirely structures his fantasy life."[30] We are thus led to ask whether, even on the far side of the Oedipus complex, the play of fantasy that lures desire, the very stuff of sublimation, does not retain the stamp of the body image that originally structured imaginary identity.

Conclusion

The task of clarifying Lacan's treatment of castration is of value both as it enables us to recognize how Lacan's return to Freud gathers together and integrates Freud's own concepts and as it affords us a special insight into the relations between the three Lacanian registers of Imaginary, Symbolic, and Real.

Despite his insistence on the indispensability of the castration complex to the psychoanalytic theory, Freud never integrated castration with the larger scheme of his metapsychology. Lacan, by contrast, conceives castration in a way that links it not only with the Oedipus complex, but with other key concepts of Freud's thought. For example, Lacan is able to make good Freud's suggestion that castration anxiety is paradigmatic of anxiety in general. Freud was convinced that anxiety signaled danger to the ego but, lacking a theoretical account of the unity of the ego, he was unable to specify the nature of the danger. "What it is that the ego fears from the external and from the libidinal danger cannot be specified," he said. "We know that the fear is of being overwhelmed or annihilated; but it cannot be grasped analytically."[31] Lacan's conception of the imaginary origin of the ego enables him to ground the unity of the ego on the perceptual gestalt of the body-image and allows him in turn to explain why the fantasy of bodily dismemberment constitutes a privileged manifestation of anxiety. In addition, from a Lacanian point of view a profound connection emerges between the castration complex and Freud's otherwise enigmatic hypothesis of a death instinct. Castration anxiety becomes itself an expression of the death instinct. As a tendency toward repetition of trauma, the death instinct can be said to constitute a deeply motivated predisposition to anxiety. In Lacanian terms, such a predisposition to anxiety implies a tendency toward violation of the imago of the human body—a tendency that, for reasons reviewed earlier, is especially liable to realize itself in the fantasy of castration.

Of course, although Lacan's reconstruction of castration can be seen to extend the direction of Freud's own thinking in these respects, Lacan's conclusions also mark certain discontinuities with Freud. First, a Lacanian view requires that Freud's supposition of a death instinct must be interpreted not biologically but psychologically. "Freudian biology," Lacan insists, "has nothing to do with biology."[32] The "death" demanded by the death drive is not that of the biological organism but rather that of the imaginary ego. Second, where Freud continued to refer castration to the contingency of a parental threat of punishment, Lacan maintains that the human being is internally motivated toward the fantasy of bodily dismemberment. Castration anxiety arises in the subject's passage toward the assumption of its own desire.

Our examination of Lacan's approach allows castration to emerge as a key concept, perhaps *the* key concept by which the three Lacanian categories of Imaginary, Symbolic, and Real may be integrated. Castration functions to bring the three registers into dynamic relation with one another.[33] This is especially prominent in the relation of the Imaginary to the Symbolic, inasmuch as Lacan's theory locates the birth of the symbolic function in relation to a certain deconstruction of the Imaginary. The fantasmatic violation of the body imago effected by castration furnishes a precondition for the unfolding of the capacity for signification. It is upon the site of the body image, or better, upon the *sight* of its dismemberment, that the insertion of the subject into the symbolic order begins. The first movements of signification find their material support in the parts of the fragmented body. But if castration thus forms the hinge between Imaginary and Symbolic, it may also be said to offer a new possibility of relation to the Real. Castration functions to short-circuit the disjunction between the Imaginary and the Real, propelling the subject beyond the bounds of narcissism. Castration establishes the anticipation of difference in the subjective economy, enabling a transformed ego to sustain the presence of genuine otherness. By inaugurating the subject's submission to the law of the symbolic order, castration opens a new, symbolically mediated contact with the Real. In doing so, castration opens new access to the movement of desire. For Lacan, castration therefore involves a two-sided process of imaginary refusal and symbolic registration, the effect of which is to permit a limited approach to the Real. The outline of such a process can be glimpsed in Lacan's otherwise puzzling assertion that "castration means that *jouissance* must be refused, so that it can be reached on the inverted ladder [*l'échelle renversée*] of the Law of desire."[34]

The density and difficulty of this conclusion is hard to avoid in such a brief statement. However, the challenge for our understanding arises in part from the subject matter itself. Indeed, it is perhaps at this point that the enigmatic character of Lacan's entire construction may be most striking, as we are faced with the conclusion that castration anxiety is ultimately motivated by and accepted in the name of desire. We are forced to come to grips with the idea that, from a Lacanian point of view, the density of desire in the human being is inextricably bound up with its most profound experiences of fear. It is with respect to castration that some of the most mysterious aspects of Freud's discovery impress themselves upon us, aspects that Lacan emphasizes in his claim that "[Freud] questioned life as to its meaning, and not to say that it has none... but to say that it has only one meaning, that in which desire is borne by death."[35] With that, however, we understandably may be vexed by new perplexity. We may be moved to ask again, for example, about the nature of the imaginary structuration of identity that alienates desire. As I have read Lacan, it is the alienation constitutive of the imaginary ego that sets in motion the whole dynamic of the castration complex. Looking back over Lacan's account of castration, are we not inclined to ask why, ultimately, the solidarity of the imaginary ego is taken to be inimical to desire? Or perhaps even more pressingly, are we not given to wonder again what, in fact, Lacan means by *desire?*

But those are other questions.

Appendix

I offer the following series of children's drawings merely as a suggestive illustration of what Lacan means by imaginary castration. The drawings were made by a young boy—my son, in fact—at various intervals between the ages of 3½ and 5½ years old.

In the first two drawings (Figures 1 and 2), made about age 3½, we find a feature that is typical of body representations made by children of that age: there is great attention to detail, especially to the inclusion of appendages like fingers and toes. Indeed, so zealous is the artist to account for all the fingers and toes that he includes at least five, sometimes seven or even ten, on each limb. This penchant for detail seems to betoken a concern for the body's wholeness that a Lacanian understanding of the pre-Oedipal child would lead us to predict. Is the obsessiveness of that concern a reflection of a dawning anxiety about the body's integrity?

In Figure 3, made about a year and a half later, around age 5, we are surprised to find one eye depicted as flying out of the face. What is going on here? The model for this drawing was a toy called a *Madball.* A popular gimmick at the time, a Madball is a rubber ball fashioned in the form of a distorted and disfigured face, complete with lolling tongue, gouged-out eye, stitched wounds, bulging veins, and so on; in short, a toy whose magic consists in its capacity to generate the squirmy excitement of "grossing out" people. Whatever its proximate source of inspiration, however, the drawing seems motivated by a more general interest in bodily dismemberment, for it is just one of a large number of drawings made over a year-long period that explore all manner of bodily partitionings and violations. In the midst of that period, my son asked me for a stack of blank paper stapled together to form a sort of booklet. With this booklet in hand, he produced a special series of body-part drawings, some of which I have included here as Figures 4–10. The first of this series repeats the familiar Madball face. That image is followed, however, by a parade of body parts, each of which, I was informed, had a name. Figure 5 is fairly recognizably "Fingerman." Figure 6, with eyes placed in a forest of hairs, was dubbed "Hairman." Figure 7 is recognizable if one imagines a figure bending over and viewed from behind with a face inscribed on the buttocks; he is, of course, "Bottom-man." Figure 8 is "Scrotum-man," the buttocks-face of the previous drawing is repeated but with male genitals suspended from it instead of legs. Figures 9 and 10 are "Handman" and "Footman," drawn by the artist, incidentally, as rough tracings of his own hand and foot.

In a striking way, these drawings present a phantasmagoria of what Lacan calls the *corps morcelé*. They constitute a veritable encyclopedia of the body in bits and pieces. But equally striking, each of the body parts is inscribed with a face, making it possible to ascribe to each a name. Especially when compared to the earlier drawings, which so conscientiously rendered the body's wholeness, this series seems to suggest a sort of deliberate experimentation with the body's fragmentation, as if the challenge were to see how far the body could be cut up and still retain a sense of self. It is difficult not to conclude from these drawings, especially in view of the peculiar energy and interest with which they were undertaken and by the very large number of such drawings produced, that an important developmental task was being worked out by means of them.

It is perhaps not irrelevant to note that as my son passed the 6½-year mark, the subject matter of his drawings has changed completely, shifting first to a near mania for making treasure maps and later to mixed interests in people, buildings, trees, and spaceships.

Figure 1. Person-drawing, made at age 3½

Figure 2. Person-drawing, age 3½

Figure 3. "Madball" person, age 5

Figure 4. "Madball" face, age 5½

Figure 5. "Fingerman," age 5½

Figure 6. "Hairman," age 5½

Figure 7. "Bottom-man," age 5½

Figure 8. "Scrotum-man," age 5½

Figure 9. "Handman," age 5½

Figure 10. "Footman," age 5½

18

Postmodern *Différends*

Our society produces schizos the same way it produces Prell shampoo or Ford cars, the only difference being that the schizos are unsalable.[1]

Différend I: Preliminary Remarks

The pretext for my comments is *The Postmodern Condition.*[2] I will refer to and comment on the text by Jean-Francois Lyotard that goes by that title. Always engaged in an *explication de texte,* analogous to the kind of exegesis performed in Friedrich Nietzsche's *On the Genealogy of Morals,* I will proceed by commenting on a passage from Lyotard's *Le Différend:* "Reality relays the *différend.*"[3] It is an exegesis that will describe the postmodern condition by working through the agonistics of language that characterize the phrase *the postmodern condition* and the strategies used in response to this condition to comprehend and phrase it.

My working hypothesis is this: from the very outset, "the postmodern condition" *is* "schizo." From the moment of its initial "phrasing," from the site of its initial posting, "the postmodern condition"—the knowledge it reports and the strategies of thinking and acting it requires—*will have signified* or *will have been* (the) "schizo." Indeed, the schizo conditions Lyotard's conception and articulation of the postmodern. The modern is always and already *post,* it bears the postmodern; in its nascent state, the post is always and already *modern.* The postmodern is the *différend* of the modern; a part of the modern, it (has) become(s) the modern always dissembling itself. In a similar fashion, the modern is the *différend* of the postmodern, it (has) become(s) the postmodern through its own internal conflicts. As such, the modern and the postmodern can be comprehended as identities of one another, that is, as *différends* of one another. They are contiguous: the one never dominates the other but always presents itself articulating the other, speaking the language of the other, and always bearing the possibility of becoming the other.

The postmodern condition, then, can be understood only in terms of the agonistics of language, its *différends*. The *différend* simultaneously designates a singularity and a plurality: it can be understood only as a condition of language and knowledge; a characteristic of language and knowledge that can be understood only from the perspective of paganism, the desire to experiment with phrasings, with the links made between language and reality, so-called. And, finally, the pagan can be understood only as an attempt to account for the heterogeneity and multiplicity of phrasings, in short, an attempt to account for the pragmatic context (of dissension and difference) in which the postmodern is identified and, as such, engendered.

Différend II: Becoming Socrates, Becoming Pagan...

In spite of its nominal designation as a "condition" *(condicio* and *condicere),* the postmodern does not present a situation in which agreement is possible. It is not anything essential upon which agreement has been reached; nor is it a provision—a requirement prior to any performance—about which we have come to together to talk in order to reach an agreement or a consensus. In fact, there is no agreement about the postmodern: there is no agreement concerning its significance, if any; what it constitutes, whether it is an "occasion," an "awareness," or even a "turn" or "sensibility."⁴ Because of the heterogeneity it names, because of the pragmatics that define the postmodern, Lyotard claims that "consensus is a horizon never reached" (PC 61). Consensus "has become outmoded and suspect" (PC 66); it has been "rendered impossible" (DIF para. 92).

To be sure, the postmodern has no unique identity; it presents no unified mentality, nor systematic, ordered perspective: it presents multiple, disjointed identities, none of which naturally is dominant, all of which fissure and conflict with one another at the moment of their initial (and subsequent) appearance. As such, it is a condition of internal dissension, of cleavages, rifts, gaps, and fragmentation; it is a condition of the incessant generation of multiple positions, situations, "selves," and stories *we* tell to and about *selves.* In this way, "the postmodern condition" is a sign, a name, indicating "that something which should be able to be put into phrases cannot be phrased in the accepted idioms" (DIF para. 93; compare para. 22–23).

For Lyotard, the postmodern condition *is* and, as such, *presents* the possibilities of "paganism." The postmodern condition signifies that situation in which, as Lyotard claims in *Just Gaming,* "one judges without criteria" not only in "matters of truth, but also in matters of beauty (aesthetic efficacy) and in matters of justice, that is, of politics and ethics."⁵ It is the condition of "opinion" and "experimentation" (JG 28–34). As such, it is the condition of the *phrase,* the condition of the links or connections drawn between "language" and "reality."

Furthermore, for Lyotard the postmodern presents the necessity of recognizing that in whatever domain, whatever field of inquiry, in whatever phrasic network, one is without a rule, one already judges without criteria. That is to say, one is without recourse to a metalanguage, a *"grand récit."* And yet one understands that in whatever domain, whatever field of inquiry, in whatever phrasic network, "one must decide" (JG 17). Indeed, one must decide. But how can one decide without criteria? without rules? without appeal to a grand narrative? How can one decide, how can one litigate and adjudicate under these conditions? One can decide, ironically enough, only in recognizing the wisdom of *the philosopher*—albeit a pagan wisdom rendered by a pagan philosopher: Plato's Socrates.

One can decide by making new links beyond old forms, that is, by creating new links or new rules for linking phrases, for making links to other, different genre of discourses or "families of phrases" (DIF para. 21) because "it is impossible to know" the state or condition of one's knowledge, especially knowledge about one's selves without the linkage to other idioms (PC 13; see also DIF para. 102, 190, and 192), without breaking with certain "régimes of phrases."⁶ Is this not the wisdom of Plato's Socrates? Is this wisdom not known already? Is it not already all-too-familiar? And yet, because of its familiarity, because of what might be called its immanence (for lack of another phrase), because it borders the grand speculative systems of Western thought in a legendary fashion, has it not become unbelievable? Has it all-too-easily and all-too-carelessly been forgotten? Here let us recall, momentarily, the pagan wisdom narrated and staged so effectively by Plato's Socrates: one (the philosopher perhaps?) does not know what one knows nor what one does not know. And yet—in spite of and because of this underlying agonistic—one must decide, one must find different idioms, different ways of speaking, writing, and acting to present the unpresentable, to pursue "the unknown"—that is, for Socrates, Plato, and Lyotard, to pursue the desire for justice.⁷

To the extent that the postmodern condition doubles, intermixes, interlaces the Socratic-Platonic and pagan-experimental (Sophistic?) voices—in effect, links their strategic networks—and thus separates the Socratic-Platonic and the pagan-experimental from their own "proper" idiograph (or signature), it signifies the *différend.* The *différend* is "the unstable state and instant of language wherein something which must be able to be put in phrases cannot yet be" (DIF para. 22). The relation between the Socratic-Platonic and the pagan-experimental in Lyotard's work can be likened to the relation between the Apollinian and the Dionysian articulated by Nietzsche in *The Birth of Tragedy:* "The intricate relation of the Apollinian and the Dionysian in tragedy may really be symbolized by a fraternal union of the two deities: Dionysus speaks the language of Apollo; and Apollo, finally [speaks] the language of Dionysus; and so the highest goal of tragedy and of all art is attained."[8] Here the Dionysian requires the Apollinian idiom to speak and to be heard; and, in order to speak, the Apollinian requires the Dionysian allusion (to the truth?). Moreover, the Apollinian must speak the language of the Dionysian in order to present the wisdom of Dionysus *as if* it were Apollo's. In other words, the Apollinian must translate the Dionysian idiom in such a way as to supply the illusion that the idiom and the Dionysian wisdom will have been already Apollo's. Here Apollo and Dionysus are twins. Their fraternal union constitutes a unity of appositives, a unity that differs from itself and and defers itself. It creates, as Lyotard would note, a *différend*, a conflict of faculties. Even when one speaks the language of the other, they do not speak in unison; they do not speak univocally, nor uniquely. The recitation, the performance supplies the illusion of speaking the same identical idiom. But the performance, the recitation, the rephrasing transfigures its object. Their idioms remain discordant; their idiographs, their identities remain differ*a*nt and, Nietzsche notes at times, unknown and forgotten. In other words, at times it is of little significance *who* speaks, only that something is said or phrased, a value declared, for example, that demands a response.

In Lyotard's works, the Socratic "desire for justice" and "the desire for the unknown"—otherwise taken as analogues of the unpresentable—are presented in the name of, in the disguise of the pagan-experimental. Here the pagan-experimental speaks the language of, speaks in the name of, Socratic-Platonic values so as to demonstrate the precarious and violable nature of the boundaries that separate these classical worlds. The relation between the Apollinian and the Dionysian, as well as the relation between the Socratic-Platonic and the pagan-experimental, is one of contiguity. They come into contact with one another in a localized fashion; they use one another for specific purposes within a particular context. But their *différend*, their differences as it were, or their internal conflicts are never abated, never withdrawn. As a result, in terms of the pursuit of justice and the desire for the unknown, the postmodern condition *or* the *différend or* the pagan can be phrased as presenting a continuum of desire, "[a continuum of contiguities] with shifting limits that are always displaced."[9] Because of this condition, one (again, the philosopher?) is always faced with having to pursue the desired object through another kind of material, another idiom, a different phrasing. In this way, Lyotard's recitation of the Socratic narrative or idiom rephrases or translates its wisdom.

However, this reiteration is no mere repetition of the same. Plato's Socratic wisdom and values are displaced in the recitation—detached from the site of their "initial declaration," diverted from the path assigned and transmitted by the grand narratives that have become the history of philosophy. Recast according to the demands of the postmodern condition—that is, in accordance with the agonistics and idioms of paganism— the desire for justice and the desire for the unknown have become "pragmatic" once again. The desire for justice and the desire for the unknown are no longer singular or separate. They have become obverse sides of one another, a duality. This dual desire, these desires that interfere with one another, that intrude upon and intervene in the workings of one another, can no longer postulate a unity, systematize and identify problems in advance of the agonistics—that is, the *différend(s)* that define(s) the practical context, indeed, the reality—in which it is (or they are) expressed. The pertinence of their phrasing in relation to reality is at issue, where "reality" names the future, not the present deferred in the reference to facts and absorbed in the narratives of the past.

With the postmodern, the desire for justice and the desire for the unknown have been recontextualized—given a new form or formed again *(anamorphose)*—by the very fact that they have been (and will have been) recited, recalled *(anámnesis)*, ana-lyzed according to an anagogic *(anagogie)* process.[10] Such a process entails, for Lyotard, an "initial forgetting [*oubli initial*]" that takes shape only according to a different articulation, an idiom that *différends,* or that "schizzes," to recite a phrase from Deleuze and Guattari's *Anti-Oedipus* (AO 244). In other words, forgetting takes shape in the linkage of phrases that conflicts with the initial declaration or articulation, and breaks with the form of the original, the accepted idiom and sensibility. It is a practice of "writing," to invoke a Derridean signature, that resembles the "minor literatures" recalled by Deleuze and Guattari in their *Kafka:* it "begins by expressing itself and doesn't conceptualize until afterward" (K 28). With expression comes the rupture of forms, dispersal of boundaries. And "to reconstruct the content. . . will necessarily be part of a rupture in the order of things" (K 28). (One experiences the effects of this common practice of displacement throughout the *Dialogues* of Plato.)

To this end, boundaries become the "stakes" and "provisional results"; so Lyotard claims in *The Postmodern Condition.* The boundaries identifying and segmenting the Socratic-Platonic and the pagan-experimental, as well as the modern and postmodern, are horizons toward which experiments work. Thus, Lyotard does not valorize what Plato condemns;

there is no "simple" reversal of Platonic values, as Philippe Lacoue-Labarthe claims.[11] But there is always, as Lyotard notes in *Just Gaming,* the desire to "keep open the 'abyss' between the two worlds" (JG 89).

Différend III: Image Schizzes...Relays

Keeping open the abysses between worlds, between phrases is the condition of language according to Lyotard. It is, as one might expect, *the postmodern condition of language.* Recitation, reiteration, (re-)phrasing, linkage are possible only where the *différend* is signaled or entailed—as Lyotard notes in *Le Différend,* "Reality relays [*comporte:* carries, calls for, requires] the *différend*" (DIF para. 92). And the *différend*—the agonistics of idioms that deliver themselves over to the order of desire—is the condition for subsequent linkage. But it is a condition that cannot be conceptualized: it cannot be brought under the determination of a current descriptive or prescriptive regime or idiom. As such it is not something to be identified, because it is not presentable as such—it "schizzes" in its presentation. It circulates and breaks with the signs that code it (compare AO 243).

But the schizzes are allusions or phrasings signaling something that is constantly not yet because it is (in) a state of constant transfiguration; that is, because it constantly delivers itself over to the order of desire. Such is the *différend,* if I may recite the line from Lyotard once again: "the unstable state and instant of language wherein something which must be able to be put into phrases cannot yet be" (DIF 22). In other words, the presentations, the schizzes of any "object"—reality, nature, meaning, interpretation, indeed the postmodern—are the determinations of that object. It is this point that *Le Différend* demonstrates. Lyotard says *"Le Différend* (1983) tries to give an ontological and linguistic (or, better yet, 'sentential,' 'phrasic') status" to what, in *Peregrinations,* he calls *the blank.*[12] Lyotard continues:

> It's the emptiness, the nothingness in which the universe presented by a phrase is exposed and which explodes at the moment the phrase occurs and then disappears with it. The gap separating one phrase from another is the "condition" of both presentation and occurrences, but such a "condition" remains ungraspable in itself except by a new phrase, which in turn presupposes the first phrase. This is something like the condition of Being, as it is always escaping determination and arriving both too soon and too late. (PER 31–32)

As the condition of language, the postmodern presents the "not yet," the "unpresentable"—that which cannot be thought, said, or done according to the preestablished categories and familiar principles of a grand or metanarrative, the idioms of systems. As the language of that unstable condition, the postmodern signifies that now (and always) the so-called philosopher, the artist, and the writer work without rules; it signifies that the rules and categories remain to be articulated within specific pragmatic contexts (PC 81).[13] In this respect, the postmodern designates what Deleuze and Guattari call "the revolutionary condition for every literature within the heart of what is called great (or established) literature" (K 18). For Lyotard, the schizo-idioms, schizo-realities characteristic and constitutive of the postmodern insist upon the destruction of "narrative monopolies" (IP 86) through the "introduction of a foreign, minor *historiette"* (IP 84) or the "multiplication of small narratives" (JG 59) for the purpose of plotting those "territories of language" that fall under the rubric "minority" (JG 95). At stake here is not the issue of boundaries but, rather, the issue of idioms that differ from and defer the totalitarian *use* of language. "What is at stake," writes Lyotard, "in a literature, in a philosophy, in a politics perhaps, is to bear witness to *différends* by finding new idioms for them" (DIF para. 22). At stake is the recognition (again, a form of wisdom expressed by Plato's Socrates perhaps?) "that what remains to be phrased exceeds what they [existing idioms] can phrase at the present, and that they must be allowed to institute idioms that do not yet exist" (DIF para. 23).

The incessant generation of idioms, idiographs, and identities—or the "multiplication of small narratives" where "there is no finality [no hierarchy] in the field of opinions" or the fields of multiplicities, as Lyotard states in *Just Gaming* (59, 81)—demonstrates that for Lyotard the postmodern, the *différend,* or the pagan cannot provide (a) master narrative(s). As a condition of language, a condition of being, the postmodern has no language of its own; as a characteristic of language, a characteristic of being, the *différend* is not in itself a unifying category; and as a strategy for action, a style of being, the pagan is only one phrasic link in a network of phrases, it has no language or reality of its own. What Lyotard says about the political and the *différend* applies to the postmodern:

> The political is the threat of the *différend.* It is not a genre; it is the multiplicity of genres, the diversity of ends, and above all the question of linkings [*l'enchaînement:* concatenation, chain, series, connection]. ...It is, if you wish, the state of language, but it does not have *a* language. And the political consists of a language that is not a language, but phrases, or [it is] being that is not being, but the *there is.* (DIF para. 190)

There is no-thing prior to the determination of linkages, and there is no necessity governing the determination of linkages.

In tandem with this or any other determination of the links comes rupture, because there can never be anything but more links, more schizzes, more interlinking and separation of "heteromorphous classes of utterances (denotative, prescriptive, performative, technical, evaluative, etc.)" (PC 65). As such, there is no "metaprescriptive" common to all of these networks of idioms. There is no "common measure" nor "procedure" that can mediate the *différend* of idioms (JG 50–51; DIF para. 36). That is, there is no "common code" that can be deciphered (PER 44); no code that has been or will have been "instituted to establish" a reality underlying all determinations. As Lyotard remarks, this is why there is only the *différend* (PER 44).[14] There is only the link, the phrase, the creation of new idioms. "That there is no phrase is impossible: it is, instead, *and a phrase* is necessary. It is necessary to link [*Il faut enchaîner*]. . . . To link is necessary, but how to link is not" (DIF para. 102). There is only the necessity of *that which is not yet,* that which will have been presented by the phrase. Whence being!

The postmodern condition is an issue of *différends,* differences, the apposition and opposition of multiplicities—idioms and desires. One might say that the postmodern, the *différend,* and the pagan present, albeit in a sublime fashion, "thresholds" not yet determined, not yet fixed, not yet "present." To this extent, the postmodern, the *différend,* and the pagan—as an ensemble or an assemblage of phrases, or as individual links— introduce(s) the generation of Ideas (and concepts); for Lyotard, Kantian (regulative) Ideas. It is important to note that these Ideas are paraphrased by Lyotard as "Kantian Ideas." They supply the most familiar hooks or links, the most familiar ways of phrasing the schizzes of a new idiom. Why? Because "like all Kantian Ideas, it is simply a pushing to the limit, the maximization of a concept" (JG 46). The schizzes of the postmodern, that is, the ways—the ideas, the concepts, or the images—used to identify the postmodern as such, whether presented in terms of the *différend* or the pagan, cannot be demonstrated nor derived; they cannot be articulated nor deduced.

> It is simply the idea [of a society], that is, ultimately, of a set of diverse pragmatics (a set that is neither totalizable nor countable, actually). . . . They cannot be synthesized into a unifying metadiscourse. (JG 58; compare DIF para. 177–79)

> Ideas are not operators or categories, but horizons of thought.[15]

The ideas and "concepts" (for lack of a different idiom) that Lyotard puts to work in his texts present "images" of themselves analogous to those images encountered in the cinema.[16] An image defines its own limits, marks out the boundaries of its field, of the objects it (re-)presents, and orients the background and foreground of comprehension. Comprehended in these terms, the "identity" of the postmodern *or* the *différend or* the pagan eludes apprehension; each is and will be fragmented—(the) schizo—because the issue is itself a self-dismantling process. According to Deleuze in *Cinema I: L'Image-Mouvement,* to recognize that concepts, images, or Ideas define their limits, one must acknowledge an "out-of-field [*le hors-champ*]" (CIN 15–16; 28). Here, the *out-of-field* is not a negation. Instead, it "refers to what is neither seen nor understood, but is nevertheless perfectly present" (CIN 16; 28). It refers to the unpresentable, that which cannot "fit" within the limits of a frame—that which "does not belong to the order of the visible" (CIN 17; 30). The *out-of-field* refers to that which has withdrawn into and has been dispersed across the structures of thought, action, and discourse.

In a rather cryptic and telegraphic fashion, one might say that the postmodern *and* the *différend and* the pagan—individually as phrases of one another, and assembled as links within a discursive chain that does not constitute a unified discourse or grand narrative—each presents and is its own model: a glimpse of its selve*s* given in and through its schizzes and determinations. In effect, this is to say there is no model for presentation. As such, fields of possibilities (for the presentations of the unpresentables) are fabricated through the concatenation of phrases. And yet, the postmodern, the *différend,* and the pagan do not anchor a foundation, a transcendental category, or a necessary principle. As a condition of knowledge and language, as a characteristic of that condition, as a strategy for acting within this condition or context, the postmodern, the *différend,* and the pagan, respectively, cannot be comprehended, if comprehended at all, as Derrida remarks in *La Carte Postale,* according to a Heideggerian *epoch* of Being where it would be submitted to a transcendental interrogation, a questioning that takes it "'beyond every genre.'"[17] Instead, the schizzes of and that identify the postmodern, the *différend,* the pagan, or . . . present a series of relays or switching points "to mark there is never anything but relays" (CP 191–92; 206) or "transit points" (compare JG 59).

Différend IV: Multiplying Schizzes . . . Double Binds

A picture cannot . . . place itself outside its representational form.[18]

We can foresee only what we ourselves construct.[19]

Nothing can be said about reality that does not presuppose it. (DIF para. 47)

The first two propositions, taken from Wittgenstein's *Tractatus Logico-Philosophicus,* are incorporated already into Lyotard's comment, into his attempt to present the postmodern condition of language, thought, and action—that is, the *différend* and the pagan. Nothing can be said about the modern, the "postmodern," the *différend,* the pagan, metanarratives, speculative philosophy, techno-science, art, and so on without presupposing that these "entities" can be talked about in this or that way. When apposing the postmodern to the modern, particularly in "Apostille aux récits" and in "Response to the Question: What Is the Postmodern?" Lyotard claims that, though the postmodern does not entail an abandonment or a forgetting of the modern (project), it does entail a destruction and "liquidation" of the modern domain.[20] But this happens from *within* the modern: the postmodern (condition) is "undoubtedly part of the modern" as its *différend* (PC 79).[21] In fact, according to Lyotard, the postmodern does not announce the end of the modern or the end of "history" as such.[22] Instead, it presents itself as the modern "in the nascent state," a state or condition that is "constant" (PC 79). The postmodern is the modern at that "unstable state and instant of language wherein something which must be able to be put into phrases cannot yet be."

If the postmodern is "undoubtedly part of the modern," indeed the modern in a constant nascent state of difference and deferral, then "undoubtedly" the idiom that presents the "postmodern condition" (or the *différend* or the pagan) as such is situated in the modern as well. Indeed. And this paradox does not escape Lyotard's attention. One cannot help but be caught in between idioms, "in the middle." Or as Lyotard states in *Just Gaming,* one cannot help being "modern," because to be modern is to be "in-between" the traditional and the "not yet" (JG 11). Here one always finds oneself having to create an audience (à la Nietzsche). Here, at the instant of the *différend,* one finds "substitutions in the pragmatic system of narration, permutations of the author with the narrator, of the narratee with the speaker and with the one who is spoken of in the narrative, and so on..." (JG 12). One might say, with Lyotard, Deleuze and Guattari, and Derrida, that one is always caught in a "double bind" (DIF para. 8 and AO 79–80).[23] One (again, the philosopher?) always finds them-selves schizzing between the Platonic-Socratic and the pagan-experimental, and the modern and the postmodern.

> The fact that I myself speak of this plurality does not imply that I am presenting myself as the occupant of a unitary vantage point upon the whole set of these games....(JG 51)

> We are always within opinion, and there is no possible discourse of truth on the situation. And there is no such discourse because one is

caught up in a story, and one cannot get out of this story to take up a metalinguistic position from which the whole could be dominated. We are always immanent to stories in the making, even when we are the ones telling the story to the other. (JG 43)

Moreover, and finally, Lyotard does not underestimate the degree to which metaphysical complicity is inescapable. In *Discours, Figure,* Lyotard declares that even though language is found and placed everywhere, and even though once there is a phrase there is another, this does not mean that one "breaks with metaphysics."[24] This is part and parcel of the agonistics of language, the *différend*, of what Lyotard takes to be one of the schizzes of language. Even though there is no model for making links, with each phrase, with each link made by rephrasing or recollecting the sense of one sentence in the presentation of another sentence, *there is* the presentation of a "universe" (DIF para. 111). Just as there are many forms of presentations (that is, a multiplicity of schizzes), there are many universes. And there can be no synthesis, no presentation of a totality. However, regardless of its form and its intent, a phrase (a sentence, a proposition) always entails, involves, and relays a "there is" (DIF para. 111–12). In this way the "unpresentable" is presented. Presentation always involves an ontological, a metaphysical, and an epistemological move or transmission—as Wittgenstein claims in the *Tractatus,* a presentation of "what is the case."

As such, a phrase (or a text, a narrative, a discourse, a pagan vision) is at once a point of convergence or condensation—where themes and issues are brought together—and a point of rupture—where boundaries are ignored and redrawn. The permutations are limited only by the pragmatics of context and desire. As an appeal to the etymology of "knowledge" ("science") would show, an appeal to more phrases and more stories, the permutations of the knowledge we report about our conditions is limited only by the stories we tell our selves about selves, about our desires, our needs, and our goals. *Skhizein,* meaning "to split" into many parts, and the root for "schizo" and "schism," is related to, perhaps as the appositive of, *scire,* meaning "to know." *Scire* and *skhizein* are derivatives of *skei* which means "to cut" or "to split." Knowledge, then, so-called, is the ability or skill to separate one thing from another, "to discern." It is the ability to discern differences. But in order to systematize, to pronounce order, to identify a condition, or even to recollect, one must produce different idioms. For Lyotard, *these phrases* are the only *givens.*

But these stories are just other stories waiting to be inserted into a practical domain so as to be validated. And yet, it seems that the condition of this validation will remain schizo. If, as William James declares in the lectures on *Pragmatism,* "the world is full of partial stories that run parallel to one another, beginning and ending at odd places," stories that mutually interlace and interfere (exclude one another) at certain points, then "we cannot unify them completely in our minds."[25] Universal knowledge, or a so-called objective standard or foundation, remains a fictive Idea— another presentation of schizzes...It remains another presentation that schizzes, another presentation that recalls the paganism of Peirce's "pragmaticism": "there is no distinction of meaning so fine as to consist in anything but a possible difference of practice."[26]

Notes

Chapter 1. Husserl's Concept of the World

1. Letter quoted in R. Hirsch, "Edmund Husserl und Hugo von Hofmannsthal. Eine Begegnung und ein Brief," in *Sprache und Politik: Festgabe für Dolf Sternberger,* ed. C. J. Friedrich (Heidelberg: Lambert Schneider Press, 1968), pp. 108–15.

2. For this early conception of world view see E. Husserl, "Philosophie als strenge Wissenschaft," first published in *Logos* 1 (1911): 289–341, esp. pp. 323–41; published in the collection, *Aufsätze und Vorträge (1911–1921),* ed. T. Nenon and H.-R. Sepp, Husserliana no. 25 (Dordrecht: Martinus Nijhoff, 1987), pp. 1–62, esp. pp. 41–62; English translation: "Philosophy as Rigorous Science," in Husserl, *Phenomenology and the Crisis of Philosophy,* trans. Q. Lauer (New York: Harper & Row, 1965), pp. 71–147, esp. pp. 122–47.

3. E. Husserl, *Ideen zu einer reinen Phänomenologie und phänomenologischen Philosophie. Erstes Buch: Allegemeine Einführung in die reine Phänomenologie,* ed. K. Schuhmann, Husserliana no. 3/1 (The Hague: Martinus Nijhoff, 1976), sect. 49. Subsequent references to this volume will be indicated in the text by "IdI," followed by section and page number. Compare the English translation: *Ideas Pertaining to a Pure Phenomenology and to a Phenomenological Philosophy. First Book: General Introduction to a Pure Phenomenology,* trans. F. Kersten (The Hague: Martinus Nijhoff, 1983).

4. E. Husserl, *Zur Phänomenologie der Intersubjektivität. Texte aus dem Nachlass. Dritter Teil: 1929–1935,* ed. I. Kern, Husserliana no. 15 (The Hague: Martinus Nijhoff, 1973), p. 621. This text comes from 1933. Subsequent references to this volume will be indicated in the text by "ZPh," followed by the page number; translations are my own.

5. E. Husserl, *Ideen zu einer reinen Phänomenologie und phänomenologischen Philosophie. Zweites Buch: Phänomenologische Untersuchungen zur Konstitution,* ed. M. Biemel, Husserliana no. 4 (The Hague: Martinus Nijhoff, 1952), sect. 48–64.

Subsequent references to this volume will be indicated in the text by "IdII," followed by section and page number; translations are my own.

6. E. Husserl, *Cartesianische Meditationen und Pariser Vorträge,* ed. S. Strasser, Husserliana no. 1 (The Hague: Martinus Nijhoff, 1950), sect. 45, p. 130; my translation. See as well ZPh 492.

7. Husserl, *Cartesianische Meditationen,* sect. 55; see also ZPh 133–70, 613–27.

8. M. Heidegger, *Sein und Zeit* (Tubingen: Max Niemeyer Verlag, 1977), p. 187; my translation. Compare English translation: *Being and Time,* trans. J. Macquarrie and E. Robinson (New York: Harper & Row, 1962), pp. 231–32. Subsequent references to *Sein und Zeit* will be indicated by "SZ" followed by page number; translations are my own. References to *Being and Time,* indicated by "BT," that follow a reference to SZ, are for comparison.

9. See the excellent article of J. F. Courtine, "L'idée de la phénomènologie et la problématique de la réduction," in *Phénomènologie et métaphysique* (Paris: Presses Universitaires de France, 1984), pp. 211–45; see esp. pp. 232–33.

10. For Heidegger's account of such a "shaping" of the world see especially M. Heidegger, *Die Grundbegriffe der Metaphysik. Welt—Endlichkeit—Einsamkeit,* vols. 29–30 of Heidegger, *Gesamtausgabe* (Frankfurt am Main: Vittorio Klostermann, 1983), pp. 397–532: "der Mensch ist weltbildend."

11. E. Husserl, *Phänomenologische Psychologie,* ed. W. Biemel, Husserliana no. 9 (The Hague: Martinus Nijhoff, 1962), pp. 274–75, 601. Heidegger summarizes their different approaches when he asks Husserl: "Does not a world in general belong to the essence of the pure ego?" (p. 274, n. l.).

12. E. Levinas, *De l'existence à l'existant* (Paris: Vrin, 1978), pp. 109–10. Compare English translation: *Existence and Existents,* trans. A. Lingis (The Hague: Martinus Nijhoff, 1978), pp. 65–66.

13. J. Patocka, *Le monde naturel comme problème philosophique* (The Hague: Martinus Nijhoff, 1973), p. 175. The next quote is from p. 176.

14. The pregivenness of the world therefore should not be confused with the pregivenness of the sensuous "hylé"; unlike the hylé which precedes constitution, the world is for Husserl always a constituted world.

Chapter 2. A Critique of Husserl's Notion of Crisis

1. Martin Heidegger, *Being and Time,* trans. J. Macquarrie and E. Robinson (New York: Harper & Row, 1962), p. 23.

2. Umberto Eco, "On the Crisis of the Crisis of Reason," in *Travels in Hyperreality* (New York: Harcourt Brace, 1986), p. 126.

3. Edmund Husserl, *The Crisis of European Sciences and Transcendental Phenomenology*, trans. D. Carr (Evanston: Northwestern Univ. Press, 1970), sect. 15.

4. Husserl-Archive manuscript A.IV.17.

5. Edmund Husserl, *Ideen zu einer reinen Phänomenologie und phänomenologischen Philosophie. Zweites Buch: Phänomenologische Untersuchungen zur Konstitution*, ed. M. Biemel, Husserliana no. 4 (The Hague: Martinus Nijhoff, 1952).

6. Edmund Husserl, *Formal and Transcendental Logic*, trans. D. Cairns (The Hague: Martinus Nijhoff, 1978). See especially the introduction.

7. Husserl-Archive manuscript B.II.23/8a.

8. Karl Schuhmann, *Husserl-Chronik: Denk- und Lebensweg Edmund Husserls*, Husserliana Dokumente vol. 1 (The Hague: Martinus Nijhoff, 1977), p. 7.

9. Edmund Husserl, *Philosophie der Arithmetik*, Husserliana no. 12 (The Hague: Martinus Nijhoff, 1970).

10. Robert Sokolowski, *The Formation of Husserl's Concept of Constitution*, Phaenomenologica no. 18 (The Hague: Martinus Nijhoff, 1970), p. 35.

11. Theodorus de Boer, *The Development of Husserl's Thought*, trans. T. Plantinga, Phaenomenologica no. 76 (The Hague: Martinus Nijhoff, 1978), p. 120.

12. Husserl, *Formal and Transcendental Logic*, pp. 86–87.

13. Edmund Husserl, "Philosophie als strenge Wissenschaft," in *Aufsätze und Vorträge (1911–1921)*, ed. T. Nenon and H.-R. Sepp, Husserliana no. 25 (Dordrecht: Martinus Nijhoff, 1987), p. 4: "Ich sage nicht, Philosophie sei eine unvollkommene Wissenschaft, ich sage schlechthin, sie sei noch keine Wissenschaft."

14. Herbert Spiegelberg, *The Phenomenological Movement*, Phaenomenologica no. 5/6 (The Hague: Martinus Nijhoff, 1982), pp. 74–75.

15. Edmund Husserl, *Vorlesungen über Ethik und Wertlehre (1908–1914)*, ed. Ulrich Melle, Husserliana no. 28 (Dordrecht: Kluwer Academic Pub., 1988), p. 62.

16. See *Vorlesungen über Ethik*, pp. 204–8. For an excellent discussion of Husserl's distinction between objectifying and non-objectifying acts, see an article by the editor of Husserliana no. 28, Ulrich Melle, "Objektivierende und nicht-objektivierende Akte," published in *Husserl-Ausgabe und Husserl-Forschung*, Phaenomenologica no. 115 (Dordrecht: Kluwer Academic Pub., 1989), pp. 35–49.

17. Husserl, "Philosophie als strenge Wissenschaft," p. 7.

18. Letter found under Husserl-Archive signature R. I. Bell, 13.XII 1922: "Ich bin zwar Millionär an Jahresgehalt—fast 1.5 millionen pro anno—herrlich! Aber

leider steht der Dollar auf ca. 8.300 Mark und so sind es knapp 160 Dollar, nach kaufwert in Lande kaum 300, also kaum 1/10 von meinem alten amtlichen Einkommen."

19. The articles written for *Kaizo* in 1922–24, along with unpublished manuscripts relating to this theme of *Erneuerung* (renewal), appear in Edmund Husserl, *Aufsätze und Vorträge (1922–1937)*, Husserliana no. 27 (Dordrecht: Kluwer Academic Pub., 1989).

20. Husserl, *Crisis*, p. 167.

21. Letter found under Husserl-Archive signature R. I. Ingarden, 19.III 1930: "modische Schwenkung zu einer Philos. der 'Existenz', Preisgabe der Philosophie als strenge Wissenschaft."

22. Martin Heidegger, *History of the Concept of Time: Prolegomena*, trans. T. Kisiel (Bloomington: Indiana Univ. Press, 1985), pp. 1–2.

23. Heidegger, *History*, p. 2.

24. Heidegger, *Being and Time*, pp. 20–30.

25. Husserl, *Crisis*, p. 6.

26. Heidegger, *History*, p. 3.

27. Martin Heidegger, *The Basic Problems of Phenomenology*, trans. A. Hofstadter (Bloomington: Indiana Univ. Press, 1982), sect. 3.

28. Martin Heidegger, *Die Grundbegriffe der Metaphysik: Welt—Endlichkeit —Einsamkeit*, vols. 29–30 of Heidegger, *Gesamtausgabe* (Frankfurt am Main: Vittorio Klostermann, 1983), sect. 18.

29. Martin Heidegger, *Introduction to Metaphysics*, trans. R. Manheim (New Haven, Conn.: Yale Univ. Press, 1959), p. 35.

30. Martin Heidegger, "Only a God Can Save Us," *Der Spiegel* interview (1966), in *Heidegger: The Man and the Thinker*, ed. T. Sheehan (Chicago: Precedent Pub., 1981), p. 64.

31. Heidegger, "Only a God," p. 56.

Chapter 3. The Myth of Absolute Consciousness

1. Aron Gurwitsch, *Marginal Consciousness*, ed. Lester Embree (Athens, Oh.: Ohio Univ. Press, 1985), chap. 1.

2. Edmund Husserl, *Zur Phänomenologie des inneren Zeitbewusstseins*, ed. Rudolf Boehm, Husserliana no. 10 (The Hague: Martinus Nijhoff, 1966), p. 73. Subsequent references to this volume will be indicated in the text by "ZPZ,"

followed by page or section number. Compare the English translation, *The Phenomenology of Internal Time Consciousness,* trans. James S. Churchill (Bloomington: Indiana Univ. Press, 1964), p. 98; translation altered. Subsequent references to this volume will be indicated in the text by "PhT," followed by page or section number. It should be noted that the Churchill translation of *The Phenomenology of Internal Time-Consciousness* is very unreliable. A new translation, which will include all of the texts in Husserliana no. 10, is being prepared by John Brough and is forthcoming from Kluwer Academic Publishers.

3. Thomas Seebohm, *Die Bedingungen der Möglichkeit der Transzendental-Philosophie* (Bonn: H. Bouvier und Co. Verlag, 1962). Subsequent references will be indicated by "BMT." John Brough, "The Emergence of an Absolute Consciousness in Husserl's Early Writings on Time-Consciousness," in *Husserl: Expositions and Appraisals,* ed. Frederick Elliston and Peter McCormick (Notre Dame, Ind.: Univ. of Notre Dame Press, 1977). Subsequent references will be indicated by "EAC." Robert Sokolowski, *Husserlian Meditations* (Evanston, Ill.: Northwestern Univ. Press, 1974), chap. 6. Subsequent references will be indicated by "HM."

4. John Brough has emphasized that the account of absolute consciousness is "primarily and unambiguously a theory of the *experiencing* of immanent temporal objects" (EAC 92). He is certainly right in this, but already the manner in which he (following Husserl) brings together the concepts of "experiencing" *(erleben* or living through) and "immanent temporal *objects"* indicates that the model for *erleben* will be perceptual consciousness. This will turn out to be of great importance.

5. Edmund Husserl, *Logische Untersuchungen,* vol. II.1 (Tubingen: Max Niemeyer Verlag, 1968), p. 532. Subsequent references will be indicated by "LU." Compare the English translation: *Logical Investigations,* vol. 2, trans. J. N. Findlay (New York: Humanities Press, 1970), p. 540; translation altered. Subsequent references will be indicated by "LI." The Findlay translation reads "between the experience or conscious content," an error taken over by Sokolowski (HM 128).

6. ZPZ 127/PhT 177, translation modified; my emphasis. On this, see HM 132. Sokolowski dates this text as "written after 1911."

7. See BMT 112–13, 125n, which refers to the Husserl manuscript C 15, page 6 (undated).

8. See BMT 112–13. Seebohm seems to be misreading the text he refers to (ZPZ 25/PhT 45). Husserl distinguished between describing "the *manner* in which the immanent-temporal object 'appears' in a continual flow" (my emphasis) and describing "the appearing temporal duration itself." The phenomenology of time consciousness concerns the former. But Seebohm's point can be restated in these terms.

9. Compare Jean-Paul Sartre, *Being and Nothingness,* trans. Hazel Barnes (New York: Washington Square Press, 1966), p. 20; Aron Gurwitsch, *The Field of Consciousness* (Pittsburgh: Duquesne Univ. Press, 1964), pp. 265–72.

10. See Rudolf Bernet's introduction, "Einleitung," to Edmund Husserl, *Texte zur Phänomenologie des inneren Zeitbewusstseins (1893–1917)*, ed. Rudolf Bernet (Hamburg: Felix Meiner, 1985), p. xxxv.

11. This analysis has been taken to be definitive: "Since the former impressional consciousness is kept alive as a primary memory, the phase correlative to it is also kept around in the present, but in a new profile, in a new mode of temporal orientation, as just past" (HM 153). Peter McInerney has recently claimed that this is Husserl's general account of retention, in "What Is Still Valuable in Husserl's Analyses of Inner Time-Consciousness?" *Journal of Philosophy* 85, no. 11 (November 1988): 613. Husserl does suggest it, but not consistently. It is contradicted by, for example, ZPZ 371.

12. There would be at least two alternative accounts of the retention of a transcendent time phase if we allow that there is a retentional phase to the perceptual act itself.

13. This sentence is part of a manuscript that seems to present Husserl's actual discovery of the non-temporal status of absolute consciousness (see Sokolowski, HM 133). In it things have not yet been sorted out clearly, since remembering and perceiving do not belong on the level of absolute consciousness; on Husserl's considered account they are rather constituted by absolute consciousness.

14. Although this might seem to confirm Derrida's deconstruction in *La Voix et le Phénomène* (Paris: Presses Universitaires de France, 1967); references indicated by "VPh"—compare the English translation, *Speech and Phenomena*, trans. David Allison (Evanston, Ill.: Northwestern Univ. Press, 1973); references indicated by "SPh"—the appearance is misleading. Derrida's account depends on his interpretation of Husserl's claim that "the acts in question are themselves experienced [*erlebt*] by us at that very moment [*Augenblick*]" (LU II.1, 37/LI 1, 280). Several comments are in order here: (i) Derrida interprets *"Augenblick"* to mean "instant" in the sense of a very strict punctuality, but he offers no justification for this reading. The fact that Husserl read William James's *The Principles of Psychology* in 1891–92 and 1894 and had thus encountered the idea that the present is, as James put it, "a saddle-back, with a certain breadth of its own" (quoted in Bernet, "Einleitung," xxii), makes that reading anything but automatic. (ii) Derrida exploits the metaphor of the *"Augenblick"* by reading it as the "blink of an eye [*clin d'oeil*]" (VPh 66/SPh 58), although the word would suggest rather something like the "glance of an eye." This would easily lead into an analysis of *erleben* in terms of a perceptual model—which is just what Husserl tends to do. But if one does not assume a punctual interpretation of the "moment," it might also give us reason to view the "blind spot" as the condition of the duration of the glance (as opposed to the blink) and thus of the opening of the eye of consciousness, not its closing (see VPh 73/SPh 65). In this connection, note the effect of including the functioning of protention (which I shall discuss shortly) in the analysis. I shall investigate Derrida's deconstruction in a book entitled *Strategies of Deconstruction*.

15. This would provide partial confirmation of Alfred Schutz's claim that reflection is always post facto. But it does not mean that reflection on conscious life

presupposes "an expired, an *entwordenes,* finished, in short a past experience"; *Der sinnhafte Aufbau der sozialen Welt* (Vienna: Springer Verlag, [1932] 1960), p. 49. In addition, if Husserl's analysis of the phenomenon of double intentionality is correct, Schutz is wrong in claiming that a meaningful experience as such is always a finished object of subsequent reflection. A Husserlian analysis contradicts the Bergsonian presuppositions of this principle; the flow of experience as marginally constituted prior to all reflection *is* meaningful.

16. Rudolf Boehm, "Bewusstsein als Gegenwart des Vergangenen," *Monist* 59 (1975-76): 24.

17. Bernet, "Einleitung," lii. If I understand him correctly, Bernet argues that the same is true of the transition from one phase of the temporal object to another (lii), which does not seem to be correct. However, other remarks seem to go in a different direction (see liii).

18. Emmanuel Levinas, "Intentionalité et sensation," *En découvrant l'existence avec Husserl et Heidegger* (Paris: Libraire Philosophique J. Vrin, 1982), p. 155. Subsequent references to this text will be indicated by "DHH."

19. See Ludwig Landgrebe, "Das Problem der Teleologie und der Leiblichkeit in Phänomenologie und Marxismus," in *Phänomenologie und Marxismus,* vol. 1, ed. Bernhard Waldenfels, Jan M. Broekman, and Ante Pazanin (Frankfurt: Suhrkamp, 1977), p. 96; compare the English translation, "The Problem of Teleology and Corporeality in Phenomenology and Marxism," *Phenomenology and Marxism,* ed. Waldenfels, et al., trans. J. Claude Evans (London: Routledge & Kegan Paul, 1984), p. 74. There are two errors here, one in the English translation and one in Landgrebe's original text. *Triebintentionalität* is translated as "instinctive intentionality" and the Husserl text that Landgrebe quotes as *"des ichlosen Strebens* [egoless striving]" reads *"des ichlosen Strömens* [egoless flowing]."

20. Edmund Husserl, *Zur Phänomenologie der Intersubjektivität,* part 3, ed. Iso Kern (The Hague: Martinus Nijhoff, 1973), p. 595; my emphasis. Subsequent references to this text will be indicated by "ZPI."

21. It may well also have implications for the understanding of memory: memory is most originally the recollection of what we have *done,* where this would include the activity of seeing things. The first time my niece, Rachel Lee Evans, clearly talked about a past event, it concerned "going down to see the peacocks" during a visit to her grandmother. This recollected field of action, charged with anticipation and hesitation, cannot be analyzed in terms of a clear-cut inner (her perceiving of the peacocks) vs. outer (the peacocks taken simply as things seen).

22. Edmund Husserl, *Ideen zu einer reinen Phänomenologie und phänomenologischen Philosophie,* Book Two, ed. Marly Biemel (The Hague: Martinus Nijhoff, 1952), sect. 36.

23. See, for example, Edmund Husserl, *Phänomenologische Psychologie,* ed. Walter Biemel (The Hague: Martinus Nijhoff, 1968), pp. 292-95.

24. Edmund Husserl, *Der Krisis der europäischen Wissenschaften und die transzendentale Phänomenologie,* ed. Walter Biemel (The Hague: Martinus Nijhoff, 1962), p. 82; subsequently referred to as "Kr." Compare the English translation, *The Crisis of European Sciences and Transcendental Phenomenology,* trans. D. Carr (Evanston, Ill.: Northwestern Univ. Press, 1970), p. 178; subsequently referred to as "Cr."

25. Letter to Alfred Schutz, November 30, 1954. See Alfred Schutz and Aron Gurwitsch, *Briefwechsel 1939–1959,* ed. Richard Grathoff (Munich: Wilhelm Fink Verlag, 1985), p. 369; compare the English translation, *Philosophers in Exile: Alfred Schutz and Aron Gurwitsch—Correspondence 1939–1959,* trans. J. Claude Evans (Bloomington: Indiana Univ. Press, 1989).

26. The author thanks Herbert Spiegelberg and Jill Petzall for helpful comments on an earlier draft of this essay and P. Holley Roberts for excellent editing.

Chapter 4. Husserl's Complex Concept of the Self and the Possibility of Social Criticism

My thanks to Rick Scott and Charles Pinches for helpful comments on an earlier version of this paper, and to the University of Central Arkansas for a research grant that aided in its production.

1. Michael Sandel, *Liberalism and the Limits of Justice* (Cambridge; New York: Cambridge Univ. Press, 1982), p. 11.

2. George Herbert Mead, *Mind, Self, and Society* (Chicago: Univ. of Chicago Press, 1934). Thomas Nagel, *The View from Nowhere* (Oxford: Oxford Univ. Press, 1986). Michel Foucault, *The Order of Things: An Archaeology of the Human Sciences* (New York: Vintage Books, 1973).

3. Here I borrow freely from Michael Sandel's argument on pp. 20–21 of *Liberalism and the Limits of Justice.* I then use the argument to deal with a slightly different issue than he does, namely, the issue of *the conditions for the possibility* of social criticism.

4. See, e.g., Paul Natorp, *Einleitung in die Psychologie nach kritischer Methode* (Freiburg, 1888) sect. 4, pp. 11–12; quoted in part by Husserl in *Logical Investigations,* trans. J. N. Findlay (London: Routledge & Kegan Paul, 1977), pp. 548–49. Also see Edmund Husserl, *Ideas Pertaining to a Pure Phenomenology and to a Phenomenological Philosophy,* trans. Fred Kersten (The Hague: Martinus Nijhoff, 1982), pp. 132–33, 190–92.

5. Michael Walzer, *Interpretation and Social Criticism* (Cambridge, Mass.: Harvard Univ. Press, 1987), p. 39. Subsequent references to this work will be indicated in the text by "ISC" followed by page number.

6. Habermas's initial criticism of Gadamer's hermeneutic position can be found in *Zur Logik der Sozialwissenschaften* (Tubingen: J.C.B. Mohr, 1967), pp. 149–80; compare English translation: *On the Logic of the Social Sciences,* trans. S. W. Nicholsen and J. Stark (Cambridge, Mass.: MIT Press, 1988). Gadamer's response, "Rhetorik, Hermeneutik und Ideologiekritik," has been translated by Richard Palmer as "The Scope and Function of Hermeneutical Reflection," in *Philosophical Hermeneutics,* ed. David E. Linge (Berkeley: Univ. of California Press, 1976), pp. 18–43. Habermas responds to Gadamer in "The Hermeneutic Claim to Universality," in *Contemporary Hermeneutics: Hermeneutics as Method, Philosophy and Critique,* ed. and trans. Josef Bleicher (London: Routledge & Kegan Paul, 1980), pp. 181–211.

7. Jean-Francois Lyotard, *The Postmodern Condition: A Report on Knowledge,* trans. Geoff Bennington and Brian Massumi (Minneapolis: Univ. of Minnesota Press, 1984). Richard Rorty, "Postmodernist Bourgeois Liberalism," *Journal of Philosophy* 80 (1983): 583–89; "Habermas and Lyotard on Postmodernity," *Praxis International* 4, no. 1 (April 1984): 32–44; "Solidarity or Objectivity?" in *Post-Analytic Philosophy,* ed. John Rajchman and Cornel West (New York: Columbia Univ. Press, 1985), pp. 3–19; *Contingency, Irony, and Solidarity* (Cambridge; New York: Cambridge Univ. Press, 1989), esp. part I.

8. In the more strictly Anglo-American context of this debate, what Rorty and Lyotard have been to Habermas, so Michael Walzer has been to Thomas Nagel. Although in each case the first half of the pairing (Rorty and Lyotard, Walzer) acknowledges the actuality of social criticism, each also denies their interlocutor's claim to a privileged perspective, a world-purified "view from nowhere" that makes such criticism possible.

9. Rorty, "Postmodernist Bourgeois Liberalism," p. 214.

10. Husserl, *Logical Investigations,* pp. 541, 551.

11. Husserl, *Cartesian Meditations,* trans. Dorion Cairns (The Hague: Martinus Nijhoff, 1977), pp. 65–67.

Chapter 5. Crisis and Life-World in Husserl and Habermas

1. This is evident even in the English translation of the title of the second volume, *Lifeworld and System: A Critique of Functionalist Reason,* trans. Thomas McCarthy (Boston: Beacon Press, 1987). The notion of the life-world has, however, always been implicit in Habermas's model of interpretive social science—see, in particular, *Zur Logik der Sozialwissenschaften* (Tubingen: J. C. B. Mohr, 1967); English translation, *On the Logic of the Social Sciences,* trans. Shierry Weber Nicholsen and Jerry A. Stark (Cambridge, Mass.: MIT Press, 1988). Although earlier he preferred to speak of the "institutional framework of society," this notion is functionally equivalent to that of the sociocultural life-world in his later writings; compare "Technology and Society as 'Ideology'," in *Toward a Rational Society,*

trans. Jeremy Shapiro (Boston: Beacon Press, 1970), pp. 81–122, especially p. 94. Further references to *The Theory of Communicative Action,* vols. 1 and 2, will be abbreviated as TCA 1 or 2.

2. "The object domain of the social sciences encompasses everything that falls under the description 'element of a lifeworld.' What this expression means can be clarified intuitively by reference to those symbolic objects that we produce in speaking and acting, beginning with immediate expressions (such as speech acts, purposive activities, and cooperative actions), through the sedimentations of these expressions (such as texts, traditions, documents, works of art, theories, objects of material culture, goods, techniques and so on), to the indirectly generated configurations that are self-stabilizing and susceptible of organization (such as institutions, social systems, and personality structures)" (TCA 1: 108).

3. *The Crisis of European Sciences and Transcendental Phenomenology,* trans. David Carr (Evanston, Ill: Northwestern Univ. Press, 1970), p. 299; italics in the original. Hereafter abbreviated as CES.

4. Max Weber, *The Protestant Ethic and the Spirit of Capitalism,* trans. Talcott Parsons (New York: Scribner's, 1958), p. 181; see TCA 1: 143–271.

5. For a discussion of the various aspects of this theoretical crisis, see the essays collected in *Lebenswelt und Wissenschaft in der Philosophie Edmund Husserls,* ed. Elisabeth Stroeker (Frankfurt: Klostermann, 1979). In speaking of a "theoretical crisis," I do not mean to suggest that this is a separate crisis, but rather a more specific manifestation of the same general crisis of reason.

6. See Maurice Natanson, "Phenomenology and the Social Sciences," in *Phenomenology and the Social Sciences,* ed. M. Natanson (Evanston, Ill.: Northwestern Univ. Press, 1973), p. 26; compare also CES 152.

7. Husserl discusses the distinction between the natural and humanistic (or social) sciences in "The Attitude of Natural Science and the Attitude of Humanistic Science" (Appendix 3 to CES, pp. 315–34). It seems to me that, like Alfred Schutz after him, Husserl wants to claim that, via an act of "pure" theoretical abstraction from the interests of everyday life, the social sciences can attain a type of universality and objectivity analogous to that of the natural sciences; see CES 323.

8. Merleau-Ponty, "The Philosopher and Sociology" in *Signs,* trans. Richard C. McCleary (Evanston, Ill.: Northwestern Univ. Press, 1964), p. 110; the notion of "reciprocal envelopment" is discussed on p. 102.

9. See A. Schutz, "The Problem of Transcendental Intersubjectivity in Husserl," in Schutz, *Studies in Phenomenological Philosophy,* vol. 3 of *Collected Papers* (The Hague: Martinus Nijhoff, 1962–66), p. 83; *Collected Papers* hereafter abbreviated as CP; and Natanson, "Phenomenology and the Social Sciences," p. 28.

10. Schutz, "Phenomenology and the Foundations of the Social Sciences," CP 3: 47–48; and "Phenomenology and the Social Sciences," in CP 1, *The Problem of Social Reality,* pp. 122–25.

11. Schutz, "Concept and Theory Formation in the Social Sciences," CP 1: 62.

12. By *preestablished harmony* I wish to describe the same position expressed by Natanson: "If phenomenology moves in a different philosophical direction from empiricism, it does not challenge the legitimacy of empirical work in the sciences. It would be a disastrous misinterpretation of Husserl to think that he sought to replace empirical science with phenomenological science. No such replacement is conceivable because phenomenology and empirical science operate at qualitatively different levels. They relate to but do not contradict each other" (Natanson, "Phenomenology and the Social Sciences," p. 34).

13. See Habermas, "Philosophy as Stand-in and Interpreter," in *After Philosophy: End or Transformation?* ed. Kenneth Baynes, James Bohman, and Thomas McCarthy (Cambridge, Mass.: MIT Press, 1987), pp. 296–315. This strategy must, however, be conceived at a quite formal and procedural level, which thus distances it from Merleau-Ponty's notion of reciprocal envelopment.

14. These two different meanings are discussed by Ulrich Claesges, "Zweideutigkeiten in Husserls Lebenswelt-begriff," in *Perspektiven transzendentalphaenomenologischer Forschung,* ed. Ulrich Claesges and Klaus Held (The Hague: Martinus Nijhoff, 1972), pp. 85–101; and by Ludwig Landgrebe, "Life-World and the Historicity of Human Existence," in *Phenomenology and Marxism,* ed. B. Waldenfels, J. Broekman, and A. Pazanin, trans. J. Claude Evans (London: Routledge & Kegan Paul, 1984), pp. 167–204.

15. CES 147. For a discussion of the ambiguities in Husserl's concept of the life-world, see David Carr, *Phenomenology and the Problem of History* (Evanston, Ill.: Northwestern Univ. Press, 1974), esp. chap. 8.

16. CES 142, 173; see also David Carr's discussion, *Phenomenology and the Problem of History,* esp. p. 171; and Ludwig Landgrebe, "Regions of Being and Regional Ontologies," in *The Phenomenology of Edmund Husserl,* ed. Donn Welton (Ithaca, N.Y.: Cornell Univ. Press, 1981), p. 152.

17. See L. Landgrebe, "Life-World and the Historicity of Human Existence," pp. 194–97.

18. See Habermas, *On the Logic of the Social Sciences,* pp. 112–13.

19. For a discussion of some of these criticisms of Husserl's return from the life-world to transcendental philosophy, see Bernhard Waldenfels, *In den Netzen der Lebenswelt* (Frankfurt: Suhrkamp, 1985), esp. chaps. 1 and 2.

20. See Schutz, *The Phenomenology of the Social World,* trans. George Walsh and Frederick Lehnert (Evanston, Ill.: Northwestern Univ. Press, 1967) and, with Thomas Luckmann, *The Structures of the Life-World,* trans. Richard Zaner and H. Tristram Engelhardt, Jr. (Evanston, Ill.: Northwestern Univ. Press, 1973).

21. "The descriptive phenomenology of the *Lebenswelt* is ultimately based on the phenomenological method of radical reduction and attention to the experience of intentional acts in originary evidence. It is thus philosophically legitimated by a

critically reflexive account of the knowledge of experience. In other words, the descriptive phenomenology of the natural attitude in everyday life has its methodological foundation in phenomenology as a transcendental critique of knowledge." Thomas Luckmann, "Philosophy, Science and Everyday Life," in *Phenomenology and the Social Sciences,* ed. M. Natanson, pp. 179–80.

22. Fred Dallmayr has developed this criticism in "Genesis and Validation of Social Knowledge: Lessons from Merleau-Ponty," in *Phenomenology and the Social Sciences: A Dialogue,* ed. Joseph Bien (The Hague: Martinus Nijhoff, 1978), pp. 74–106, esp. pp. 89–90; see also the critical remarks of Ronald Cox, *Schutz's Theory of Relevance: A Phenomenological Critique* (The Hague: Martinus Nijhoff, 1978), pp. 218–28.

23. This criticism is developed by John Heritage in *Garfinkel and Ethnomethodology* (New York: Polity Press, 1984), pp. 61–66; compare Schutz's remarks on the "postulate of rationality," CP 2, *Studies in Social Theory,* pp. 86–87.

24. TCA 1: 82. Habermas suggests that the aspect of the life-world as a resource is emphasized by the phenomenological approach of Husserl and Schutz, whereas the aspect of the life-world as that about which we negotiate is emphasized in ethnomethodological approaches; see his "Remarks on the Concept of Communicative Action," in *Social Action,* ed. G. Seebass and R. Tuomela (Boston: Reidel, 1985), p. 160. For a critical discussion of this dual aspect of the life-world in Habermas, see Ulf Matthiesen, *Das Dickicht der Lebenswelt und die Theorie des kommunikativen Handelns* (Munich: Fink, 1983).

25. Habermas, "Remarks," p. 167; also TCA 2: 135.

26. Habermas, *The Philosophical Discourse of Modernity,* trans. Frederick Lawrence (Cambridge, Mass.: MIT Press, 1987), p. 343; hereafter abbreviated as PDM.

27. PDM 343; this set of differentiations is obviously also intended to parallel Talcott Parson's distinction among the three general social systems of action.

28. For example, the differentiation of society and culture means that the institutional system is less dependent on world views; the differentiation of society and personality means an extension of the scope of contingency for interpersonal relations; and the differentiation of culture from personality means that the renewal of tradition depends more and more on the individual readiness to criticize and ability to innovate (see TCA 2: 145).

29. Habermas's argument is, in this respect, similar to the sort of transcendental argument that Donald Davidson makes in "On the Very Idea of a Conceptual Scheme," in *Inquiries into Truth and Interpretation* (Oxford: Clarendon Press, 1984), pp. 183–98. The speech and action of others will simply be unintelligible to us unless we attribute to them the same rationality assumptions that we employ. For a further comparison of the interpretive method in Habermas and Davidson, see my "Rational Reconstruction and Social Criticism: Habermas's Model of Interpretive Social Science," *Philosophical Forum* 21 (Fall–Winter 1989–90): 122–45.

30. For some of these criticisms, see Axel Honneth, *Kritik der Macht* (Frankfurt am Main: Suhrkamp, 1985), pp. 328–34; Thomas McCarthy, "Complexity and Democracy, or the Seducements of Systems Theory," *New German Critique* 35 (1986): 27–53; and Nancy Fraser, "How Critical Is Critical Theory? The Case of Habermas and Gender," *New German Critique* 35 (1986): 97–131. Despite these objections, I believe that Habermas must retain some form of a functionalist or systems-theoretic approach to society if anything like Marx's analysis of the reifying effects of capitalist production and the bureaucratic state is to be maintained; see my "Rational Reconstruction and Social Criticism: Habermas's Model of Interpretive Social Science."

Chapter 6. Feminist Politics and Foucault: The Limits to a Collaboration

1. I would like to thank the following people for their helpful comments on this paper as well as for their encouragement: Richard Schmitt, Sandra Bartky, Nancy Fraser, Seyla Benhabib, and Kelly Oliver.

2. See, for example, Sandra Bartky, "Foucault, Femininity, and the Modernization of Patriarchal Power," in *Feminism and Foucault,* ed. Irene Diamond and Lee Quinby (Boston: Northeastern Univ. Press, 1988), pp. 61–86; Susan Bordo, "Anorexia Nervosa: Psychopathology as the Crystallization of Culture," *Philosophical Forum* 17, no. 2 (Winter 1985): 73–104; *Female Sexualization,* ed. Frigga Haug, trans. Erica Carter (London: Verso, 1987).

3. See, for example, Jana Sawicki, "Foucault and Feminism: Toward a Politics of Difference," *Hypatia* 1, no. 2 (1986): 23–36; and "Identity Politics and Sexual Freedom," in *Feminism and Foucault,* pp. 177–92; Irene Diamond and Lee Quinby, "Introduction," and "American Feminism and the Language of Control," in *Feminism and Foucault,* pp. ix–xx and 193–206; and Chris Weedon, *Feminist Practice and Post-Structuralist Theory* (New York: Basil Blackwell, 1987).

4. For examples of these lines of criticism, see Nancy Fraser, "Michel Foucault: A 'Young Conservative'?" *Ethics* 96 (October 1985): 165–84, and "Foucault on Modern Power: Empirical Insights and Normative Confusions," *Praxis International* 1 (October 1981): 272–87. See also Richard Rorty, "Foucault and Epistemology"; Michael Walzer, "The Politics of Michel Foucault"; Charles Taylor, "Foucault on Freedom and Truth"; and Jurgen Habermas, "Taking Aim at the Heart of the Present"—all included in *Foucault: A Critical Reader,* ed. David Hoy (New York: Basil Blackwell, 1986).

5. Michel Foucault, "Two Lectures," in *Power/Knowledge: Selected Interviews and Other Writings, 1972-1977,* ed. Colin Gordon, trans. Colin Gordon et al. (New York: Pantheon, 1980), pp. 97, 98; the collection is hereafter cited as P/K.

6. See Michel Foucault, "The Subject and Power," in Hubert L. Dreyfus and Paul Rabinow, *Michel Foucault: Beyond Structuralism and Hermeneutics,* 2d ed.

(Chicago: Univ. of Chicago Press, 1983), p. 208; also see Colin Gordon, "Afterword," in P/K, p. 239; and Peter Dews, "Power and Subjectivity in Foucault," *New Left Review* no. 144 (March–April 1984): 72–95.

7. Foucault, "The Subject and Power," p. 212.

8. Foucault, "The Subject and Power," p. 216.

9. This may seem an odd question to ask. After all, if Foucault's claims are empirically valid, the question of their political ineffectivity is moot. In the absence of decisive means to establish empirical validity, however, the use of political criteria to evaluate philosophical claims is not inappropriate. And it is arguable that in the case of philosophical claims, decisive empirical validation is always lacking. In this case philosophy may be understood as a discipline in which theory choice is constrained by plausibility, explanatory value, and positive political effects.

10. See, for example, Weedon, *Feminist Practice and Post-Structuralist Theory;* Sawicki, "Foucault and Feminism: Toward a Politics of Difference"; and Diamond and Quinby, "American Feminism and the Language of Control."

11. Weedon, *Feminist Practice,* p. 125.

12. Nor is it clear whether Foucault's own very late pronouncements toward this end can be made consonant with the political ontology he constructs in his major texts. For example, in an interview in 1984 Foucault expresses a conception of the subject that sounds almost word for word like Weedon's; see *The Final Foucault,* ed. James Bernauer and David Rasmussen (Cambridge, Mass.: MIT Press, 1988), p. 11. But of course, on Foucault's own advice we cannot give privilege to such "final texts" as being the authority on Foucault's "real" views. Nor can we privilege Foucault's own pronouncements that his account of subjectivity is consistent with some degree or type of agency. The issue here is not over Foucault's own beliefs or political commitments but over whether the political ontology to be found in his major texts theorizes subjectivity persuasively or adequately, and whether it allows for any significant degree of agency. However, it does seem to be the case that in his later works Foucault moved away from the one-sided analysis of subjectivity characteristic of his work in the 1960s and 1970s. Perhaps, if he had lived, his next works would have developed theoretically the declaration he made shortly before his death that we need new forms of subjectivity.

13. He says we are bodies "totally imprinted by history"; "Nietzsche, Genealogy, History," in *Language, Counter-Memory, Practice,* ed. Donald Bouchard (Ithaca, N.Y.: Cornell Univ. Press, 1977), p. 148.

14. Foucault, *Discipline and Punish,* trans. Alan Sheridan (New York: Random House, 1979), p. 28.

15. See for example, Foucault, "Two Lectures," P/K 81–82.

16. On this point see Stephen David Ross, "Foucault's Radical Politics," *Praxis International* 5 (2 July 1985): 135; Dews, "Power and Subjectivity in Foucault," p.

79; and Haug, *Female Sexualization,* p. 196. The sense of "oppressor" and "oppressed" I wish to invoke here and throughout this paper is the sense in which differential amounts of responsibility and blameworthiness can be assigned throughout the population. And as I shall argue, differential categories of responsibility require differential access to power.

17. Foucault, "The Eye of Power," P/K 156, emphasis added; see also "Power and Strategies," P/K 142.

18. Foucault, "Introduction" to *Herculin Barbarin: Being the recently discovered memoirs of a nineteenth-century French hermaphrodite,* trans. Richard McDougal (New York: Pantheon Press, 1980), p. 208; quoted in Sawicki, "Foucault and Feminism," p. 30. This sounds disturbingly like Hobbes!

19. Foucault, "History of Systems of Thought," in *Language, Counter-Memory, Practice,* pp. 200-210.

20. See Haug, *Female Sexualization,* especially chap. 1.

21. Haug, *Female Sexualization,* p. 59.

22. Bell hooks, "Critical Integration, Talking Race, Resisting Racism," Toni Morrison Lecture, Cornell University, April 23, 1989.

23. The point of contention here is not whether in some extradiscursive reality we "really are" subjects. Foucault and I would agree on this point: of course, we all think and speak as if we are subjects and therefore in an important sense we are subjects. The disagreement is over whether we should resist the discourse of subjectivity.

24. The macro-historical thesis of Hegel contradicts this to the extent that the individual's view does not represent truth, but it is still the case that the full development of subjectivity on Hegel's account involves achieving a recognition by others of one's own values and self-understanding.

25. Adorno and Horkheimer asked the same questions but answered them with a dialectical account of subjectivity. See their *Dialectic of Enlightenment,* trans. John Cumming (New York: Continuum, 1987), and Adorno's "Subject and Object," in *The Essential Frankfurt School Reader,* ed. Andrew Arato and Eike Gebhardt (New York: Continuum, 1982). Peter Dews contrasts Adorno's and Horkheimer's approaches with Foucault's in his *Logics of Disintegration* (New York: Verso, 1987), esp. pp. 150-61.

26. See, for example, Teresa de Lauretis, "Feminist Studies/Critical Studies: Issues, Terms and Contexts," in her edited anthology, *Feminist Studies/Critical Studies* (Bloomington: Indiana Univ. Press, 1986), pp. 1-19; see also Biddy Martin and Chandra Talpade Mohanty, "Feminist Politics: What's Home Got to Do with It?" same volume, pp. 191-212; and my "Cultural Feminism versus Post-Structuralism: The Identity Crisis in Feminist Theory," *SIGNS* 13 (Spring 88): 405-36.

27. Many feminist social scientists have rejected the discourse of expertise and instrumentality without having to jettison the concept of the subject. See Dorothy Smith, *The Everyday World as Problematic* (Boston: Northeastern Univ. Press, 1987); Renate Duelli Klein, "How to Do What We Want to Do: Thoughts about Feminist Methodology," in *Theories of Women's Studies,* ed. Gloria Bowles and R. Duelli Klein (London: Routledge & Kegan Paul, 1983), pp. 88–104; and Maria Mies, "Towards a Methodology for Feminist Research," same volume, pp. 117–39.

28. Another major problem with humanism and concepts of the subject based on humanism involves essentialism and false universalism: posing a generic human with some essential characteristics as representing all humanity. There is no such generic human or essential humanity, and we may want to reject the tradition of humanism to avoid its resultant erasure and denial of difference. But, again, this does not require a rejection of subjectivity: subjectivity need not entail essentialism. See note 26.

29. Foucault, "The Subject and Power," p. 221.

30. Diamond and Quinby, "American Feminism and the Language of Control," p. 195.

31. See Fraser, "Foucault on Modern Power: Empirical Insights and Normative Confusions," and Ross, "Foucault's Radical Politics." Also see Foucault's conversation with Gilles Deleuze published as "Intellectuals and Power," in *Language, Counter-Memory, Practice,* pp. 205–17.

32. Foucault asserts in one of his last interviews that patterns of domination can persist in perpetual asymmetry, and he uses the relations between men and women as an example of this. This is an important acknowledgment on his part, never made in his major writings. However, his account of power relations cannot explain the persistence of such asymmetry: it cannot be characterized as a structural hierarchy or as an institution of male supremacy because power cannot be "possessed" and so cannot be possessed exclusively or primarily by anyone. Therefore it is difficult to see how Foucault's account of power could make any sense of a perpetual asymmetrical pattern of domination; only chance could explain it, like a game of dice in which one person mysteriously always wins. Many feminists understandably are inclined to say more than this about the domination of women. See *The Final Foucault,* ed. Bernauer and Rasmussen, p. 12.

33. See Foucault, "Power and Strategies," P/K 142. Also see "The Subject and Power," pp. 222–24; and *Discipline and Punish,* pp. 26–27.

34. Foucault, "Intellectuals and Power," p. 216.

Chapter 7. Derrida and Habermas on the Subject of Political Philosophy

1. Jurgen Habermas, *The Philosophical Discourse of Modernity,* trans. Frederick Lawrence (Cambridge, Mass.: MIT Press, 1987); hereafter cited as "PDM."

2. To chart Habermas's career is to follow the course of a series of academic "conflicts." This is not an inconsequential observation, suggesting as it does a certain style of writing, a direction of reading, and continuity with a long and venerable tradition in German academics. To play out this theme of argumentation, of adversarial posturing, of the centrality of strife and (the) war in Habermas's thought would require an essay in a style I have purposely rejected here, for the sake of producing something that Habermas perhaps would accept as an argument. Suffice it to say that the issue abbreviated in this note would be *the* issue, if one were to pursue the (post)modernity debate from what Habermas's style determines to be the "other" side (of the Rhine).

3. Habermas reads Lukacs, and then Horkheimer and Adorno, as a development of Weber's account of rationality. See Jurgen Habermas, *The Theory of Communicative Action,* trans. Thomas McCarthy, 2 vols. (Boston: Beacon Press, 1984), 1: 345–46; hereafter cited as "TCA" followed by volume and page numbers.

4. See also "Life-forms, Morality, and the Task of the Philosopher," an interview with Perry Anderson and Peter Dews, in *Habermas: Autonomy and Solidarity,* ed. Peter Dews (London: Verso Press, 1986), pp. 195–265.

5. In this view, at issue is not the epochality or historicality of the different forms that philosophy had given to Being; rather, the process of making sense here and now of meaning, as a historical phenomenon, is the central question of Heidegger's account of the history of Being. Habermas consistently and stubbornly reads Heidegger's shift from temporality to history as a shift from the temporal form of something like "will" in *Being and Time* to something like an idealized Being as the omnipotent and ineffable motor of history. It is less interesting that this reading is inadequate than that, for Habermas, everything depends upon it. Habermas's argument would be inadequate if there were some other position besides the two alternatives of staying within or leaving behind the modernity-as-rationality debate. There might be another possibility for reading-writing the meaning of modernity as a form of reason developed in Heidegger's transformation of the question of temporality into a question of history. The suggestion I am pursuing is that Habermas's own style of argumentation in his reading of deconstruction, in fact, is an example of just such a form of reading-writing; though, of course, he lacks the tools to acknowledge the possibility. I developed these suggestions in "Politology" (Ph.D. diss., SUNY—Stony Brook, 1989).

6. On the theory of argumentation see TCA 1: 22–42. See as well *Habermas: Autonomy and Solidarity,* p. 162.

7. See Georg Lukacs, *History and Class Consciousness,* trans. Rodney Livingstone (Cambridge, Mass.: MIT Press, 1971), pp. 205–6.

8. On system and life-world and Habermas's translation of that dichotomy out of the theoretical problematics of the Frankfurt School see Chapters 4, 5, and 6 of TCA.

9. The complex relationship between Habermas's pragmatic logic and Kant's transcendental logic is evident. Both are logics of the actual use of a competence—speech for Habermas, intuition for Kant.

10. See Max Horkheimer, "Traditional and Critical Theory," in *Critical Theory*, trans. M.J. O'Connell (New York: Seabury Press, 1972).

11. Jurgen Habermas, "A Reply to My Critics," in *Habermas: Critical Debates*, ed. J.B. Thompson and D. Held (Cambridge, Mass.: MIT Press, 1982), pp. 261–62.

12. *Habermas: Autonomy and Solidarity*, p. 207.

Chapter 8. Dasein and the Analytic of Finitude

1. Martin Heidegger, *Being and Time*, trans. John Macquarrie and Edward Robinson (New York: Harper & Row, 1962), p. 428; hereafter cited as "BT."

2. Michel Foucault, *The Order of Things* (New York: Pantheon Books, 1970), pp. 312–35; hereafter cited as "OT."

3. In their book, *Michel Foucault: Beyond Structuralism and Hermeneutics* (Chicago: Univ. of Chicago Press, 1982), Hubert Dreyfus and Paul Rabinow issue a warning on understanding the relationship between Heidegger and Foucault that applies here as well: "There is no way to make Heidegger's position clear and Foucault's critique plausible short of writing a book on Division II of *Being and Time*, so let the reader beware," p. 38, n. 4. Dreyfus and Rabinow's discussion of the relationship between Heidegger and Foucault is rather rudimentary, although it can serve as a point of departure for a more extensive treatment. In this chapter, I occasionally refer to their discussion.

4. The notion of "hinge" is borrowed from Jacques Derrida, *Dissemination*, trans. Barbara Johnson (Chicago: Univ. of Chicago Press, 1981).

5. A more sophisticated version of this is found in the Marxian notion of *Kritik*, which depends on a fundamental separation of crisis and critique, of criticism and revolution.

6. Compare: There is a "close affinity between the early Foucault and the early Heidegger, for Heidegger's most pervasive concern in *Being and Time* is precisely with circumventing...the subject-object dichotomy," Alan Megill, *Prophets of Extremity: Nietzsche, Heidegger, Foucault, Derrida* (Berkeley: Univ. of California Press, 1985), p. 200; and, "Both [Foucault and Heidegger] attempt to disengage and relate the 'factical' principles which structure the space governing the emergence of objects and subjects," Dreyfus and Rabinow, *Michel Foucault*, p. 57.

7. The phrase *culminating example* actually comes from Dreyfus and Rabinow.

8. Dreyfus and Rabinow, *Michel Foucault*, p. 38.

9. Dreyfus and Rabinow, *Michel Foucault*, p. 39.

10. Martin Heidegger, "Letter on Humanism," in *Basic Writings*, trans. David Krell (New York: Harper & Row, 1977), p. 210.

11. Reiner Schurmann, "Anti-Humanism: Reflections on the Turn towards the Post-Modern Epoch," *Man and World* 12 (1979): 172.

12. Heidegger, "Letter on Humanism," p. 208.

13. Heidegger, "Letter on Humanism," p. 239.

14. Michel Foucault, *The Archaeology of Knowledge*, trans. A. M. Sheridan Smith (New York: Pantheon Books, 1972), p. 121. See also Dreyfus and Rabinow, *Michel Foucault*, p. 57.

Chapter 9. Foucault's Analytics of Power

1. Research for this paper was made possible in part by a Faculty Research Grant from Northeast Missouri State University for the summer of 1987.

2. Michel Foucault, *The History of Sexuality: An Introduction*, vol. 1 of *The History of Sexuality*, trans. Robert Hurley (New York: Vintage Books, 1978), pp. 92–102.

3. Michel Foucault, "Truth and Power" and "Power and Strategies," in *Power/Knowledge*, ed. Colin Gordon (New York: Pantheon Press, 1980), pp. 109–33 and 134–45, respectively.

4. Michel Foucault, "Afterword: The Subject and Power," in Hubert Dreyfus and Paul Rabinow, *Michel Foucault: Beyond Structuralism and Hermeneutics* (Chicago: Univ. of Chicago Press, 1982), pp. 208–26. Also significant are several interviews in Michel Foucault, *Politics, Philosophy, Culture*, ed. Lawrence Kritzman (New York: Routledge, Chapman, Hall, 1988).

5. Mark Philip, "Foucault on Power: A Problem in Radical Translation?" *Political Theory*, 11, no. 1 (February 1983): 29–52.

6. We cannot distinguish occurrences of force from other occurrences on Foucault's "model," because all events are valent; all events are occurrences of power. Therefore, in Foucault's view, one cannot even speak of an event that is not a force-event. Apparently Philip is interested in preserving a liberal domain of legitimacy in which people are not "forced" to behave as they do. But to do that will require that Philip maintain a liberal concept of ahistorical subjectivity, that is, of a subjectivity not wholly produced within force networks. Since Philip is not prepared to place in question the notion of such a subjectivity, his project is simply alien to Foucault's and cannot stand as a critique of it.

7. This seems to be the thrust of Nicos Poulantzas's criticisms in *State, Power, Socialism*, trans. Patrick Camiller (London: NLB, 1978), p. 149, where he writes, "It is often said that one can deduce from Foucault nothing more than a guerilla war and scattered acts of harassment of power; but in fact, no kind of resistance is possible if we follow Foucault's analyses. For if power is always already there, if

every power situation is immanent in itself, *why should there ever be resistance? From where* would resistance come, and *how would it even be possible?"*

8. This is Nancy Fraser's criticism in "Michel Foucault: A 'Young Conservative'?" *Ethics* 96 (October 1985): 165–84.

9. Foucault, "Afterword: The Subject and Power," p. 209.

10. See Foucault, "Truth and Power," p. 111.

11. Foucault, "Afterword: The Subject and Power," p. 217. See also p. 219, where Foucault writes that "something called Power, with or without a capital letter, which is assumed to exist universally in a concentrated or diffused form, does not exist."

12. For an important discussion of the differing movement of discourse in Nietzsche, Heidegger, and Foucault, see Charles E. Scott, *The Language of Difference* (Atlantic Highlands, N.J.: Humanities Press, 1987).

Chapter 10. The Call of Conscience and the Call of Language: Reflections on a Movement in Heidegger's Thinking

1. Martin Heidegger, *Sein und Zeit* (Tubingen: Niemeyer, 1986), p. 290. Where an English translation of this work is cited using "SZ" (followed by page number), the translation is my own; other translations cited with "BT" (followed by section number) refer to Joan Stambaugh's unpublished translation.

2. In Heidegger, *Poetry, Language, Thought,* trans. A. Hofstadter (New York: Harper & Row, 1971), p. 199; hereafter cited as "PLT," followed by page number.

3. P. 59 of Heidegger, "The Nature of Language," in *On the Way to Language,* trans. Peter Hertz (New York: Harper & Row, 1971), pp. 57–108; hereafter cited as "WL," followed by page number. "The Nature of Language" is a translation of "Das Wesen der Sprache," from Heidegger, *Unterwegs zur Sprache* (Pfullingen: Neske, 1986), pp. 157–216, which will be cited hereafter as "US," followed by page number.

4. P. 142 of Heidegger, "Words," in WL 139–56. "Words" is a translation of "Das Wort," from US 217–38.

5. P. 206 of Heidegger, "Language," in PLT 187–210. "Language" is a translation of "Die Sprache," from US 9–34.

6. Charles E. Scott, *The Language of Difference* (Atlantic Highlands, N.J.: Humanities Press, 1987), p. 166 n. 50.

Chapter 11. Heidegger and Aristotle:
Dasein and the Question of Practical Life

1. Martin Heidegger, *Aristoteles, Metaphysik Theta 1-3: Von Wesen und Wirklichkeit der Kraft,* vol. 33 of Heidegger, *Gesamtausgabe* (Frankfurt am Main: Klostermann, 1981), p. 137; translation is my own.

2. Martin Heidegger, *Basic Problems of Phenomenology,* trans. Albert Hofstadter (Bloomington: Indiana Univ. Press, 1982), p. 327.

3. In the *Ethics,* at 1170a2 and after, Aristotle says that the supremely happy person will need friends since such a person chooses a *theōria* of actions that are good and that are one's own, and such are the actions of a good person who is a friend.

4. Martin Heidegger, *Being and Time,* trans. J. Macquarrie and E. Robinson (New York: Harper & Row, 1962), p. 347.

5. Heidegger, *Being and Time,* p. 344.

Chapter 12. Economies of Production: Heidegger
and Aristotle on *Physis* and *Technē*

1. Martin Heidegger, *Aristoteles, Metaphysik Theta 1-3,* vol. 33 of Heidegger, *Gesamtausgabe* (Frankfurt am Main: Klostermann, 1981), p. 146. "Where [there is] world—there [is] work." The translation is mine. In subsequent citations of translated texts, if an existing translation has been cited, that translation is listed first in the note, followed by the reference to the original text; if the translation there is my own, then the original text is listed first, followed by the English translation, if one exists. The Aristotle translations here are my own; however, they follow McKeon's translations very closely. Compare R. P. McKeon, *Basic Works of Aristotle* (New York: Random House, 1970, 1941).

2. Heidegger, *Aristoteles,* p. 137.

3. Martin Heidegger, *Wegmarken* (Frankfurt am Main: Klostermann, 1978), p. 242. See translation: "On the Being and Conception of *Physis* in Aristotle's *Physics* B, 1," trans. T. Sheehan, in *Man and World* 9 (1976): 224.

4. The question of that analogy and exchange is one that Heidegger persists in raising and then postponing. See, for instance, *Einführung in die Metaphysik* (Tübingen: Niemeyer Verlag, 1966), p. 13, where, after noting that, thanks to the Greeks, we think *"physis* constricting itself in opposition to *technē,"* Heidegger says, in a parenthesis, "(the essentially Same in *physis* and *technē* could be made clear only in a special study)." Translation: *Introduction to Metaphysics,* trans. R. Manheim (New Haven, Conn.: Yale Univ. Press, 1959), p. 16.

5. The importance of the word *poĺemos* for Heidegger, especially its political importance, should be noted. It is not only one of the key words in "Origin of the Work of Art" and *Einführung*, but, according to Heidegger's own self-interpretation in "Tatsache und Gedanken," it also names the central concern of "Die Selbstbehauptung der deutschen Universität," Heidegger's rectorial address. What is more remarkable about that claim is that in the address *poĺemos* is thought as *Kampf*—a word that could not be spoken as the central thought of a political address in 1933 Germany without unmistakable echoes. See *Die Selbstbehauptung der deutschen Universität* (Frankfurt am Main: Klostermann, 1983), pp. 28–29.

6. Martin Heidegger, *Nietzsche*, vol. 2 (Pfüllingen: Neske Verlag, 1961), p. 228.

7. See my "Belonging to the Discourse of the Turn," in *Heidegger Studies* 5 (1989): 201–11, for a more complete discussion of the character of this topological and tropological step and shift, especially as it concerns the possibility of its own discourses.

8. See Heidegger, *Einführung*, p. 12; *Introduction*, pp. 15–16.

9. For a treatment of this issue in Plato and Nietzsche see my "Poetry and the Political," in *Festivals of Interpretation: Essays on Hans-Georg Gadamer's Work*, ed. K. Wright (Albany: SUNY Press, 1990); also see Christopher Prendergast, *The Order of Mimesis* (Cambridge: Cambridge Univ. Press, 1986), esp. pp. 9–23.

10. Heidegger, *Aristoteles*, p. 142. This is the point from which it becomes necessary to engage in a critique of the entire notion of "fore-structure" at work in *Sein und Zeit*, if the issue at hand is to be thought through in its widest scope for Heidegger. One productive way this might be pursued leads to the remark by Paul de Man, who claims that "poetry is the foreknowledge of criticism," in *Blindness and Insight* (Minneapolis: Univ. of Minnesota Press, 1983), p. 31.

11. Heidegger, *Wegmarken*, p. 287; "Being and Conception," p. 260.

12. Immanual Kant, *Kritik der Urteilskraft* (Berlin: Walter de Gruyter, 1968), Ak. 374. Translation: *Critique of Judgment*, trans. W. Pluhar (Indianapolis: Hackett Publishing Co., 1987), pp. 253–54. The translation is cross-referenced with the Ak. page numbers, so no other number is given in subsequent citations.

13. See Hannah Arendt, *Kant's Political Philosophy* (Chicago: Univ. of Chicago Press, 1982).

14. Kant, *Kritik der Urteilskraft*, Ak. 303.

15. Martin Heidegger, *Holzwege* (Frankfurt am Main: Klostermann, 1972), p. 8. Translation: "Origin of the Work of Art," in *Poetry, Language, Thought*, trans. A. Hofstadter (New York: Harper & Row, 1971), p. 18. See my "Circles— Hermeneutic and Otherwise," in *Writing the Future*, ed. D. Wood (London: Routledge, 1989), pp. 67–77, for a discussion of the way in which the image of the circle works in Heidegger, Hegel, Bloch, and Gadamer.

16. Heidegger, *Aristoteles*, p. 138.

17. This is another point at which Kant's third critique offers interesting avenues for further reflections—here along the line that thinks the meaning of "purposeless purposivity," that is, the relation of nature and play.

18. Heidegger, *Wegmarken*, pp. 295–96; "Being and Conception," p. 266. See also *Einführung*, p. 100; *Introduction*, p. 131: "For the opinionated life is only life. Death is for them death and only that. But the being of life is at the same time death. Everything that enters life begins to die with that entry, to head to its death is at the same time life." Heidegger continues that passage with reference to Heraclitus's fragment 8. The context of that passage directs it not only to the notions of return, struggle, and restraint, but also to the Greek sensitivity to the relation between beauty and death. This is equally an element in Hölderlin; see for instance the final line of "In lieblicher Bläue...".

19. Heidegger, *Wegmarken*, p. 295; "Being and Conception," p. 266.

20. Heidegger, *Wegmarken*, p. 294; "Being and Conception," pp. 265–66.

21. Translation: "physis likes to encrypt [itself]."

22. The enormity, of course, is what Kant refers to as the "mathematically sublime" (see Ak. 248–60). The power of nature, on the other hand, is its dynamic sublimity that "reveals itself aesthetically only through sacrifice" (Ak. 271).

23. See Jacques Derrida, "Economimesis," in Sylviane Agacinski et al., *Mimesis des Articulations* (Paris: Aubier-Flammarion, 1975), pp. 70–71. Translation: "Economimesis," trans. R. Klein, *Diacritics* 11 (1981): 7.

24. Martin Heidegger, *Vorträge und Aufsätze* (Pfullingen: Neske Verlag, 1978), p. 12. Translation: *The Question concerning Technology,* trans. W. Lovitt (New York: Harper & Row, 1977), p. 10.

25. Full treatment of this relation requires attention to Freud's theory of the unconscious and repression. See Odo Marquard, "On the Importance of the Theory of the Unconscious for a Theory of the No Longer Fine Art," in *New Perspectives in German Literary Criticism: A Collection of Essays,* ed. Richard E. Amacher and Victor Lange, trans. David H. Wilson et al. (Princeton: Princeton Univ. Press, 1979), pp. 260–78.

26. It is worth asking about the parallels of this reflection with Lacan's description in a psychoanalytical context of the "mirror stage."

27. Heidegger, *Einführung*, p. 122; *Introduction*, p. 159.

28. Theodor Adorno, *Aesthetic Theory,* trans. C. Lenhardt (London: Routledge & Kegan Paul, 1984), p. 193. Original: *Aesthetische Theorie* (Frankfurt am Main: Suhrkamp Verlag, 1970), p. 200.

29. Heidegger, *Holzwege*, p. 64; "Origin," p. 77.

30. Kant, *Kritik der Urteilskraft*, Ak. 302.

31. The social-political dimensions of Kant's theory of mimesis are conflicted like all else in the *Kritik der Urteilskraft*. One of the more interesting ways to draw together such a theory is by developing a reading that follows references to bird songs, blades of grass, and desert islands. See Akademie Edition pages 371–72, 378, 400, 409 for remarks about blades of grass; pages 205, 297, 299, 367–68 for remarks about desert islands. Derrida indicates only one line animating the third critique when he says "a paradigmatics of the flower orients the third critique." See J. Derrida, *La vérité en peinture* (Paris: Flammarion, 1978), p. 97. Translation: *Truth in Painting*, trans. G. Bennington and I. McLeod (Chicago: Univ. of Chicago Press, 1987), p. 85.

32. This is most evident in the first version of Heidegger's "Origin of the Work of Art." See "Vom Ursprung des Kunstwerkes: Erste Ausarbeitung," *Heidegger Studies* 5 (1989): 5–22.

33. Heidegger, *Holzwege,* p. 67; "Origin," p. 80. See also Heidegger's later self-interpretation of that remark on that decision in his letter to Rudolf Krämer-Badoni in *Studien zur neueren französischen Phänomenologie* (Freiburg: Alber Verlag, 1986), pp. 175–82.

34. See Marquard, "Theory of the Unconscious," pp. 260–61.

35. Heidegger, *Holzwege,* p. 253. Translation: "Anaximander's Fragment," in *Early Greek Thinking,* trans. D. F. Krell and F. Cauzzi (New York: Harper & Row, 1975), p. 20.

36. That remark leads to Georges Bataille; see especially his *La part maudite: Précédé de la Notion de dépense* (Paris: Editions de Minuit, 1967). English translation: *The Accursed Share: An Essay on General Economy,* trans. Robert Hurley (New York: Zone Books, 1988-).

Chapter 13. The *Deinon* of Yielding at the End of Metaphysics

1. See David Farrell Krell, *Intimations of Mortality: Time, Truth, and Finitude in Heidegger's Thinking of Being* (University Park: Pennsylvania State Univ. Press, 1986); Christopher Fynsk, *Heidegger: Historicity and Thought* (Ithaca, N.Y.: Cornell Univ. Press, 1986); Werner Marx, *Is There a Measure on Earth? Foundations for a Non-Metaphysical Ethics,* trans. Thomas J. Nenon and Reginald Lily (Chicago: Univ. of Chicago Press, 1987); and Gerald Bruns, *Heidegger's Estrangements: Language, Truth, and Poetry in the Later Writings* (New Haven, Conn.: Yale Univ. Press, 1989).

2. The clearest discussion of the notion of *Grundstimmung* in the later Heidegger is to be found in the neglected lecture, "What Is Philosophy?" published in English as *What Is Philosophy?,* trans. William Klubak and Jean T. Wilde (New York: Twayne, 1958), hereafter abbreviated "WP." I am currently at work on an essay on this lecture that will examine Heidegger's treatment of the relation between *Stimmung and Bestimmung.*

Quotations from frequently cited works by Heidegger are given in the text using the following abbreviations:

EM   *Einführung in die Metaphysik* (Tubingen: Max Niemeyer Verlag, 1966).

IM   *An Introduction to Metaphysics,* trans. Ralph Manheim (New Haven, Conn.: Yale Univ. Press, Anchor Books Edition, 1961).

N   *Nietzsche III: Will to Power as Knowledge and as Metaphysics,* ed. David Farrell Krell, trans. Joan Stambaugh (New York: Harper & Row, 1987).

SA   "The Self-Assertion of the German University: Address, Delivered on the Solemn Assumption of the Rectorate of the University of Freiburg" and

R   "The Rectorate 1933–34: Facts and Thoughts," trans. Karsten Harries, *Review of Metaphysics* 38 (1985): 467–502.

3. In Martin Heidegger, *Discourse on Thinking,* trans. J. M. Anderson and E. H. Freund (New York: Harper & Row, 1966), pp. 54–55. In what follows I will consider only *Gelassenheit.*

4. Just what is the force of Heidegger's saying that "presumably" a fundamental attunement is at work today? One could object that if the dispersion of attunements that Heidegger notes *is* the "fundamental attunement" of thought today, then the very notion of a *Grund,* a fundamental attunement, is called into question. This objection marks one place in which Heidegger confronts Derrida. It is a place needing reflection that goes beyond the limits of this chapter; but it should be noted that Heidegger does not use the word *dispersion,* and that my use of it already indicates the influence of Derrida.

5. At this juncture one could ask, Is not your attempt to determine the *Grundstimmung* of thought at the end of metaphysics itself governed by the very "modern attunement" you have just described? Does it not seek to think *about* a fundamental attunement rather than think *from* it? The answer to such questions will be worked out in seeing what happens when we follow the *deinon* of yielding in *Antigone.* The question then will become how we listen to the saying of that text.

6. Martin Heidegger, *Poetry, Language, Thought,* trans. Albert Hofstadter (New York: Harper & Row, 1971), p. 10.

7. See IM 121–22.

8. John Caputo has objected to the implication here that the Nazi members of Heidegger's audience at his rectorial address did not recognize his words as in tune with the revolution at hand; for while some may have objected to his "private" Nazism, that is very different from saying that his call was spoken "into the wind." My point in quoting Heidegger here is not somehow to absolve him of the responsibility for his address. Indeed I tend to see an important relation between Heidegger's address and Creon's refusal to yield, though I will not directly develop it in what follows. The point for Heidegger in 1945 is that his audience in 1933 *could not* heed his attempt to lead the Nazi party to a genuine recognition of its historical mission, not simply because of the failings of its leaders, but because of the abandonment by Being of man. Heidegger sees himself as having undergone that same abandonment: he does so in making his call—which as a call cannot listen to its own situation—and so, in this other sense, is "spoken into the wind."

9. The translations of *Einführung in die Metaphysik* (EM) that follow are mine, but utilize the previous work of Ralph Manheim in *Introduction to Metaphysics* (IM).

10. I am indebted to conversations with Karin Ahbel for suggestions used in this brief etymology.

11. Line 915. Line numbers for the text of *Antigone* follow R. D. Dawe's edition, *Sophoclis Tragoediae* (Leipzig: B. G. Teubner Verlags-gesellschaft, 1979). Translations are my own but make use of several different translations, especially that by Richard Braun: Sophocles, *Antigone* (New York: Oxford Univ. Press, 1973). I also wish to thank my colleague, Dana Burgess, for suggestions with the translations.

12. Of course, the time for such an opportunity has already passed; Creon has already passed by two opportunities to yield to the claim of either the human or the divine.

13. A place to begin would be with Heidegger's own comments on the relation between dread and awe in his "Postscript" to the lecture "What Is Metaphysics?" published in English in *Existence and Being,* ed. Werner Brock (Chicago: Regnery-Gateway, 1949), pp. 385–87. Werner Marx takes up these comments in *Is There a Measure on Earth?* but in a way that fails to develop the late Heideggerian notion of *Stimmung* as presented in *What Is Philosophy?.* A good examination of the limitations of Marx's work is David Farrell Krell's review, *"Is There a Measure on Earth?:* A Discussion of Werner Marx's 'Nonmetaphysical Ethics',*" Journal of the British Society for Phenomenology,* 16, no. 2 (May 1985): 196–201.

I want to thank Charles Scott, Robert Bernasconi, John Caputo, Dennis Schmidt, Holley Roberts, Sherah Stacy, and Peter Warnek for comments on different drafts of this paper.

Chapter 14. Appetite and Violability: Questioning a Platonic Metaphor

1. Plato, *Phaedo,* trans. Harold North Fowler (Cambridge, Mass.: Harvard Univ. Press, Loeb Library Edition, 1977). Subsequent references are to this edition and are cited in the text by title and Stephanus number.

2. Plato, *Phaedrus,* trans. Harold North Fowler (Cambridge, Mass.: Harvard Univ. Press, Loeb Library Edition, 1977). Subsequent references are to this edition and are cited in the text by title and Stephanus number.

3. James Hillman, *Re-Visioning Psychology* (New York: Harper & Row, 1975), p. 90. Subsequent references are cited in the text by "RVP" and the page number.

4. See "...Poetically Man Dwells..." in Martin Heidegger, *Poetry, Language, Thought,* trans. Albert Hofstadter (New York: Harper & Row, 1971), pp. 222–26

especially. Subsequent references are cited in the text by "PLT" and the page number.

Chapter 15. Monstrous Reflection: Sade and Masoch— Rewriting the History of Reason

1. Gilles Deleuze, "Plato and the Simulacrum," trans. Rosalind Krauss, *October* 27 (1983): 45; cited hereafter as "PS." This text is a chapter taken from one of Deleuze's books. See Gilles Deleuze, *Logique du sens* (Paris: Editions de Minuit, 1969), pp. 292–306. Compare English translation: *The Logic of Sense*, trans. Mark Lester with Charles Stivale, ed. Constantin V. Boundas (New York: Columbia Univ. Press, 1989).

2. Plato, *Phaedrus*, trans. Walter Hamilton (New York: Penguin Books, 1983), 248 (pp. 53–54); cited hereafter as "PH."

3. Plato, *The Republic*, trans. G.M.A. Grube (Indianapolis: Hackett Publishing Co., 1974), Book 3; cited hereafter as "REP."

4. Plato, *Sophist*, trans. F.M. Cornford, in *Plato, The Collected Dialogues*, ed. Edith Hamilton and Huntington Cairns (Princeton, N.J.: Princeton Univ. Press, 1969), 236b (p. 979); cited hereafter as "SPH." In the *Sophist* Plato opposes the *ikon* to the *phantasma*.

5. Gilles Deleuze, *Masochism: An Interpretation of Coldness and Cruelty*, trans. Jean McNeil (New York: George Braziller, 1971), p. 17; cited hereafter as "MAS."

6. See Gilles Deleuze, *Spinoza: Philosophie pratique* (Paris: Presses Universitaires de France, 1970); translated as *Spinoza: Practical Philosophy* by Robert Hurley (San Francisco: City Lights Books, 1988), cited hereafter as "SPP." Deleuze takes up these themes in the context of what he calls Spinoza's *ethology,* an ethics that is not a moral science but "the study of the relations of speed and slowness, of the capacities for affecting and being affected that characterize each thing" (SPP 125).

7. Plato, *Statesman*, trans. J.B. Skemp, in *The Collected Dialogues of Plato,* ed. Edith Hamilton and Huntington Cairns, 300c (p. 1070); cited hereafter as "ST."

8. See Gilles Deleuze, *La Philosophie Critique de Kant* (Paris: Presses Universitaires de France, 1963); translated as *Kant's Critical Philosophy* by Hugh Tomlinson and Barbara Habberjam (Minneapolis: Univ. of Minnesota Press, 1984); cited hereafter as "KCP." In this text Deleuze investigates the nature of Law in relation to practical reason in Kant and discovers that for Kant the moral law—as the law of our intelligible existence, the form under which all rational, intelligible beings constitute their suprasensible nature—is also the basis of evil. The intelligible, moral law always includes a sphere of freedom in which we choose against the law and cease to be legislators as well as subjects (KCP 32–33). This

understanding of freedom as a fall from subjectivity, a lack of intelligibility, a refusal of Law is no doubt what is being countered in Deleuze's essay.

9. Marquis de Sade, *Juliette,* trans. Austryn Wainhouse (New York: Grove Press, 1968), p. 1163.

10. Gilles Deleuze, *Logique du sens,* p. 9; cited hereafter as "LS." The translations of *Logique du sens* cited hereafter in the text are all mine.

11. Lewis Carroll, *Alice's Adventures in Wonderland* and *Through the Looking Glass* (London: Octopus Books Ltd., 1978), p. 299; cited hereafter as "AAW."

Chapter 16. Abjection and Oppression: Dynamics of Unconscious Racism, Sexism, and Homophobia

1. Frantz Fanon, *Black Skin, White Masks* (New York: Grove Press, 1967), p. 114.

2. Anthony Giddens, *The Constitution of Society* (Berkeley: Univ. of California Press, 1984), esp. chap. 2.

3. Compare Pierre Bourdieu's concept of the *habitus* in *Outline of a Theory of Practice* (Cambridge: Cambridge Univ. Press, 1977).

4. Giddens, *Constitution,* p. 79.

5. See Charles Lawrence, "The Id, the Ego, and Equal Protection: Reckoning with Unconscious Racism," *Stanford Law Review* 39 (January 1987): 317–88.

6. Maria D. Vesperi, *City of Green Benches: Growing Old in a New Downtown* (Ithaca, N.Y.: Cornell Univ. Press, 1985).

7. Michael Omi and Howard Winant, "By the Rivers of Babylon: Race in the United States, Part 1," *Socialist Review* 71 (September–October 1983): 31–66. They discuss how racism is covert in much contemporary policy discussion, such as affirmative action discussion.

8. See Lawrence, "The Id, the Ego."

9. Julia Kristeva, *Powers of Horror* (New York: Columbia Univ. Press, 1982). Quotations from this work will be cited in the text with the abbreviation "PH," followed by page number.

10. Julia Kristeva, "Le sujet en procès," *Polylogue* (Paris: Editions du Seuil, 1977), pp. 55–106.

11. See Marilyn Frye, "On Being White: Toward a Feminist Understanding of White Supremacy," *The Politics of Reality: Essays in Feminist Theory* (Trumansburg, N.Y.: Crossing Press, 1983), pp. 110–27.

12. Thomas Cole, "Putting Off the Old: Middle Class Morality, Antebellum Protestantism, and the Origins of Ageism," in *Old Age in a Bureaucratic Society,* ed. David Van Tassel and Peter N. Stearns (New York: Greenwood Press, 1986).

Chapter 17. Lacanian Castration: Body-Image and Signification in Psychoanalysis

1. P. 60 of Jacques Lacan, "The Seminar on the 'Purloined Letter'," *French Freud: Structural Studies in Psychoanalysis,* trans. Jeffrey Mehlman, Yale French Studies no. 48 (New Haven, Conn.: Yale Univ. Press, 1972), pp. 38–72. See also note 18.

2. P. 323 in Jacques Lacan, "The Subversion of the Subject and the Dialectic of Desire in the Freudian Unconscious," *Ecrits: A Selection,* trans. Alan Sheridan (New York: W.P. Norton Press, 1977), pp. 292–325; hereafter cited as "ES," followed by page number.

3. P. 287 in Jacques Lacan, "The Signification of the Phallus" (ES 281-91).

4. "La relation de l'enfant au phallus est essentielle en tant que la phallus est l'objet du désir de la mère." Lacan, Le Séminaire V, "Formations de l'inconscient," unpublished seminar of 1957–58, quoted by Joel Dör, *Introduction à la lecture de Lacan* (Paris: Editions Denoël, 1985), p. 102.

5. Lacan, "The Subversion of the Subject" (ES 320).

6. See Lacan's remark: "[The woman] finds the signifier of her own desire in the body of him to whom she addresses her demand for love. Perhaps it should not be forgotten that the organ that assumes this signifying function takes on the value of a fetish." "The Signification of the Phallus" (ES 290).

7. Catherine Clément, *Lives and Legends of Jacques Lacan,* trans. Arthur Goldhammer (New York: Columbia Univ. Press, 1983), pp. 100-101.

8. Philippe Julien, *Le rétour à Freud de Jacques Lacan, L'application au miroir* (Toulouse: Editions Erès, 1985), p. 225; my translation.

9. P. 17 in Jacques Lacan, "Aggressivity in Psychoanalysis" (ES 8–29).

10. Jacques Lacan, *The Seminar of Jacques Lacan. Book II: The Ego in Freud's Theory and in the Technique of Psychoanalysis,* ed. Jacques-Alain Miller, trans. Sylvana Tomaselli and John Forrester (New York: W.P. Norton Press, 1988), p. 326.

11. Lacan, "Aggressivity in Psychoanalysis" (ES 19–20).

12. P. 42 in Jacques Lacan, "The Function and Field of Speech and Language in Psychoanalysis" (ES 30–113).

13. Compare Lacan's discussion on pp. 128–29 of "The Freudian Thing, or the Meaning of the Return to Freud in Psychoanalysis" (ES 114–45).

14. Jacques Lacan, *Four Fundamental Concepts of Psychoanalysis,* ed. Jacques-Alain Miller, trans. Alan Sheridan (New York: W.P. Norton Press, 1981), p. 45.

15. Serge Leclaire, *Psychoanalyser, essai sur l'ordre de l'inconscient et la pratique de la lettre* (Paris: Editions du Seuil, 1968), quoted by Anika Lemaire, *Lacan,* trans. D. Macey (London: Routledge & Kegan Paul, 1977), p. 167.

16. Lacan, "The Subversion of the Subject" (ES 302).

17. Sigmund Freud, *The Standard Edition of the Complete Psychological Works of Sigmund Freud,* ed. and trans. James Strachey, Anna Freud, et al., 24 vols. (London: Hogarth Press & the Institute for Psycho-Analysis, 1955), 19: 26.

18. *"Beyond the Pleasure Principle*...is the work of Freud that many of those who authorize themselves with the title of psychoanalyst do not hesitate to reject as a superfluous, indeed chancy speculation...insofar as the supreme antimony which results from it, the *death instinct,* becomes unthinkable for them....It is difficult, however, to take as an excursion, still less as a mistake of the Freudian doctrine, the work which is precisely the prelude to the new topography represented by the terms ego, id, and superego, which has become as prevalent in its theoretical usage as in its popular diffusion." Pp. 44–45 in Jacques Lacan, "Le Séminaire sur 'La Lettre Volée'," *Écrits* (Paris: Editions du Seuil, 1966), pp. 11–61; my translation.

19. Jacques Lacan, "Some Reflections on the Ego," *International Journal of Psycho-analysis* 34 (1953): 16.

20. See appendix for an illustration of this point.

21. Lacan, "The Subversion of the Subject" (ES 315).

22. See Roman Jakobson and Krystyna Pomorska, *Dialogues* (Cambridge, Mass.: MIT Press, 1983), pp. 93–98.

23. See Lacan, "The Signification of the Phallus" (esp. ES 287).

24. *Entry into language* does not here mean a minimal capacity to use words in more or less appropriate ways. The pre-Oedipal child of two already possesses a certain degree of speech competence but has not entered into language in Lacan's sense. By entry into the symbolic function, Lacan has in mind an ability to dwell in language, to rely on the structure of language for the guidance of thought and action, to genuinely appropriate language and be appropriated by it. In and through the Oedipus complex, the subject comes into being by becoming *subject* to language.

25. It is worthwhile to quote at length Helen Keller's account of the incident:

"One day, while I was playing with my new doll, Miss Sullivan put my big rag doll into my lap also, spelled 'd-o-l-l' and tried to make me understand that 'd-o-l-l' applied to both. Earlier in the day we had had a tussle over the words 'm-u-g' and 'w-a-t-e-r.' Miss Sullivan had tried to impress it upon me that 'm-u-g' is *mug* and that 'w-a-t-e-r' is *water*, but I persisted in confounding the two. In despair she had dropped the subject for the time, only to renew it at the first opportunity. I became impatient at her repeated attempts and, seizing the new doll, I dashed it upon the floor. I was keenly delighted when I felt the fragments of the broken doll at my feet. Neither sorrow nor regret followed my passionate outburst. I had not loved the doll. In the still, dark world in which I lived there was no strong sentiment of tenderness. I felt my teacher sweep the fragments to one side of the hearth and I had a sense of satisfaction that the cause of my discomfort was removed. She brought me my hat, and I knew I was going out into the warm sunshine. This thought, if a wordless sensation may be called a thought, made me hop and skip for pleasure.

"We walked down the path to the well-house, attracted by the fragrance of the honeysuckle with which it was covered. Some one was drawing water and my teacher placed my hand under the spout. As the cool stream gushed over one hand she spelled into the other the word *water*, first slowly, then rapidly. I stood still, my whole attention fixed upon the motions of her fingers. Suddenly I felt a misty consciousness of something forgotten—a thrill of returning thought; and somehow the mystery of language was revealed to me. I knew then that 'w-a-t-e-r' meant the wonderful cool something that was flowing over my hand. That living word awakened my soul, gave it light, hope, joy, set it free! There were barriers still, it is true, but barriers that could in time be swept away.

"I left the well-house eager to learn. Everything had a name, and each name gave birth to a new thought. As we returned to the house every object which I touched seemed to quiver with life. That was because I saw everything with the strange, new sight that had come to me. On entering the door I remembered the doll I had broken. I felt my way to the hearth and picked up the pieces. I tried vainly to put them together. Then my eyes filled with tears; for I realized what I had done, and for the first time I felt repentance and sorrow." Helen Keller, *The Story of My Life* (New York: Grosset & Dunlap, 1905), pp. 22–24.

26. Plato, *Phaedrus* 264c, *Collected Dialogues of Plato,* ed. Edith Hamilton and Huntington Cairns (Princeton, N.J.: Bollingen Press, 1973), p. 510.

27. "One cannot stress too strongly the irreducible character of the narcissistic structure. . . . This narcissistic moment in the subject is to be found in all the genetic phases of the individual." "Aggressivity in Psychoanalysis" (ES 24).

28. A concept coined by Lacan during a period of especially intense Heideggerian influence, *empty speech* calls to mind Heidegger's notion of "idle chatter" in *Being and Time.* Although Heidegger does not specifically link idle talk with the body or its imago, a link can be made indirectly through the complementary notion of "equipmentality" that characterizes the everydayness of *Dasein.* Is it not precisely something on the order of Heideggerian equipmentality that Freud points to in *Civilization and Its Discontents* when he designates all tools as extensions of

the body (Freud, *Standard Edition,* 21: 90–92)? The ego locates itself in the world by means of the body and defines the objects with which it deals as furthering or hindering the body's powers of motion and position.

29. For Lacan's treatment of Freud's famous case study of *Senatspräsident* Schreber, see Lacan, *Le Séminaire, Livre III, Les Psychoses,* ed. Jacques-Alain Miller (Paris: Editions du Seuil, 1981).

30. Jacques Lacan, *The Seminar of Jacques Lacan, Book I, Freud's Papers on Technique, 1953–54,* ed. Jacques-Alain Miller, trans. John Forrester (New York: W.P. Norton Press, 1988), p. 79.

31. Freud, *Standard Edition,* 19: 57.

32. Jacques Lacan, *The Seminar, Book II,* p. 75.

33. Lacan often stresses the inseparability of Imaginary, Symbolic, and Real, comparing them to the three rings of a Borromean knot. No doubt it is with this intertwining of the three registers in mind that Lacan proposes that "the unconscious castration complex has the function of a knot." "The Signification of the Phallus" (ES 281).

34. Lacan, "The Subversion of the Subject" (ES 324).

35. P. 277 in Jacques Lacan, "The Direction of the Treatment and the Principles of Its Power" (ES 226–80).

Chapter 18. Postmodern *Différends*

1. Gilles Deleuze and Felix Guattari, *Anti-Oedipus: Capitalism and Schizo-phrenia,* trans. Robert Hurley, Mark Seem, and Helen R. Lane (New York: Viking Press, 1977), p. 245; hereafter cited as "AO," followed by page number.

2. Jean-Francois Lyotard, *The Postmodern Condition: A Report on Knowledge,* trans. Geoff Bennington and Brian Massumi (Minneapolis: Univ. of Minnesota Press, 1984); hereafter cited as "PC," followed by page number.

3. Jean-Francois Lyotard, *Le Différend* (Paris: Editions de Minuit, 1983), paragraph 92; hereafter cited as "DIF," followed by paragraph number. All translations are mine unless otherwise noted.

4. In addition to the practices that go by the name *postmodern* or *post-modernism* in architecture, film, dance, painting, literary criticism, historiography, and psychoanalysis—especially as accounted for in the works of Daniel Bell, Paolo Portoghesi, Heinrich Klotz, and Charles Jencks—one should note the more recent accounts that parallel Lyotard's vision of the "postmodern."

See for example, William V. Spanos, *Repetitions: The Postmodern Occasion in Literature and Culture* (Baton Rouge and London: Louisiana State Univ. Press,

1987), especially chap. 5, "Postmodern Literature and Its Occasion: Retrieving the Preterite Middle," pp. 189–276. Spanos writes: "The measure of postmodern occasion form is, in other words, the differential measure of diaspora: not the inseminating Patriarchal Word that establishes a dynastic relationship between the temporal words, but of the disseminating words of contemporary man's [sic] orphanage, not of the One but of the many, not of unity but of dispersal, not of Identity but of ontological difference..." (p. 234).

In the introduction to *Deconstruction in Context* (Chicago: Univ. of Chicago Press, 1986), Mark Taylor says, "Postmodern awareness is born of the recognition that the past that never was present eternally returns as the future that never arrives to displace all contemporaneity and defer forever the presence of the modern" (p. 34).

And finally, see Ihab Hasan, *The Postmodern Turn: Essays in Postmodern Theory and Culture* (Columbus: Ohio State Univ. Press, 1987). Hassan identifies the following characteristics of the "postmodern sensibility": "the decenterment of man," "the vitality of the new," "the demystification of reason," "the refusal of unity,""the empty subject,""the liminality of language,""thinking in fictions,""the denial of origins," "the energetics of value," "ludic arts, the metaphysics of play," and "the collapse of being and becoming, a new ontology" (pp. 46–51).

5. Jean-Francois Lyotard and Jean-Loup Thebaud, *Just Gaming,* trans. Wlad Godzich (Minneapolis: Univ. of Minnesota Press, 1985), p. 16; hereafter cited as "JG," followed by page number.

6. Lyotard, "Memorandum sur la légitimité," *Le Postmoderne expliqué aux enfants* (Paris: Editions Galilee, 1986), p. 71; hereafter cited in the notes as "PEE," followed by page number.

7. Many links can be drawn to traverse the heterogeneity and multiplicity of Lyotard's texts, but for present purposes the most significant link is between the phrase or idiom used, in a particular context and of course for particular purposes, to describe, designate, and, thus, prescribe the desire for the unknown or the unpresentable. See Lyotard, DIF para. 22–24; PC 65–67.

8. Friedrich Nietzsche, *The Birth of Tragedy Out of the Spirit of Music,* trans. Walter Kaufmann (New York: Vintage Books, 1967), section 21.

9. Gilles Deleuze and Felix Guattari, *Kafka: Toward a Minor Literature,* trans. Dana Polan (Minneapolis: Univ. of Minnesota Press, 1986), p. 51; hereafter cited as "K," followed by page number.

10. Lyotard, "Note sur les sens de 'post-'" (PEE 126).

11. Philippe Lacoue-Labarthe, "Talks," trans. Christopher Fynsk, *Diacritics* 14, no. 3 (Fall 1984): 34. In this context, Lacoue-Labarthe claims that Lyotard is like Nietzsche: both valorize everything Plato condemns.

12. Jean-Francois Lyotard, *Peregrinations: Law, Form, Event* (New York: Columbia Univ. Press, 1988), p. 31; hereafter cited as "PER," followed by page number.

13. Jean-Francois Lyotard, *Instructions païennes* (Paris: Editions Galilee, 1977), p. 16; hereafter cited as "IP," followed by page number.

14. See also, Lyotard, "Memorandum sur la légitimité" (PEE 70).

15. Jean-Francois Lyotard, "Interview," trans. Georges Van Den Abbeele, *Diacritics* 14, no. 3 (Fall 1984): 20.

16. See Gilles Deleuze, *Cinema I: L'Image-Mouvement* (Paris: Editions du Minuit, 1983), pp. 46–61 and 243–89; compare the English translation, *Cinema 1: The Movement Image,* trans. Hugh Tomlinson and Barbara Habberjam (Minneapolis: Univ. of Minnesota Press, 1986), pp. 29–40 and 178–215. Hereafter cited as "CIN," followed by the page number of the English translation and then that of the original.

17. Jacques Derrida, *The Post Card: From Socrates to Freud and Beyond,* trans. Alan Bass (Chicago: Univ. of Chicago Press, 1987), pp. 191–92; compare the original, *La Carte Postale: de Socrate à Freud et au-delà* (Paris: Flammarion, 1983), p. 206. Hereafter cited as "CP," followed by the page number of the English translation and then that of the original.

18. Ludwig Wittgenstein, *Tractatus Logico-Philosophicus,* trans. D.F. Pears and B.F. McGuinness (London: Routledge & Kegan Paul, 1961), 2. 174.

19. Wittgenstein, *Tractatus,* 5. 556.

20. Lyotard, "Apostille aux récits" (PEE 38).

21. Lyotard, "Response to the Question: What Is the Postmodern?" trans. Regis Durand (PC 71–82). For the purposes of referring to this article, I have altered, significantly, Durand's translation of the French title. See "Réponse à la question: qu'est-ce que le postmoderne" (PEE 12–34). Durand translates the title, in a rather misleading fashion, as "What Is Postmodernism?"

22. See Gianni Vattimo's critique of Lyotard on the question of the "end of history" in "The End of (Hi)story," *Chicago Review* 35 no. 4 (1987): 20–30. Despite what seems to be a desire to talk in postmodern phrases, Vattimo dismisses Lyotard on the grounds that his narrative (and Habermas's narrative as well) does not go as far in the dissolution of the *metarécits* as Heidegger's attempt to rethink the *Geschick das Sein* according to the demands of *Verwindung.* See especially pp. 25–27.

23. Also see Jacques Derrida, *Of Grammatology,* trans. Gayatri Chakravorty Spivak (Baltimore: Johns Hopkins Univ. Press, 1975), especially the discussion of the "hinge," pp. 65–73.

24. Jean-Francois Lyotard, *Discours, Figure* (Paris: Klincksieck, 1971), p. 14.

25. William James, *Pragmatism* and *The Meaning of Truth* (Cambridge, Mass.: Harvard Univ. Press, 1978), p. 71.

26. Charles Sanders Peirce, *Collected Papers,* ed. Charles Hartshorne and Paul Weiss (Cambridge, Mass.: Harvard Univ. Press, 1931–35), 5.400.

Contributors

Linda Alcoff is assistant professor of philosophy at Syracuse University in New York. She has written several articles on feminism and on Foucault's philosophy. She is at work on a manuscript relating Foucault's and Gadamer's accounts of knowledge to the tradition of coherence epistemology.

Kenneth Baynes is assistant professor of philosophy at the State University of New York at Stony Brook. He is the author of articles on Kant's political philosophy, the liberal-communitarian debate, and Habermas's social theory. He is co-editor (with J. Bohman and T. McCarthy) of *After Philosophy: End or Transformation?* (1987).

Rudolf Bernet is ordinary professor at the University of Louvain, Belgium, and a member of the board of directors of the Husserl Archives. He has edited and translated works by Husserl and Derrida and written numerous articles on Husserl, Heidegger, Derrida, Freud, and Lacan, dealing with such topics as time, language, and imagination. His most recent publication (in collaboration with I. Kern and E. Marbach) is *Edmund Husserl: Darstellung seines Denkens* (F. Meiner, 1989).

Richard P. Boothby is assistant professor of philosophy at Loyola College in Baltimore, Maryland. In addition to his degree in philosophy he holds a master's degree in counseling psychology. He is the author of a book on Jacques Lacan's treatment of the Freudian death instinct, forthcoming from Routledge, Chapman, and Hall.

Walter A. Brogan is associate professor of philosophy at Villanova University in Pennsylvania. He has written several articles on Greek and continental thought, including an essay in *Continental Philosophy in America* (1983) on Derrida's reading of Plato. He is currently translating Heidegger's 1931 lecture course on Aristotle.

R. Philip Buckley is a scientific assistant in the Husserl Archives at the Institute of Philosophy of the University of Louvain, Belgium. He has studied philosophy at the University of Toronto and the University of Louvain.

Michael Clifford is instructor in philosophy at Washington State University. He received his degree from Vanderbilt University in 1989, and his dissertation is a study of Foucault on the problem of political subjectivity. He has written several articles, including a contribution to *The Question of the Other* (1989).

Arleen B. Dallery is associate professor of philosophy at La Salle University in Philadelphia, Pennsylvania. She served as executive co-director of the Society for Phenomenology and Existential Philosophy from 1986 to 1990. Her most recent publications include two articles on French feminist theory: "Sexual Embodiment: Beauvoir and French Feminism" and "The Politics of Writing (the) Body: *Ecriture féminine.*"

Thomas A. Davis is assistant professor of philosophy at Whitman College in Walla Walla, Washington. He has written book reviews on Nietzsche, Derrida, and Heidegger, and an article on Heidegger in the forthcoming volume, *Heidegger and the Earth: Essays in Environmental Philosophy* (1990). He is currently working on a book on Heidegger and Greek tragedy.

J. Claude Evans is assistant professor of philosophy at Washington University in St. Louis, Missouri. He is the author of *The Metaphysics of Transcendental Subjectivity: Descartes, Kant, and W. Sellars* (B. R. Grüner, 1984) and essays on Plato, Kant, Husserl, Habermas, and Derrida, and is the translator of several works in phenomenology. He is currently at work on a manuscript, "Strategies of Deconstruction."

Charles Harvey is associate professor of philosophy at the University of Central Arkansas in Conway, Arkansas. He is the author of *Husserl's Phenomenology and the Foundations of Natural Science* (1989).

Jane Love received an M.A. in philosophy from Vanderbilt University. She is currently pursuing doctoral studies in critical theory at the University of Florida.

Ladelle McWhorter is assistant professor of philosophy at Northeast Missouri State University in Kirskville, Missouri. She is the editor of *Heidegger and the Earth: Essays in Environmental Philosophy* (1990) and has written articles on Foucault, including an essay in *The Question of the Other* (1989).

Dorothea Olkowski is assistant professor of philosophy at the College of Charleston in South Carolina. She has written several articles on art and postmodern thought, including an essay on the sublime in *The Question of the Other* (1989). She is currently at work on a book, "The Limits of Representation."

Gayle L. Ormiston is associate professor in the department of philosophy and the Institute for Applied Linguistics at Kent State University in Ohio. He is the editor of several volumes of essays, most recently of *From Artifact to Habitat: Studies in the Critical Engagement of Technology*

(1990) and (with R. Sassower) of *Prescriptions: The Dissemination of Medical Authority* (1990). He is the author of numerous articles in continental thought and (with Sassower) of *Narrative Experiments: The Discursive Authority of Science and Technology* (1989).

P. Holley Roberts is a graduate student in philosophy at Vanderbilt University, where she is completing her dissertation on Gadamer's hermeneutics. She served as assistant editor for the journals *Soundings* and *Quarterly Review* and is editor (with C. Finn and D. Ravitch) of *Challenges to the Humanities* (1985).

Jane Kelley Rodeheffer is assistant professor of philosophy at St. Mary's College of Minnesota. She completed her degree at Vanderbilt University in 1989. The title of her dissertation is "Beyond Narrative Discourse: The Role of Poetry in Heidegger's Understanding of Time."

Dennis J. Schmidt is associate professor of philosophy at State University of New York at Binghamton. He is the author of *The Ubiquity of the Finite: Hegel, Heidegger, and the Entitlements of Philosophy* (1988) and numerous articles, and is the translator of Ernst Bloch's *Natural Law and Human Dignity* (1986). He is also editor of the SUNY Press Series in Continental Philosophy.

Charles E. Scott is professor of philosophy at Vanderbilt University in Nashville, Tennessee. He served as executive co-director of the Society for Phenomenology and Existential Philosophy from 1986 to 1989. He is the author of *The Language of Difference* (1987) and, most recently, of *The Question of Ethics: Nietzsche, Foucault, Heidegger* (1990).

Thomas R. Thorp is instructor in philosophy at the University of Colorado at Colorado Springs. He received his Ph.D. in 1989 from the State University of New York at Stony Brook, and his dissertation is on Kant's first critique. He is currently working (with Brian Seitz) on a book on the politics of representation.

Iris Marion Young is associate professor of public and international affairs at the University of Pittsburgh and has taught philosophy most recently at Worcester Polytechnic Institute. Her books include *Justice and the Politics of Difference* (1990) and *Throwing Like a Girl and Other Essays in Feminist Philosophy and Social Theory* (1990).